STUDIES IN ENGLISH LITERATURE

Volume LXXXIV

THE LOVE THAT FAILED

Ideal and Reality in the Writings of E. M. Forster

by

RICHARD MARTIN

Rheinisch-Westfälische Technische Hochschule
Aachen

1974

MOUTON

THE HAGUE · PARIS

© Copyright 1974 in The Netherlands
Mouton & Co. N.V., Publishers, The Hague

LIBRARY OF CONGRESS CATALOG CARD NUMBER: 73-79280

Printed in The Netherlands by Mouton & Co., The Hague

ACKNOWLEDGEMENTS

For their assistance in providing copies of articles and in allowing me to make full use of their facilities, I would like to thank the librarian and staff of the University Library in Cambridge, without whose co-operation this study would not have been possible.

My warmest thanks go also to all the following who, by making available further material, answering queries, reading the manuscript and making helpful suggestions, aided and encouraged me in the completion of this work:

Prof. Quentin Bell, University of Sussex
Prof. Ulrich Broich, Ruhr University Bochum
Prof. Willi Erzgräber, Freiburg University
Dr. K. W. Gransden, University of Warwick
Prof. Frederick P. W. McDowell, University of Iowa
Prof. Reinhold Schiffer, Ruhr University Bochum
Prof. Wilfred Stone, Stanford University
Dr. Dieter Zeh, Frankfurt University

CONTENTS

CONTENTS

FOREWORD

> I strove with none, for none was worth my strife;
> Reason I loved, and, next to Reason, Doubt;
> I warmed both hands before the fire of life;
> And put it out.
>
> E. M. Forster[1]

When E. M. Forster died in June 1970, reports of his death and lengthy obituary notices (*The Times* went to the almost unprecedented length of devoting nearly a complete page to his obituary) appeared in the newspapers and journals of the English-speaking world and beyond. Characteristic of the journalistic encomiums that were published on this occasion was the measure of total agreement on the place of Forster in the world of English letters – "Until today anyone's list of the greatest living British novelists would have contained the name of E. M. Forster."[2] Although Forster had for several decades been reckoned among the 'elite' of British novelists, and in spite of the long obituary notices, not one of the writers claimed for him the distinction of being the 'greatest' living novelist. This is typical of the esoteric position of Forster within the framework of contemporary English literature; a position which would appear often to owe more to his personality than to his works. Indeed it is Forster the man, the thinker, the individual, who figures most largely in the posthumous tributes. In the first place he is seen as a "last great link with Edwardian England"[3]

[1] "Landor at Sea", *New Statesman and Nation*, 6.8.1938, p. 219.

[2] David Holloway, "E. M. Forster, influence on literature", *Daily Telegraph*, 8.6.1970, p. 10.

[3] Paul D. Zimmerman, "E. M. Forster (1879-1970)", *Newsweek*, 22.6.1970, p. 60; c.f. Willy Haas, "Ein Unsterblicher stirbt", *Die Welt*, 9.6.1970.

and, as such, out of tune with the "mass age which emerged from the world war and its immediate aftermath".[4]

More important in the general estimation of Forster as an influence is the acknowledgement made by the *Times* writer of his position as a "liberal moralist",[5] since this label introduces the two traits in Forster's make-up which, it would appear, account more than anything else for his unique powers of survival in an antagonistic world and for his continued position in the English intellectual scene from which he commanded respect for a period of over forty years. He was an active supporter of liberal values (rather than a mere survivor from the creeds of a past age) and a moralist in the sense that J. S. Mill, Matthew Arnold, and even D. H. Lawrence were moralists. Not that he was concerned with the maintenance of the standards of a clearly defined moral code, but rather that he was continually occupied with the classic concerns of the moralist: what is Goodness, the Good and the best of all Goods?[6] Such a view of Forster emphasises him as a man, as a personality rather than, in the first instance, as a writer; it is this view which will dictate the line of enquiry followed in this work.

Yet to emphasise the man Forster is, at first sight, to be faced with a paradox, for Forster, as a subject for biography, presents little of interest, in the sense that he did very little; born into a respectable middle-class family in the last quarter of the nineteenth century he had an unhappy and uneventful schooling at an average English public school. He then went up to Cambridge, where he spent his time as an undergraduate in a comparatively undistinguished manner. With the financial assistance of his great-aunt he was able to live the life of a comfortable man of letters with a private income until the outbreak of the First World War. During the war he had an uneventful period with the International Red Cross in Egypt, followed by some freelance journalism, nine months in India, perhaps the most eventful period of his life, as private secre-

---

[4] "Mr E. M. Forster, O.M.", *Times*, 8.6.1970, p. 10. Much earlier, in a review of *Abinger Harvest*, John Crowe Ransom wrote, "he has every perfect gift that the great writer needs except one: he was not born into the right age!" ("Gestures of Dissent", *Yale Review*, XXVI [1936-7], p. 181).

[5] *Ibid.*

[6] C.f. Basil Willey, *The English Moralists* (London, 1965), p. 13.

tary to a Maharajah, followed by twenty years of reviewing, broadcasting, and occasional writing. World War II brought a second
period of increased activity in these same fields, and the remaining
twenty-five years of his life were spent in semi-retirement as a
quasi-Grand Old Man of English letters in the comfort and seclusion of King's College Cambridge. The emphasis on Forster the
man is not a way of claiming that his outward biography leads us
to a more intimate understanding of Forster the writer or of his
works. The emphasis on the individual Forster is an emphasis on
the 'inner life', to use his own terminology, a turning of the focus
on the mental and intellectual development of a man who may be
taken as representative both of an age and of a particular outlook
on life. An acquaintance with the development, modification, and
change of Forster's ideas and beliefs leads us to a more complete
understanding of the particular problems that faced him as a writer
and certainly account for his popularity and influence, particularly
on the writers who came to the fore in the forties and fifties of this
century.

To the writer who chooses to concentrate upon Forster from
this point of view there emerge two central and inter-related problems. The first and, because specialised, lesser problem, is the sudden
cessation of Forster's activity as a novelist after *A Passage to India*.
The central problem, whose solution will provide the answer to the
first, is the question as to the ability of liberalism, founded upon
social stability and the middle-class ethos of Victorian and Edwardian England, to survive the onslaughts brought about by the collapse
of the social structure which nurtured it, and further, the survival
of humanism, as a belief in the essential goodness and necessary
centrality of man, in the face of two cataclysmic catastrophes in
1914 and 1939. Forster's 'inner biography' would appear to provide
clues to the answering of these questions. For now, it may be sufficient to hint firstly at his mental resilience and adaptability, and at
a faith, which he himself has characterised as "a stiffening process,
a sort of mental starch",[7] in certain fundamental necessities which
centre upon the emotions *and* upon reason.

[7] *Two Cheers for Democracy* (London, 1951), p. 77.

By now the assertion that Forster was a liberal needs no further documentation. However, the very term 'Liberal' and the notion of liberalism are in themselves vague and can mean much or nothing depending on who uses the terms or of whom they used are. This can be seen from the *Daily Telegraph*'s obituary notice which refers to Forster's "wishywashy Leftish liberalism"[8] and Forster's own remark in 1955: "...if I say I am a liberal the answer is: 'You can't be; only Socialists and Tories.'"[9]

On the one hand it is clear that in using the term 'liberal' we are not refering to adherence to a specific political party, nor, necessarily, to their underlying beliefs. Yet, on the other hand, the term is rooted in a fundamentally political movement with its own roots in the nineteenth century and it is, as we shall see, just these roots which Forster has in common with those of his contemporaries who felt their allegiance to be political rather than philosophical. Lionel Trilling has expressed this double-sideness of the term as follows: "The word liberal is a word primarily of political import, but its political meaning defines itself by the quality of life it envisages, by the sentiments it desires to affirm."[10]

It is this express linking of political belief with a quality of life that brings us to Forster. Moreover, it is the view of liberalism, which Trilling puts forward, as a tendency rather than a body of doctrine,[11] that leads to the inherent vagueness and occasional weaknesses in quite a lot of what Forster, and his critics, have to say in this direction. Essentially, Forster's liberalism is concerned with the emotions and with the organisation of the emotions, in an atmosphere of freedom, into a clear expression of belief which may counteract the rootlessness and illiberalism of a later age.

In the study which follows, a particular theme has been followed which in its use of terminology, especially of the concept of 'reality', may be felt to be open to further charges of vagueness or looseness. Although this approach will be clarified at a later stage,[12] we may,

8 Holloway, *Daily Telegraph*, 8.6.1970, p. 10.

9 'A Letter', *Twentieth Century*, CLVII (1955), p. 99.

10 Lionel Trilling, *The Liberal Imagination* (1950) (London, 1961), p. xi.

11 *Ibid.*

12 See particularly chapter 4 below.

perhaps, attempt to explain it briefly here. Forster inherited a tradition which, on the one hand, looked back to the strictly rational liberalism of Mill, with its insistence on freedom, individuality, and community feeling relieved by a somewhat euphoric belief in the imagination and its products, and, on the other hand, to Arnold's stolidly Victorian expression of a desire for human perfection rooted in culture. Added to this tradition was the discovery, made at Cambridge, of a concept of the Good as that which is centered in personal relations and aesthetic satisfaction. The union of tradition with Moore/Bloomsbury ethics provided Forster with a vision of what we shall call the Ideal. Elements and facets of this ideal are to be found in varying degrees of intensity in each of Forster's five novels, but in each case the ideal comes into conflict with circumstances or ways of life which are opposed to it. Even on the evidence of the novels alone, we could form the hypothesis that Forster was testing his ideal against the background of life and society as he had encountered them, and was, as a result, forced into compromising the ideal in order to preserve it. That which opposes the ideal in this way we have called, following Forster's own terminology, 'reality'; reality, that is, seen as everyday life, the experience of life. However, the problem arises when we are confronted, in Forster's own writings, by a second concept of reality as the 'ultimate reality', that which is truly real, lasting. In other words, our approach is centered upon three concepts: an untried, hypothetical Ideal, reality as experience which tests the ideal and modifies it into a valid and acceptable postulate, and finally reality as that to which adherence to the Ideal will aim. This second 'reality' may also be seen, as Forster in fact sometimes does see it, as closely related to the more troublesome term, 'truth'.

It is this theme together with the already mentioned concern with Forster the man rather than with Forster the novelist that has led us to pay particular attention to that large body of uncollected articles, reviews, and letters which are to be found scattered through the newspapers and periodicals of sixty years. For it is this material in particular that, together with some of the items in *Abinger Harvest*, provides us with insight into Forster's pre-occupations during the fourteen year period between his fourth and last novels, and thus forms the evidence on which any solution of the problem of his renunciation of fiction must be based.[13] In addition, a consideration of this material[14] provides us with a consistent and continuous view of Forster as an active and public man of letters over a period of sixty years. The most important reason for paying such attention to Forster's non-fiction is, however, that here one may justifiably claim to be able to detect what has been called the 'Forsterian voice'. That is, without the considerable, carefully documented evidence of the non-fictional writings, we would not be in a position to detect similar manifestations of Forster's own voice in the novels. The claims that will be made that certain characters in the novels are projections of Forster's own concerns, or that events and judgements made within a fictional framework are closely related to or identical with the author's opinions are made only after Forster's position has been established on the basis of his articles, reviews, and letters.[15]

Sufficient has now been pointed out about the approach to Forster and the material studied to enable us to proceed a step further and indicate the extent to which we believe that this study departs from others and may be regarded as a valid contribution to Forster criticism. Of the seventeen full-length studies of Forster

[13] The essays in *Pharos and Pharillon* and Forster's history of Alexandria are by no means as revealing, although they do give indications of an interest in the early history of Christianity and Islam. This is, however, a concern dictated more by milieu than by personal interest. Forster's previously unpublished novel, *Maurice*, appeared after this study had been completed. However, it adds little to the picture we have formed of Forster's concerns in the period 1910-1924 and will be referred to at the relevant time.

[14] It should be noted that the uncollected items far outnumber those which were collected in Forster's lifetime. Compared to 60 items in *Abinger Harvest* and a further 69 in *Two Cheers*, we have had access to a further 348 miscellaneous pieces which have formed the foundation of this study.

[15] In the course of this study no mention will be made of Forster's short stories. This does not mean that the theme of ideal and reality may not be traced in them, for several of the stories (e.g. "Albergo Empedocle" or "The Road from Colonus") are very clearly related to this main concern of Forster's. Rather the focus has been directed upon Forster's non-fiction in order to establish his preoccupations and then the novels, as the most considerable part of Forster's opus, have been re-examined in the light of these findings. A further chapter on the short stories would not have brought any new material or ideas to light, and would thus have only unnecessarily lengthened an already lengthy work.

written between 1938 and 1969, we may immediately set aside those
written simply as contributions to series of such works.[16] The first
full-length study of Forster, by his contemperary and fellow-novel-
ist Rose Macaulay,[17] was concerned almost exclusively with the
novels and again with one aspect of them, namely that of social
comedy, and it was not until Wilfred Stone's monumental study
of 1966 that any serious attempt was made to integrate the non-
fiction into a total view of Forster,[18] yet even here the chapters on
the 1910-1924 period and the post-*Passage to India* years remain
unsatisfactory, since little more is done than to present a survey of
what Forster was doing without integrating this into the over-all
thesis of the study as a whole. Of the intervening seven studies of
Forster,[19] only two stand out as attempting to present a coherent
and integrated account of the writer and his pre-occupations:
Lionel Trilling's, by now classic, study (1944), which like his earlier
study of Matthew Arnold (1939) betrays the critic's sympathies and
his identification of himself with the concerns of his subject by concentrating on a moral approach to Forster as fellow liberal; and
Frederick Crews' study (1962) of the nineteenth century sources of
Forster's attitudes and the revelation of his sceptical humanism
throughout the novels. After the formidable trio of Trilling, Crews,
and Stone, it seemed that there was really little more to be said on
the subject of the novels alone; one did not expect further revelations in the form of lengthy interpretations or investigations of
Forster's style and technique and yet four further studies appeared
during the next two years,[20] three of which remain undistinguished

[16] C.f. Rex Warner, *E. M. Forster* (London, 1950); K. W. Gransden, *E. M.
Forster* (London, 1962); Harry T. Moore, *E. M. Forster* (New York, 1965).
[17] Rose Macaulay, *The Writings of E. M. Forster* (London, 1938).
[18] Wilfred Stone, *The Cave and the Mountain* (Stanford and London, 1966).
[19] Lionel Trilling, *E. M. Forster* (London, 1944); James McConkey, *The
Novels of E. M. Forster* (Ithaca, 1957); H. J. Oliver, *The Art of E. M. Forster*
(Melbourne, 1960); J. B. Beer, *The Achievement of E. M. Forster* (London,
1962); Frederick C. Crews, *E. M. Forster: The Perils of Humanism* (London
and Princeton, 1962); Alan Wilde, *Art and Order. A Study of E. M. Forster*
(New York, 1964); David Shusterman, *The Quest for Certitude in E. M.
Forster's Fiction* (Bloomington, 1965).
[20] Norman Kelvin, *E. M. Forster* (Carbondale, 1967); George H. Thomson,
The Fiction of E. M. Forster (Detroit, 1967); Laurence Brander, *E. M. Forster:*

and the fourth, by Professor Thomson, concerns itself with an archetypal study of the novels.

In contrast to the continual interest in Forster among English and American critics, the bulk of Forster studies in the German-speaking countries has, perhaps understandably, been small. Apart from the half-dozen or so articles which are quoted in the text of this study, mention should be made of the handful of doctoral dissertations which have appeared in Germany and Austria over the last twenty years.[21] In them, the interest is centered almost exclusively on Forster's fiction either as revealing directly his view of life or, by way of an examination of specific themes and techniques, as supplying an insight into certain personal attitudes of their author. Whereas earlier works (e.g. Junker, Jungel, and Postel) are in many ways unsatisfactory both in method and in the conclusions reached, Stebner's carefully documented study of the presentation of death in Forster's fiction is of greater relevance to our concern here. Stebner shows how the abrupt intrusion of death in the novels, by emphasising the reality of death opens the way to a presentation of the mystery of life. However, useful and interesting as this approach is, it still largely ignores Forster's very extensive non-fiction. A much more recent study, that of Dieter Zeh, although thematically related to this present work, in so far as Zeh is concerned with Forster's presentation of life and reality, approaches Forster's novels from a different angle. Here the focus is upon the structure of Forster's fiction and upon the relation between the complexity of these structures and Forster's attempt to understand reality in terms of meaningful relationships. Within the present context, such an approach to Forster by way of themes and techniques in the novels can only be of peripheral interest, since here we are concerned

---

A Critical Study (London, 1968); Denis Godfrey, *E. M. Forster's Other Kingdom* (London, 1968).
[21] See Renate Jungel, "Die Zeitstruktur in den Romanen E. M. Forsters", Diss., Graz, 1953; Rochus Junker, "Studien zur Romanwelt von E. M. Forster", Diss., Münster, 1949; Elisabeth Postel, "Symbol und Leitmotiv in den Romanen E. M. Forsters", Diss., Kiel, 1959; Gerhard Stebner, "Das Phänomen des Todes im Werke E. M. Forsters", Diss., Marburg, 1960; Dieter Zeh, "Studien zur Erzählkunst in den Romanen E. M. Forsters", Diss., Frankfurt, 1970.

with building up a framework of preoccupations within which the novels may be set in order to be seen as the fictional extension of a tradition of thought, behaviour, and attitudes which Forster embodied.

As early as 1965, that invaluable bibliographer of Forster criticism, Professor McDowell, suggested three lines which future works on Forster could profitably follow:

First, the critic should consider his subject from a well-defined approach so that aspects of Forster's work, difficult to search out in a general study, will be seen more clearly. Second, the critic must also attempt to assimilate the vast body of existing commentary and build upon that rather than repeat, without acknowledgement, points previously made by others. He must determine, in short, those matters on which there is agreement and those cruxes upon which opinion is still divided. Third, the critic should use, for the illumination they provide, the uncollected essays and, as they become available, previously unpublished materials.[22]

The present study of Forster has been an attempt to work along these lines. The approach to Forster and his writings and the uses of the material have been delineated above; the novels although of necessity centrally placed in this study are seen continually both in the light of Forster's statements and pre-occupations elsewhere and are discussed at length only where there is seen to be relevance to the over-all theme of the work. Forster criticism is consulted at every point along the way, and, particularly in the case of the last two novels, a survey is given of critical points of view to indicate the wide spectrum of critical views which exist in spite of apparent general agreement of the position and concerns of Forster himself.

Although the aims motivating this study have been set out above, one could still legitimately ask whether the problem discussed here is central to the concerns of the literary critic or literary historian, and, further, whether this study is thought to represent a radically new approach leading to correspondingly new findings, or rather

[22] Frederick P. W. McDowell, "Forster's Most Recent Critics", *English Literature in Transition*, VIII (1965), p. 49. Prof. McDowell's own book on Forster, which appeared in 1969, appears to have been somewhat restricted by the limitations imposed upon it as one of a well-known series of introductory studies of English authors. C.f. *E. M. Forster*, Twayne's English Authors Series (New York 1969).

does it simply bring to light new details to fill out a well-known frame. In so far as any writer and any work of literature is formed by the age in which he lives and the work is produced, such an approach is valid for both the critic and the historian of literature. Moreover, where, as will be shown in Forster's case, there exists a clear relation between historical events, personal experience, and literary development, such an approach is not only valid, but necessary for a fuller elucidation of the writings of the author in question. As to the findings of this study, the final judgement as to their value rests, naturally, with the reader. We would claim that certain areas of Forster's work are illuminated more clearly than they have been in the past, and that the suspicions and intuitive judgements of other critics have been substantiated or, on the other hand, shown to be false. That which is of value is the picture which emerges of Forster, both as consistent propagator of certain views and values, and as ever aware of the necessity to maintain a relevant relation between his values and the demand of the age.

MILL, ARNOLD, AND THE LIBERAL TRADITION

I too am a Victorian.

E. M. Forster[1]

1

English Liberalism, which developed out of the philosophical speculations of the 17th and 18th centuries, emerged as a political and social doctrine in the early 19th century, closely related to the Utilitarian speculations of Bentham and James Mill, and to the economic and social theories of Ricardo and Malthus. Essentially, liberalism was a libertarian doctrine which advocated the maximum freedom of individuals to think, believe, express and discuss views, to organise in parties, to find employment, buy and sell, to choose their rulers and their form of government.[2] Basic to such a creed was the belief in man's reasonableness and innate goodness, and thus in man's perfectability, which was to be achieved by means of another liberal essential: education. Liberalism saw as its enemies conformity to custom and tradition, institutions and social habit. In its granting centrality to the individual, it naturally insisted, in economic and political affairs, on the principle of *laissez-faire*. When early in the 20th century liberalism as a political force collapsed and its final supporters espoused socialism as the logical

---

[1] "Portraits from Memory", *Listener*, 24.7.1952, p. 142.
[2] C.f. "Liberalism by the middle of the century, came to mean the completest individual freedom for every citizen who could contribute to the national wealth." (David Thomson, *England in the Nineteenth Century* [Harmondsworth, 1950], p. 226.)

development of liberalism as a political philosophy, this principle became dispensable. Prof. Harold Laski, who belongs to this transition phase of English Liberal-Socialism, has described at length both the history and the essential tenets of liberalism, seeing it as "a by-product of the effort of the middle class to win its place in the sun".[3] As such it becomes not only an expression of middle class optimism, but also runs the danger of turning into a vehicle for middle class complacency; at its weakest this manifests itself as an "inability to realise that great possessions mean power over men and women as well as over things".[4] That is to say that liberalism is not only rooted in a specific class, but owes much to that class's freedom from economic worry, which expresses itself in an inability to understand or fully comprehend the plight of those in a less fortunate position.[5] On the other hand, Liberalism had a number of positive virtues which one cannot overlook; as a political and historical force it furthered international communication, religious toleration, universal suffrage and established parliamentarianism as a rule rather than merely a description of the *status quo*.[6] Under the influence of its more enlightened and more cultivated practioners, liberalism not only developed a positive concept of the sanctions and duties of the state, but became almost synonymous with the spread of education and the insistence on culture as an ideal.

This tradition has been further defined as centering on "the belief that moral independence in privileged individuals may help to secure for a changing community some measure of social justice and peace",[7] and further as speaking for "a recurrent need for the criticism of institutions and collectivities from the standpoint of the claims of human wholeness".[8] Both comments place a strong

[3] Harold J. Laski, *The Rise of European Liberalism* (1936) (London, 1962), p. 167.
[4] Laski, p. 168.
[5] C.f. the oft quoted opening of chapter 6 of *Howards End*.
[6] Laski, pp. 154-6.
[7] G. S. Fraser, *The Modern Writer and his World* (1953) (Harmondsworth, 1964), p. 95; c.f. Frederick C. Crews, *E. M. Forster: The Perils of Humanism* (London & Princeton, 1962), pp. 5-6.
[8] Malcolm Bradbury, "Two Passages to India: Forster as Victorian and

emphasis on the moral tone of liberalism and the tasks which it set itself. It is seen as a belief associated with a particular class ('privileged individuals') set, however, against conventional authority ('institutions and collectivities') in the name of individualism and for the sake of freedom, justice, and peace.

2

It has been suggested that Forster's liberalism is to be seen as an offshoot from the main 19th century tradition, and that it develops particularly out of J. S. Mill's critique of Jeremy Bentham.[9] From the beginning of Mill's essay there would appear to be a clear similarity between Mill's view of Bentham and Forster himself. Bentham is described not only as a man of great "moral sensibility" but also as staunchly opposed to fraudulent practices and abuses of authority.[10] In so far as Forster is preoccupied with the preservation of values and the nature of the good, we may insist on his moral sensibility, and his resolute stand for honest, straightforward dealing and thinking makes him an enemy of fraud and, to use his own synonym, "muddle".

In his essay on Bentham, Mill develops criteria both for the practising philosopher and moralist, and for the analysis of human behaviour. He begins by warning of the danger of generalities, and makes the very same distinction between detail and complex whole that was to play an important rôle in Forster's *Howards End*.

It is a sound maxim, and one which all close thinkers have felt (...) that error lurks in generalities: that the human mind is not capable of embracing a complex whole, until it has surveyed and catalogued the parts of which that whole is made up.[11]

Modern", *Aspects of E. M. Forster*, ed. Oliver Stallybrass (London, 1969), p. 124.

[9] C.f. Crews, pp. 24-5.

[10] *Mill on Bentham and Coleridge*, ed. F. R. Leavis (London, 1950), p. 45.

[11] *Mill on Bentham and Colerigde*, p. 49; c.f. "It is possible to see modern life steadily and see it whole, and she had chosen to see it whole." – *Howards End*, Penguin edition (Harmondsworth, 1953), p. 152.

Towards the end of his critique, Mill turns his attention to two abstractions which, for Forster, were to be of great importance: imagination and morality. The value which Mill places upon the imagination is most clearly understood against the background of his notorious upbringing. It is that element which provides the alluring escape from the dull world of fact and utilitarian learning that Dickens was so devastatingly to satirize in *Hard Times*. It is Mill's realization that man needs poetry as a source of inward joy and happiness, without which he would have remained a severe intellectual, that allies him to the artist-moralist Forster.[12]

The Imagination ... that which enables us, by a voluntary effort, to conceive the absent as if it were present, the imaginary as if it were real, and to clothe it in the feelings which, if it were indeed real, it would bring along with it. This is the power by which one human being enters into the mind and circumstances of another.[13]

When Mill, in the last sentence, sees the imagination as that which enables one man to understand and appreciate another, we are brought nearer to one of the central themes of all Forster's writings: the supremacy of personal relations.

Whereas Forster himself tends to be reticent on direct theoretical questions of morality, a number of critics have made use of the term 'Utilitarian' in their accounts of his position, either hinting at his possible attraction to Mill's modification of Utilitarianism, or at his basic similarity to Mill.[14] Later in the Bentham essay, Mill begins his discussion of morality by emphasising the relation between the individual and the society of other individuals in which he lives.

Morality consists of two parts. One of these is self-education; the training of the human-being himself, of his affections and will ... The other and co-equal part, the regulation of his outward actions, must be altogether

[12] See further: Noel Annan, "John Stuart Mill", *The English Mind*, ed. Hugh Sykes-Davies and George Watson (Cambridge, 1964), pp. 222-224.
[13] *Mill on...*, pp. 61-2.
[14] C.f. Frederick P. W. McDowell, *E. M. Forster* (New York, 1969), p. 19; Crews, *E. M. Forster: The Perils of Humanism*, p. 116 note; Peter Ault, "Aspects of E. M. Forster", *Dublin Review*, October 1946, pp. 112-3 & 128; Frederick J. Hoffmann, "*Howards End* and the Bogey of Progress", *Modern Fiction Studies*, VII (1961), p. 244.

halting and imperfect without the first: for how can we judge in what manner many an action will affect even the worldly interests of ourselves or others, unless we take in, as part of the question, its influence on the regulation of our, of their, affections and desires?[15]

Whereas the first part of the above quotation reminds one of the principles of Victorian public-school education to be lampooned by Forster later in his "Notes on the English Character", the second part, with its implied acceptance of the necessity for successful human relationships, brings us nearer, in some respects, to Forster's own position. Yet, although elsewhere Mill appears to share much of Forster's insistence on the individual,[16] he seldom divorces individual action or virtue from the total sum of community feeling and communal well-being:

The deeply-rooted conception which every individual even now has of himself as a social being, tends to make him feel it one of his natural wants that there should be harmony between his feelings and aims and those of his fellow creatures (...) This conviction is the ultimate sanction of the greatest happiness morality.[17]

It is questionable to what extent Forster shares Mill's view of man as a social being when Mill discusses this in terms of a harmony of feelings and of aims between man and his fellows. Certainly Forster affirms his "belief in the individual, and in his duty to create, and to understand, and to contact other individuals".[18] Yet, on the other hand, the way in which this belief is most often stated is as belief in an unavoidable clash of interests between the individual and the community. This latter is seen either in the form 'public life',[19] or, more clearly antithetical to Mill, as a community of non-like-minded people, or 'the herd'.

We are in a muddle. We veer from one side of human nature to the other:

[15] *Mill on...*, p. 71.
[16] Mill, *Utilitarianism, Liberty and Representative Government* (London, 1964), p. 17.
[17] Mill, p. 31.
[18] "A Letter", *Twentieth Century*, CLVII (Feb. 1955), p. 99. The punctuation has been altered according to Forster's letter in the same volume of the periodical (p. 453).
[19] "There seems to be a profound division between our private and our public outlook." ("Notes on the Way", *Time and Tide*, 2.11.1935, p. 1571).

now we feel that we are individuals, whose duty it is to create a private heaven; and now we feel we ought to sink our individuality in something larger than ourselves – something we can only partially like and partially understand.

The conviction that sometimes comes to the solitary individual that his solitude will give him something finer and greater than he can get when he merges in the multitude.[20]

Forster thus diverges from Mill in his awareness of an inevitable conflict of interests between the individual and society, but is close to Mill when he focusses his distrust on the community organised in the form of the State.

In attempting to summarise that part of Mill's writing relevant to a discussion of influence or tradition, one might suggest that Mill's insistence on individual sensitivity and reason, coupled with a willingness to submit to the visionary influence of the imagination, are an obvious starting point for a comparison with Forster, and that Mill's continual championing of the individual and his freedom comes closest to the public concerns of Forster as an active, even though unwilling moralist.[21]

3

Although much has been made by the critics of Forster's well-known statement, "I belong to the fag-end of Victorian liberalism",[22] the attempts to delineate this liberalism and its tradition have often tended to blind one to the particular representative of Victorian

[20] "The Ivory Tower", *Atlantic Monthly*, CLXIII (Jan. 1939), pp. 53 & 56.
[21] See, for example, Forster's public efforts on the part of the individual in the cases of censorship and homosexuality: "The New Censorship", *Nation and Athenaeum*, 8.9.1928, p. 726; "The Censorship of Books", *Nineteenth Century and after*, CV (1929), pp. 444-5; "Mr D. H. Lawrence and Lord Brentford", *Nation and Athenaeum*, 11.1.1930, p. 509; "Society and the Homosexual. A Magistrate's Figures", *New Statesman and Nation*, 31.10.1953, pp. 508-9; "The Swindon Classics", *Observer*, 11.3.1956, p. 17; *Report from the Select Committee on Obscene Publications*, London (HMSO) 1958; "Wolfenden Report", *Times*, 9.5.1958, p. 13; "The Consett Case", *Times* 11.12.1959.
[22] "The Challenge of Our Time", *Two Cheers for Democracy* (London, 1951), p. 67.

liberalism who seems most clearly to be Forster's predecessor: Matthew Arnold.[23] Nor has much notice been taken of Forster's own placing of Arnold, both within the 19th century tradition, and in his relevance to Forster's own attitudes.[24]

In his later years, Forster finds himself both an admirer of, and a sympathizer with Arnold. In a 1949 interview Forster couples Arnold with George Eliot as being "the most civilized of the Victorians",[25] and, more explicitly, in his broadcast talk on William Arnold, Forster claims affinity with Matthew Arnold.

Matthew Arnold is of all the Victorians most to my taste: a great poet, a civilized citizen, and a prophet who has managed to project himself into our present troubles, so that when we read him now he seems to be in the room.[26]

In both statements one is aware of the emphasis on "civilized", a term which obviously bears a close relation to Arnold's concept of 'culture', and, indeed, it is probably Arnold's *Culture and Anarchy* which has the fullest relevance to Forster and the liberal tradition.

Concluding his introduction to this book, Arnold writes: "I am a Liberal, yet I am a Liberal tempered by experience, reflection, and renouncement, and I am, above all, a believer in culture."[27]

From this modified standpoint, Arnold goes on to develop his particular conception of culture and its relation to the society and

---

[23] See, however, Crews' suggestion that Forster's "Cambridge years had predisposed him to a general sympathy with the liberalism of Arnold", and McDowell's comment that Forster "is basically indebted to Arnold's liberalism", although McDowell qualifies this by characterising this strain of liberalism as insisting "upon the need for proportion in the spiritual life". C.f. Crews, p. 31; Frederick P. W. McDowell, "'The Mild Intellectual Light': Idea and Theme in *Howards End*", *PMLA*, LXXIV (1959), p. 454. See, too, J. Delbaere-Grant, "'Who shall inherit England?' A Comparison between *Howards End*, *Parade's End* and *Unconditional Surrender*", *English Studies*, L (1969), p. 101.

[24] Prof. Stone has commented here, "This is simply not true. See my 'E. M. Forster and Matthew Arnold', *Les Langues Modernes*, Jan-Feb. 1968, pp. 65-77; and the chapter on *Howards End* in Cave. It seems to me that many critics besides myself have seen this as central" (Letter to the author). Unfortunately, Stone's article has not become available to me, nor has it been possible to trace the references in other critics which he suggests. In a letter Prof. McDowell supports the author's view.

[25] C.f. Harvey Breit, *The Writer Observed* (Cleveland, 1956), p. 55.

[26] "William Arnold" (1944), *Two Cheers for Democracy*, p. 202.

[27] Arnold, *Culture and Anarchy*, ed. J. Dover Wilson (Cambridge, 1966), p. 41.

social systems of his own day. Although in many respects similar in tone and premise to much of Forster's thinking, Arnold's basic concept is alien to the humanist side of Forster's views. Arnold bases his entire argument upon the premise of man's perfectibility, seeing culture both as a means to perfection and as "a study of perfection". To this he adds the motto under which culture is to take up its task, "To make reason and the will of God prevail."[28] This has led Prof. Trilling to characterize Arnold's concept as "religion with the critical intellect superadded".[29] Forster, on the other hand, uses the term Art more often than culture, and sees art as having to do with order, and thus revealing a possible better world, and so having a definitely humanizing influence.[30]

In the closing pages of the first chapter of *Culture and Anarchy*, Arnold, insisting on the non-materialistic nature of culture and its emphasis upon the spread of reason, demonstrates his "democratic insight";[31] that is, his own very personal view of a democracy firmly based on the universalization of culture.

Those are the happy moments of humanity, ... those are the marking epochs of a people's life, ... those are the flowering times for literature and art and all the creative power of genius, when there is a *national* glow of life and thought, when the whole of society is in the fullest measure permeated by thought, sensible to beauty, intelligent and alive.[32]

For Arnold, that is, culture, defined as a combination of lively intelligence, intellectual curiosity, and aesthetic sensibility, is independent of class distinctions and thus a democratizing principle. To this we may compare the quieter, less utopian, but equally sincere statement which Forster made in a broadcast talk during the first year of the Second World War: "When a culture is genuinely national, it is capable, when the hour strikes, of becoming

[28] Arnold, p. 45.
[29] Lionel Trilling, *Matthew Arnold* (1939) (London, 1963), p. 266.
[30] C.f. "Notes on the Way", *Time and Tide*, 2.11.1935, p. 1572; 16.11.1935, p. 1658; "I have found by experience that the arts act as an antidote against our present troubles and also as a support to our common humanity" (*Two Cheers for Democracy*, p. 7; see too pp. 70-71 and 101).
[31] Trilling, p. 269.
[32] Arnold, *Culture and Anarchy*, p. 69; c.f. "Democracy", *Mixed Essays* (London, 1883), p. 29.

super-national, and contributing to the general good of humanity."[33]

While placing a high price and high hopes upon culture, Arnold, like Forster after him, is fully aware that that class of society which, by virtue of its growing power and expansion, is destined to be the leader of society and thus, too, the potential exponent and propagator of culture, the middle class, is itself in dire need of inner reform:

The middle classes, remaining as they are now, with their narrow, harsh, unintelligent spirit and culture, will almost certainly fail to mould or assimilate the masses below them, whose sympathies are at the present moment actually wider and more liberal than theirs.[34]

On several occasions Forster asserts his adherence to the middle class: "I am actually what my age and my upbringing have made me – a bourgeois."[35] For him, the typical qualities of the intelligent, Victorian middle class are contained in his characterization of the Thornton family: "pious, benevolent, industrious, serious, wealthy, shrewd",[36] and in his other remarks on his own class position, Forster always acknowledges his place within this nineteenth century tradition.[37] It is, however, from this very position of 'belonging', that Forster begins his career as a novelist, and in his early novels English middle-class life forms the setting for the action, and provides the characters and their attitudes.[38] Moreover, although it becomes clear that within the limits provided by Forster's first three novels he is working out a critique of the middle class, his sympathies remain with that class, or at least with its best representatives.[39]

---

[33] "Culture and Freedom" (1940), *Two Cheers for Democracy*, p. 45.
[34] Arnold, "Democracy", p. 30; c.f. "The bad civilization of the English middle class" ("The Future of Liberalism", *Irish Essays and Others* [London, 1883], p. 379).
[35] "Liberty in England", *Abinger Harvest* (London, 1965), p. 79.
[36] *Marianne Thornton* (London, 1956), p. 23.
[37] C.f. "Notes on the Way", *Time and Tide*, 23.11.1935, p. 1703; "A Presidential Address", *University Humanist Federation Bulletin*, Nr. 11 (Spring 1963), p. 2.
[38] C.f. Heinz-Joachim Müllenbrock, "Gesellschaftliche Thematik in E. M. Forsters Roman *Howards End*", *Anglia*, LXXXVII (1969), p. 371. The suggestion made in this passage, that Forster is not concerned in showing up the weaknesses of the society he portrays, does not seem to me acceptable; c.f. Frederick Grubb, *A Vision of Reality* (London, 1965), p. 168.
[39] C.f. Forster's "sympathies go out to the privileged middle classes... whose

Arnold and Forster share the belief that the middle classes are the holders of promise for the future, and this very belief, coupled as it is with the qualification 'intelligent middle class', gives them cause to criticise the state of affairs within this class in their own time. And yet in the forty years which separated Arnold's *Culture and Anarchy* (1869) and Forster's *Room with a View* (1908), the Liberal ideal would appear to have had little impact upon the class it was aiming to educate up to its own utopian view of the future.

A further concept which Arnold and Forster share is a view of civilization as, in Arnold's words, "the humanization of man in society".[40] This concept pervades much of Forster's work, culminating in the well-known definition in *What I Believe*, where civilization, being creative, is opposed to force which is destructive: "All the great creative actions, all the decent human relations, occur during the intervals when force has not managed to come to the front. These intervals are what matter... I call them 'civilization'!"[41] It is this common view of civilization having to do, not with material progress and well-being, but with human intercourse and culture, that emphasises Forster's adherence to a solid tradition and leads critics to see in his works "a sense of the continuity of Europe's history and heritage – an impression of civilization in the best sense, as an enquiring rather than a positing civilization".[42]

Arnold and Forster stand watch over the ever-increasing tendency to interpret civilization as having to do with material and industrial progress, and do not hesitate to condemn, to warn, or to advise. This task was, maybe, easier for Arnold, resting in the nineteenth century's faith in progress, than for Forster, who had to watch the disintegration of established civilization and culture brought about by two world wars. Arnold calls upon the Liberal politicians of his own day:

tolerance is in no way diminished by the need to fight for economic survival" (C. B. Cox, *The Free Spirit* [London, 1963], p. 78); see too, Wolfgang von Einsiedel, "Einbildungskraft des Herzens. Der Erzähler E. M. Forster", *Merkur*, IV (1950), p. 631; Delbaere-Garant, "'Who shall inherit England'...", p. 101.
[40] "The Future of Liberalism", *Irish Essays and Others*, p. 385.
[41] *Two Cheers for Democracy*, p. 80.
[42] Elaine H. Johnson, "The Intelligent Mr Forster", *Personalist*, XXXV (Jan. 1954), p. 51.

Since the failure here in civilization comes not from an insufficient care for political liberty and for trade, nor yet from an insufficient care for conduct, but from an insufficient care for intellect and knowledge and beauty and humane life, let Liberal statesmen despise and neglect for the cure of our present imperfection no means, whether of public schools, now wanting, or of the theatre, now left to itself and to chance, or of anything else which may powerfully conduce to the communication and propagation of real intelligence, and of real beauty, and of a life really humane.[43]

In this call, the three characteristic elements of the liberal tradition are clearly heard: education ('public schools'), culture ('the theatre'), and the demand for the best rather than the second-best (*'real* intelligence', *'real* beauty').

Forster's analysis and criticism of society is often on the same lines as Arnold's, but becomes increasingly pessimistic. He is clearly aware of the contrast between himself and Arnold, between twentieth century crises and Victorian calm.

Matthew Arnold's "bad days" are Halcyon when compared with our own. He belonged to an age which was concerned with problems of faith, doubt, and personal survival; he was worried by these, but the collapse of all civilization, so realistic for us, sounded in his ears like a distant and harmonious cataract.[44]

Many of Forster's analyses of the ills of contemporary civilization still echo Arnold's concern that forms of materialism will endanger its survival. Yet even here the criticisms develop from a warning against resignation to an acceptance of hopelessness.

We are all messed up together in a civilization which is going badly askew and which may... be skewing because of the institution of private property... Yet resignation is a mistake. (1934)

The growth of secrecy and the growth of the population seem to me the twin evils that may destroy civilization, and there is little one can do against either of them. (1959)[45]

Critics have shown themselves aware of Forster's dissatisfaction

---

[43] "The Future of Liberalism", p. 402.
[44] "Notes on the Way", *Time and Tide*, 9.6.1934, p. 723. C.f. "Omega and Alpha", *New Statesman and Nation*, 10.8.1940, p. 140; "Notes to 'Arctic Summer'", *Tribute to Benjamin Britten*, ed. Anthony Gishford (London, 1963), p. 55.
[45] "Notes on the Way", *Time and Tide*, 2.6.1934, p. 696; "Nuisance Value", *Spectator*, 2.10.1959, p. 431.

with civilization, but they tend to limit this awareness to the way Forster has presented this dissatisfaction in fictional terms, unrelated, that is, to the events of the world around him.[46] Yet it is just this practical analysis that links him to the urgent concerns of such Victorian liberals as Arnold. In the end it is Forster himself who supplies the clearest analysis of the different intellectual climate which separates him from, and yet, implicitly, joins him to the nineteenth century liberal ethos:

The nineteenth century had emphasised Progress. The early twentieth century, while not rejecting progress, felt itself to be more realistic if it approached progress through problems... Disillusion and distrust of problems began back in the twenties – the most clear-sighted decade of our own half-century... Today the situation foreseen by it has occurred. Problems have disappeared, or have retreated to platforms, and worries have taken their place.[47]

That, therefore, which most clearly separates Forster from Arnold may be seen to be the former's awareness of the hollowness of the Victorian notion of progress, which, on a higher level, was implicit in Arnold's affirmation of man's desire for perfection.

4

Liberalism's belief in the individual, and the high value set upon the individual conscience and the individual's right to freedom, inevitably leads to conflict when the attempt is made to balance this belief with a theory of the state. It is just this conflict, and the attempts to resolve it, which marks the difference between the two great Victorian Liberals, Mill and Arnold.

Mill's essay *On Liberty* (1859) has as its avowed object the attempt to define the limits of individual liberty in relation to collective authority, and the limits of the state's action, or interference with relation to the individual. This leads Mill to formulate the principle upon which he operates throughout the essay: "The sole

---

[46] C.f. J. B. Beer, *The Achievement of E. M. Forster* (London, 1963), p. 49; F. R. Leavis, "E. M. Forster", *The Common Pursuit* (London, 1952), p. 262.
[47] "This worrying world", *Listener*, 22.5.1958, p. 865.

end for which mankind are warranted, individually or collectively, in interfering with the liberty of action of any of their number, is self-protection."[48] After a discussion of various forms of liberty and a theoretical account of the ideal relations between the State and the individual, Mill concludes by allowing the State no higher value that that of the individuals composing it. He shows that State tyranny and authoritarianism is not only opposed to the freedom and happiness of the individual, but is directed in the end against the State itself: "A State which dwarfs its men, in order that they may be more docile instruments in its hands even for beneficial purposes – will find that with small men no great thing can really be accomplished."[49] This we may contrast with the conclusions which Arnold reaches in *Culture and Anarchy*. In Chapter 2, "Doing as one Likes", Arnold postulates the theory that his principle of light (reason) will reveal itself as opposed to individual anarchy, and sets up as a guide and control the principle of 'right reason': "The worship of the mere freedom to do as one likes is worship of machinery,... the really blessed thing is to like what right reason ordains, and to follow her authority."[50] Only two interpretations of "right reason" are possible: either it is a principle co-existent with the deity, or it is a collective human repository of shared wisdom whose laws, like those of God, are binding. Neither concept could have been acceptable to Mill. The contrast to Mill becomes even clearer in the conclusion which Arnold draws at the end of his book. Starting from the assumption that "without order there can be no society, and without society there can be no human perfection",[51] Arnold goes on to argue as though the end (human perfection) justified the means thereto. The means for Arnold are "a State in which law is authoritative and sovereign".[52]

From the beginning of his literary career, Forster espoused those

---

[48] Mill, *Utilitarianism etc.*, pp. 72-3.
[49] *Utilitarianism etc.*, p. 170. For criticisms of Mill's libertarian rhetoric see: Maurice Cowling, "Mill and Liberalism", *Mill. A Collection of Critical Essays*, ed. J. B. Schneewind (London, 1969), pp. 330-331.
[50] *Culture and Anarchy*, p. 82. Contrast this with the conclusion of Mill's "Liberty", where Mill apostrophises the authoritarian state as "the machine", p. 170.
[51] Arnold, *Culture and Anarchy*, p. 203.
[52] *Culture and Anarchy*, p. 204.

aspects of Liberalism which most suited his own temperament and stage of intellectual development: the belief in the beneficial effects of culture, in reason and in human affection. But his allegiance was at the same time divided between inherited liberal rationalism and those aspects of human life and experience which are often beyond the immediate grasp of the conventional Liberal mind.[53] That is to say that Forster, from the very beginning, takes up the position of the sceptic and critic from within. As with his relation to his own class, so too with his relation to their beliefs, Forster is both adherent and critic.[54]

At the very heart of Forster's liberalism is his belief in the importance of the individual, and his emphasis on personal relations. Characterising himself as an individualist,[55] Forster stresses the value he attaches to the individual rather than to group, community, race or nation: "I have no mystic faith in the people. I have in the individual."[56] However, to suggest that all other elements in Forster's thinking are subsidiary to this belief in the individual is too easy a simplification.[57] What does become central to much of what Forster writes is his conviction that the individual, in so far as he is cultivated, sensitive and liberal-minded, is essentially at disharmony with organised society and, in fact, threatened by it.[58] This feeling of the insecurity of the individual underlies much of the social comedy of the novels and reaches its climax in *A Passage to India*.[59]

---

[53] C.f. Stuart Hampshire, "Two Cheers for Mr Forster", *New York Review of Books*, 12.5.1966, p. 14.

[54] C.f. F. R. Leavis, "E. M. Forster", *The Common Pursuit*, p. 276; Wilfred Stone, *The Cave and the Mountain* (Stanford & London, 1966), p. 59.

[55] C.f. "The Challenge of our Time" (1946), *Two Cheers for Democracy*, p. 67.

[56] "The Challenge etc.", p. 68. C.f. Mr Fielding in *Passage*, "I believe in teaching people to be individuals, and to understand other individuals. It's the only thing I do believe in." – *Passage to India*, Penguin edition (Harmondsworth, 1952), p. 118.

[57] C.f. David Shusterman, *The Quest for Certitude in E. M. Forster's Fiction* (Bloomington, 1965), p. 12.

[58] C.f. "The Ivory Tower", *Atlantic Monthly*, CLXIII (Jan. 1939), p. 53; compare Mill, *On Liberty*, passim.

[59] "There is in all his novels the sadness that comes from realizing how much every individual, even the most brave, cheerful, and sensitive, is at the mercy of the stupidities of his group" (G. S. Fraser, *The Modern Writer and his World*, p. 94).

The increasing pressures which Forster feels are being brought to bear upon the integrity of the individual often lead him into the defensive; a position from which he emerges, rather like D. H. Lawrence, as a champion of an individualism which is already doomed.[60]

Forster's stand on the question of the relation between the State, or society, and the individual is based not only on his inherent belief in the individual, but also on his position as a writer. For Forster, the artist is someone who must both express his own personality,[61] and one who believes "in the development of human sensitiveness in directions away from the average citizen".[62] Society, on the other hand, "can only represent a fragment of the human spirit",[63] and thus there is an inevitable conflict between artist and authority, between the writer and the State. From this it becomes clear that Forster can only follow Mill in his opposition to the State's stifling of individual initiative and liberty.

If human nature does alter it will be because individuals manage to look at themselves in a new way... Every institution and vested interest is against such a search: organised religion, the State, the family in its economic aspect, have nothing to gain, and it is only when outward prohibitions weaken that it can proceed.[64]

Forster's insistence on freedom for the individual is not simply a love of freedom for its own sake, but a belief in liberty as "a condition which occurs in human society, and the more of it there is, the more will each individual be able to do and say and think as he likes".[65] Further, Liberty is important to Forster as having particular positive functions in relation to the other values of liberalism. Liberty matters to him because it guards those values which matter above all: beauty, civilization, and culture.[66] In addition, like Mill and unlike Arnold,[67] Forster insists on the necessity of freedom to

[60] C.f. Howard N. Doughty, "The Novels of E. M. Forster", *Bookman* (New York), Oct. 1932, p. 543.
[61] C.f. "A Conversation", *Spectator*, 13.8.1937, p. 269.
[62] "The Duty of Society to the Artist" (1942), *Two Cheers for Democracy*, p. 108.
[63] "The Duty of Society...," p. 103.
[64] *Aspects of the Novel* (London, 1960), p. 157.
[65] "Efficiency and Liberty – Great Britain", *Listener*, 9.3.1938, p. 497.
[66] C.f. Rose Macaulay, *The Writings of E. M. Forster* (London, 1938), p. 294.
[67] C.f. *Culture and Anarchy*, p. 61.

the individual so that he may criticise authority and abuses of power;[68] it is here that Forster's extreme distrust of the State, both as abstract concept and as repressive reality, becomes clear.

It seems indeed likely that in the immediate future Englishmen will have to put up with less liberty of action. But all the more reason that they should jealously guard their liberty of thought and speech and while enduring the power of the State should never adore it. *The State is like death. It has to be*. And some civilizations have worshipped death.[69]

It is this particular view of the State as actively opposed to the interests of the individual that is a main preoccupation in much of Forster's writings during the ominous years of the nineteen-thirties.[70] And which, with increasing distrust and bitterness, may be found in his post-1945 essays as well.

There is a huge economic movement which has been taking the whole world, Great Britain included, from agriculture towards industrialism... It has meant organisation and plans and the boosting of the community. It has meant... the transference of power from the aristocrat to the bureaucrat and the manager and the technician. Perhaps it will mean democracy, but it has not meant it yet, and personally I hate it.[71]

The resourcefulness of Forster's liberalism is put to the test in finding possible solutions to the problem of the future of the individualist. Rather than revolting against the inhibitions of society, the characters in his novels tend to adapt themselves to conditions which, at first, seemed intolerable.[72] It has been suggested that for Forster individual conversion precedes social evolution.[73] In fact, Forster has himself pointed, somewhat wistfully, to a third possibility: a form of tolerant compromise between society and those

---

[68] C.f. Frederick P. W. McDowell, "E. M. Forster's conception of the critic", *Tennessee Studies in Literature*, X (1965), p. 96.

[69] "English Freedom", *Spectator*, 23.11.1934, p. 792 (my italics).

[70] C.f. "Seven Days' Hard", *Listener*, 14.3.1934.

[71] "English Prose between 1918 and 1939" (1944), *Two Cheers for Democracy*, p. 281. See too: "the secret which (Forster) shares with Dickinson... is a sense of the mystery of life, a hatred of all tabus and systems which would enforce a proscribed pattern" (W. H. Auden, "Lowes Dickinson", *Scrutiny*, III [Dec. 1934], p. 304).

[72] C.f. Crews, *E. M. Forster. The Perils of Humanism*, p. 4.

[73] C.f. C. Lacotte, "Études récentes sur E. M. Forster", *Études anglaises*, XX (1967), p. 428.

individuals who feel the need to opt out. The tone of the following comment is wistful, for Forster, as is implicit in the remarks we have already quoted, is aware that such a time can never come.

When the public and the private can be combined, and place can be found in the industrial and political landscapes for those symbols of personal retreat, Ivory Towers, the foundation of a New Humanity will have been laid.[74]

---

[74] "The Ivory Tower", p. 56.

2

MOORE, BLOOMSBURY, AND PERSONAL RELATIONS

It is not a popular creed – personal relations I mean.

E. M. Forster[1]

1

Nineteenth century liberalism provided Forster with the firm belief in liberty, culture and the supremacy of the individual, but Utilitarian morality was unable to transcend the world of social intercourse to point the way either to the emotions, or to the nature of supreme good. This was to be the revelation that Forster's Cambridge years at the turn of the century were to bring. Directly, or indirectly, this need was satisfied for him by the ethical propositions of G. E. Moore. J. M. Keynes, Forster's near contemporary at Cambridge, summarises what he calls Moore's religion:

The appropriate subjects of passionate contemplation and communion were a beloved person, beauty and truth, and one's prime objects in life were love, the creation and enjoyment of aesthetic experience and the pursuit of knowledge. Of these love came a long way first.[2]

It is not surprising that such ideals found ready listeners among the easily influenceable undergraduates of the first decade of this century, whom Keynes describes as being "at an age when our beliefs influenced our behaviour".[3] There is no reason to believe that Forster was not typical, and Leonard Woolf, another Cambridge

---

[1] Extract from an interview with K. Natwar-Singh in June 1962. *E. M. Forster: A Tribute*, ed. K. Natwar-Singh (New York, 1964), p. xii.
[2] John Maynard Keynes, *Two Memoirs* (London, 1949), p. 83.
[3] *Two Memoirs*, p. 81.

contemporary, lists Forster under those who "had been permanent-
ly innoculated with Moore and Moorism".[4] In his biography of
Lowes Dickinson, Forster writes of his own time at Cambridge:
"People and books reinforced one another, intelligence joined hands
with affection, speculation became a passion, and discussion was
made profound by love".[5]

Just this note of intelligence joining hands with affection may
prove to be an apt introduction to Moore's own speculations. One
of his chief contributions to modern ethics was his delineation of the
naturalistic fallacy, which he uses to confound Utilitarianism.
Moore uses the term 'naturalistic fallacy' to describe attempts on
the part of previous philosophers to deduce moral precepts from
theological, metaphysical or scientific premises. For him such attempts are fallacious "since one cannot argue from premises of one
logical type (i.e. descriptions) to conclusions of a different logical
type (i.e. prescriptions)".[6] Moore goes on to point out that even
were Mill's argumentation not fallacious, it must ultimately lead
to Egoism rather than to Naturalistic Hedonism or Utilitarianism.[7]
That is, Moore forces Mill to argue in favour of individual rather
than communal pleasure as the only thing desirable.[8]

It is, however, the last chapter, "The Ideal", which was the most
influential section of the whole of *Principia Ethica*, at least as far as
Bloomsbury was concerned.[9] In this chapter, Moore attempts to
answer the question, "What things are goods or ends in themselves?"[10] and proposes a comparative method to reach his answer.
A method which soon leads him to reject as ideals those things,
such as freedom, which are discovered to be mere means to good
and of no value in themselves.[11] Moore comes to the conclusion:

By far the most valuable things, which we know or can imagine, are

---

[4] Leonard Woolf, *Beginning Again* (London, 1964), p. 24; c.f. Crews, *E. M.
Forster. The Perils of Humanism*, p. 47.
[5] *Goldsworthy Lowes Dickinson* (1934) (London, 1962), p. 35.
[6] C.f. Richard H. Popkin and Avrum Stroll, *Philosophy* (London, 1969), p. 46.
[7] C.f. G. E. Moore, *Principia Ethica* (1903) (Cambridge, 1966), pp. 104-5.
[8] Thus Mill's 'greatest happiness morality' is modified in such a way that, with
the removal of the social principle, it becomes potentially acceptable to Forster.
[9] C.f. Stone, *The Cave and the Mountain*, p. 64.
[10] *Principia Ethica*, p. 184.
[11] *Principia*, p. 186.

certain states of consciousness, which may be roughly described as the pleasures of human intercourse and the enjoyment of beautiful objects.[12]

Moore goes one step further in his argument, to produce what is, in effect, the justification for a humanistic foundation for ethics. He proclaims that the fundamental truth of moral philosophy is that the *consciousness* of beauty is of infinitely greater value than beauty itself. Moore goes on, referring to the ideals ('goods') he has already established:

It is only for the sake of these things – in order that as much of them as possible may at some time exist – that anyone can be justified in performing any public or private duty... these complex wholes *themselves*... form the rational ultimate end of human action and the sole criterion of social progress.[13]

Thus little is left of the basis of Utilitarian morality. The place of the social principle as that which endorses human action has been taken by the twin 'goods' of personal affections and aesthetic enjoyments. These ideals are seen as including all the greatest goods that man can imagine, and so they supersede the notion that the greatest happiness of the greatest number is alone desirable.

Although Forster never read Moore,[14] and although he seems to have been somewhat of an outsider to the group of Moore's admirers at Cambridge,[15] there is little doubt that Moore's teaching had a strong influence upon him. David Garnett sees "the two fundamental tenets of *Principia Ethica* as underlying much of Forster's writing",[16] and Noel Annan expresses the nature of the influence as limited to Moore's "concern for clarity, his insistence on the importance of *states of mind* and that one must analyse *mean-*

---

[12] *Principia* p. 188.

[13] *Principia*, p. 189.

[14] C.f. "A Presidential Address", p. 4; Philip Toynbee, "E. M. Forster at Eighty", *Observer*, 28.12.1958, p. 10. Forster does note, however, that Henry James, at least, completely confused Forster and Moore when the former visited him at Ryde: "H. J. very kind. Laid his hand on my shoulder and said, 'Your name's Moore'" ("Henry James and the Young Men", *Listener*, 16.7. 1959, p. 103).

[15] C.f. Leonard Woolf, *Sowing* (London, 1960), pp. 170-171; J. M. Keynes, *Two Memoirs*, p. 81.

[16] David Garnett, "Forster and Bloomsbury", *Aspects of E. M. Forster*, ed. Oliver Stallybrass (London, 1969), p. 30.

ing".[17] If, however, we rephrase Moore's ideals – "the pleasures of human intercourse and the enjoyment of beautiful objects" – as a belief in love and personal relationships, and a belief in the value of art, we may find considerable support in Forster's writings for the wider implications of Garnett's comment.

The importance Forster attaches to love as an ideal has been subject to a considerable amount of strain and change, as we shall see later in this work. His fundamental position is contained in such statements as the following, from his history of Alexandria, where, referring to that city, he writes:

She did cling to the idea of love, and much... must be pardoned to those who maintain that the best thing on earth is likely to be the best in heaven.[18]

Or, more clearly, in relation to Forster's own position,

I myself am a sentimentalist who believes in the importance of love... I only believe that *it is important in itself* and that the desire to love and the desire to be loved are the twin anchor ropes which keep the human race human.[19]

Here the echo of Moore in the italicised phrase is clear.[20]

But for Forster love is too high and too inflexible an ideal and, from the early twenties on, it fades into the background to be supplanted by tolerance and affection. That which endures is personal relations, which Forster describes in his recollections of another Cambridge teacher, Edward Carpenter, as "the final reality".[21] His

---

[17] Noel Annan, "Books in General", *New Statesman and Nation*, 7.10.1944, p. 239.

[18] *Alexandria. A History and Guide* (1922) (New York, 1961), p. 84.

[19] "A Clash of Authority", *Listener*, 22.6.1944, p. 686 (my italics).

[20] What importance may be attached to such a belief is hinted at in a passage from *The Hill of Devi*:

"When I returned to England and he (the Maharajah) heard that I was worried because the post-war world of the twenties would not add up into sense, he sent me a message. 'Tell him', it ran, 'tell him from me to follow his heart and his mind will see everything clear.' The message as phrased is too facile: doors open up silliness at once. But to remember and respect and prefer the heart, to have the instinct which follows it wherever possible – what surer help than that could one have through life?!" – *The Hill of Devi* (1953) (Harmondsworth, 1965), p. 114.

[21] "Some Memories", *Edward Carpenter. In Appreciation*, ed. Gilbert Beith (London, 1931), p. 75.

belief in personal relations becomes almost the most constant element in his credo, together with his belief in liberty and his trust in the individual.[22]

Yet, as Forster grows older and the world he once knew disappears more and more into the oblivion of history and the mists of memory, his assertions of belief in personal relationships and human intercourse take on a resigned note. As when, expatiating sadly on the ugliness of tourism, Forster regrets the passing of "the personal approach, the individual adventure, the precious possibilities of friendship between visitor and visited".[23] Even so, the belief *is* reaffirmed, albeit in that particular prophetic tone that implies the distance of a possible time when the prophecy may come true.

It is only when personal contacts are established that the axis of our sad planet shifts and the stars shine through the ground-fog. And contacts are not easy to establish in a world that is dominated by far worse-isms than the touristic.[24]

Forster's remarks here make one aware of the pessimism which manifests itself increasingly in much of the writing of his last forty years. It is the pessimism of someone who has been granted a vision of the ideal, and a comprehension of the conditions under which the ideal may be realised, and then sees the promised time of realisation moving further out of his grasp and sight. Yet, beyond the immediate pessimism there is still a note of hope.[25]

Professor Kermode has written that "perhaps the *Principia* are never realizable except in novels";[26] a remark which both points to the possible inevitability of Forster's pessimism, and, secondly,

---

[22] C.f. "Contacts with other people are the most real thing he knows" (C. B. Cox, *The Free Spirit*, p. 80); c.f. Shusterman, *The Quest for Certitude in E. M. Forster's Fiction*, p. 210.

[23] "Tourism v. Thuggism", *Listener*, 17.1.1957, p. 124.

[24] Ibid., c.f. Natwar-Singh, ed., *E. M. Forster. A Tribute*, p. xii.

[25] C.f. "If 'logic' leads Mr Forster to pessimism, however, the profound interest of that passion is due to the fact that it springs from 'hope'. It is precisely out of his conviction of the value of human feelings and relations that he derives his continual sense of their frustration and vanity" (D. A. Traversi, "The Novels of E. M. Forster", *Arena* I [1937], pp. 30-31); c.f. F. R. Leavis, *The Common Pursuit*, p. 262.

[26] Frank Kermode, "Mr E. M. Forster as a Symbolist", *Forster* (Twentieth Century Views series), ed. Malcolm Bradbury (Englewood Cliffs, 1966), p. 94.

suggests ways in which the already noticed affinity between Moore and Forster found its expression in the works of the novelist with "the analogous aesthetic doctrine".[27] An examination of Forster's fiction limited to the attitude revealed towards personal relations discloses the disintegration of Forster's optimism and the development of a pessimism generated by frustration. Beginning with figures such as Mr Emerson in *Room with a View* ("he is kind to people because he loves them"),[28] one comes to Stephen Wonham in *The Longest Journey*, the most plainly human of the fictive embodiments of Forster's Moorism ("it wasn't a question of gentility and poverty – it was a question of two men").[29] Yet already in this novel, which works out in dramatic form a number of Forster's personal difficulties, Forster shows himself aware of the antagonists of such relationships: "Vulgarity ... had been the primal curse, the shoddy reticence that prevents man opening his heart to man, the power that makes against equality".[30] *Howards End* truly celebrates the ideal of personal relations; celebrates them for "personal intercourse, and that alone ... ever hints at a personality beyond our daily vision".[31] That is, personal relations become the means Forster sees as ideal in his constant search for what, for want of a better term, we may call the ultimate reality. It is only apt that it is Helen, the more impulsive, less rationally cautious of the two Schlegel sisters, who repeatedly insists on the reality of personal relations in comparison to the sham reality of the outer world: "I know that personal relations are the real life, for ever and ever".[32] In *Passage to India* a pessimistic tone concerning personal relations may first be heard. Although Fielding, the character nearest perhaps to Forster himself,[33] claims to believe in and be optimistic

---

[27] *Ibid.*; c.f. Donald J. Watt, "G. E. Moore and the Bloomsbury Group", *English Literature in Transition*, XII (1969), p. 127.

[28] *A Room with a View*, Penguin edition (Harmondsworth, 1955), p. 30.

[29] *The Longest Journey*, Penguin edition (Harmondsworth, 1960), p. 122.

[30] *The Longest Journey*, p. 211. In Mr Failing's differentiation between vulgarity and coareness, Forster gives us the essence of the conflict of the novel: between Rickie and Stephen, Sawston and Wiltshire.

[31] *Howards End*, Penguin edition (Harmondsworth, 1941), p. 77.

[32] *Howards End*, p. 27.

[33] Both Leavis and Glen Pedersen see in Fielding many of the characteristics of Forster's own liberal humanist position. C.f. Leavis, *The Common Pursuit*, p.

about personal relations,[34] he stands out alone against the arid background of the novel. The effect of the Marabar caves on both Mrs Moore and Adela (even after her recantation) is to reduce personal intercourse and human relationships to an almost petty insignificance; of Mrs Moore we read,

She felt increasingly (vision or nightmare) that though people are important the relations between them are not, and that in particular too much fuss has been made over marriage.[35]

As for Miss Quested, though her view is less visionary and more analytical, the effect is the same: "What is the use of personal relationships when everyone brings less and less to them?", or, "all these personal relationships we try to live by are temporary".[36]

Passage to India may thus be seen as the fictionalisation of Forster's resigned acceptance of a breakdown in personal relations as symptomatic of a changed world after the 1914-18 war. This resignation is apparent in much that he was to write in the subsequent years up to the beginning of the Second World War. Comments on human intercourse appear in his lectures on the novel, where Forster, going beyond the bounds of fiction and narrative technique, writes:

All history, all our experience, teaches us that no human relationship is constant, it is as unstable as the living beings who compose it...; if it is constant it is no longer a human relationship but a social habit.[37]

Seen within the context of Forster's earlier implicit trust in personal relations, this comment is characteristic of the new doubt, and can be seen as an attempt to find rational explanations for a failure which has been apprehended most strongly by the emotions. The attempt fails. Chapter 3 of *Aspects of the Novel* ends on the gloomy note of:

272; Glen Pedersen, "Forster's Symbolic Form", *Kenyon Review*, XXI (1959), p. 243. Even though Shusterman claims that Fielding is the true protagonist of the novel, the function of speaking with the Forsterian voice is claimed elsewhere for Professor Godbole, c.f. Shusterman, *The Quest for Certitude...*, p. 161; James McConkey, *The Novels of E. M. Forster* (Ithaca, 1957), p. 11.

[34] *Passage to India*, Penguin edition (Harmondsworth, 1936), pp. 62, 66 and 163.
[35] *Passage to India*, p. 134.
[36] *Passage to India*, pp. 193 and 257.
[37] *Aspects of the Novel*, p. 54.

We cannot understand each other, except in a rough and ready way; we cannot reveal ourselves, even when we want to; what we call intimacy is only a makeshift; perfect knowledge is an illusion.[38]

This is Forster's gentler, public voice, in private the disillusion is starker and more outspoken, and for many, perhaps, less 'Forsterian'. In a letter to T. E. Lawrence, dated 16th December 1929, he writes:

I think of a remark of mine which you once approved and which has become yours in my mind. It was about love, how over-rated and over-written it is, and how the relation one would like between people is a mixture of friendliness and lust. $F + L = \frac{L}{X}$ is the sort of thing I want you to work out, but of course have put the equation wrong. I think love has an absurd réclame: but this again may be my age. There's so much new to be said about human relationships now that the sac (sic) of lust has been dissected and been discovered to be such a small and innocuous reservoir.[39]

2

That the chief influence of Moore's *Principia Ethica* was on the various members of Bloomsbury, or Bloomsbury 'Group', is a well established fact.[40] Although, apparently, Forster does not regard himself as having belonged to the group,[41] both Gransden and Bell note larger areas of sympathy. Bell mentions that Forster was a founder member of the Memoir Club (founded 1920) together with Clive and Vanessa Bell, Lytton Strachey, Leonard and Virginia Woolf, Desmond and Molly Macarthy, Duncan Grant, Roger Fry

---

[38] *Aspects of the Novel*, p. 62.
[39] *Letters to T. E. Lawrence*, ed. A. W. Lawrence (London, 1962), p. 72. There would appear to be hints here to the unpublishable stories and unpublished novel that Lawrence mentions in a letter to Forster dated 8 September 1927. C.f. *The Letters of T. E. Lawrence*, ed. David Garnett (London, 1938), p. 537.
[40] C.f. J. K. Johnstone, *The Bloomsbury Group* (1954) (New York, 1963), pp. 20-45; Watt, "G. E. Moore and the Bloomsbury Group", p. 119 and passim.
[41] C.f. K. W. Gransden, "E. M. Forster at Eighty", *Encounter* XII (Jan. 1959), p. 77 note. Gransden mentions Forster's denial expressed in a letter to him, but goes on, "I still think he and Bloomsbury have certain things in common". In a letter to the present writer, Gransden expands this idea: "Clearly he *did* share many of their attitudes and backgrounds, yet clearly also – particularly in the 20's and after – he was increasingly aware of the limitations of B. – which Lawrence had pointed out to him forcibly". Gransden further suggests that *Passage* to a large extent repudiates Bloomsbury (the reference to D. H. Lawrence is not clear, unless Gransden is refering to an unpublished letter of Lawrence's or to some as yet unpublished remarks of Forster's).

and J. M. Keynes, but suggests that this list should not necessarily be seen as identical with membership of 'Bloomsbury'.[42] Forster is seen to differ from the other members of the group in "his essentially reverent and optimistic attitude", but ethically he was in agreement with them; aware, on the one hand of the irrationality of life, but convinced, on the other hand, of the necessity "of holding fast to reason, charity and good-sense".[43]

Bloomsbury has been seen to be, not merely a London reflection and expansion of a limited Cambridge ethos, but also a movement within an established tradition. And as such, its rationalistic and humanistic values may be seen as still relevant today, in the same way as some of the liberal values of the nineteenth century are relevant.[44] Furthermore, the social type which composed Bloomsbury was representative of that class, the middle class, and that section of that class, those with private incomes or, at least, those free from economic worries, to which Forster himself, and many of his fictional characters, belonged.[45] In his own 1929 note on Bloomsbury, Forster characterises its members as,

Essentially *gentlefolks*. Might occasionally open other people's letters, but wouldn't steal, bully, slander, blackmail, or resent generosity as some of their critics would, and have required a culture in harmony with their social position... Academic background, independent income... They are in the English tradition.[46]

[42] C.f. "The Macarthys and E. M. Forster would probably have said that while very close to Bloomsbury they were not exactly of it" (Quentin Bell, *Bloomsbury* [London, 1968], p. 14). In a letter of September 1968 to the present writer, Professor Bell reaffirms Forster's membership of the Memoir Club and states that *Marianne Thonton* contains material that was first read as a Memoir Club paper. For Forster's position on the edge of the Bloomsbury Group see too, Robert Lekachman, *The Age of Keynes* (1966), Penguin edition (Harmondsworth, 1969), p. 16.
[43] Bell, *Bloomsbury*, p. 106.
[44] C.f. Frederick P. W. McDowell, "Recent Books on Forster and Bloomsbury", *English Literature in Transition*, XII (1969), p. 140.
[45] C.f. "To be completely civilized, a man must be free from material cares, is a recurrent theme in Bloomsbury. We find it in Virginia Woolf as well as in E. M. Forster and the others" (Irma Rantavaara, *Virginia Woolf and Bloomsbury* [Helsinki, 1953], p. 51); see too, Bell, p. 117; Irma Rantavaara, "E. M. Forster ja Bloomsbury", *Valvoja*, Nr 6 (1951), pp. 257-261.
[46] "Bloomsbury, an early Note. February 1929", *Pawn*, Nr 3, November 1956, p. 10 (pages unnumbered).

These descriptions are, however, misleading in that they tend to give the impression of a homogeneous group with a unity of ideas. Bloomsbury was not only made up of novelists, several artists and art critics, an economist, scholars, an essayist and a publisher, but was in addition a mixture of "aristocratic ideals, social conscience and radical tendencies".[47] This, no doubt, accounts for the fact that its members have been seen both as representatives of socialism ("scribblers of the left"),[48] and, more accurately, as "detached from political engagement".[49] Essentially Bloomsbury was a group of intelligent, privileged, and creative people, doing their utmost to live out Moore's ethical and aesthetic ideals in an atmosphere which was in the world without being of it.[50] In this last respect they differ from Forster, who, while choosing to live very much in and with the world, finally finds his ideals becoming more and more unreal, more and more unrelated to the reality of experience.

Whatever criticisms have been made of Bloomsbury, even those critics for whom its ideals can hardly be congenial are aware of the value the group must have had.

They represent... the human tradition as it emerges from a period of "bourgeois" security... And it seems to me plain that this tradition really is, for all its weakness, the indispensable transmitter of something that humanity cannot afford to lose.[51]

And for Forster, whatever the value of the individuals who composed it, Bloomsbury was remarkable for being "the only genuine *movement* in English civilization".[52] He thus emerges on the fringes of a movement, indirectly influenced by the same teacher, sharing the same social background and privileges, but, at least in the realm of one of Moore's ideals, developing away from the group to a saddened but, perhaps, better-founded awareness of the world from which they had distanced themselves.

[47] Rantavaara, *Virginia Woolf and Bloomsbury*, p, 34.
[48] John Jewkes, *Ordeal by Planning* (London, 1948), p. 28 (quoted in Bell, p. 11).
[49] Stone, *The Cave and the Mountain*, p. 53.
[50] *Stone*, p. 43.
[51] Leavis, *The Common Pursuit*, p. 277.
[52] "Bloomsbury, an early Note".

GOD OR MAN: RELIGION AND HUMANISM

History reveals evolution, not progress.

E. M. Forster[1]

1

In the last chapter we saw how Moore in his ethical speculations added an aesthetic dimension to traditional liberal morality, and counteracted the arid rationality of Utilitarianism by placing the highest value upon an emotionally apprehendable principle. Moore, we noted,[2] hints too at a possible humanistic foundation for ethics. In this a final important element is added to Forster's legacy from the nineteenth century. The belief in man's innate goodness leads to the centrality, not only of the individual in discussions of society, but also of man in considerations of the universe and questions of faith and religious belief.

In the course of the Victorian period, a humanist attitude to life developed among the literate or intellectual members of society. This humanism was particularly concerned to obtain "recognition and acceptance of the human condition".[3] There is a clearly marked tradition of such thinking through the nineteenth century from Carlyle's concern for what the new industrial order had made for man, Ruskin's care for the human being in his wholeness, to

---

[1] "Mr Wells' Outline", *Athenaeum*, 19.11.1920, p. 690.
[2] C.f. p. 38 above.
[3] G. D. Klingopoulos, "Notes on the Victorian Scene", *Pelican Guide to English Literature*, vol VI (Harmondsworth, 1958), pp. 55-6.

William Morris' revolt against the materialism of modern civiliza-tion. Another tradition, emphasising an imaginative humanism, has its roots in Romanticism and is closest to Forster's concerns in the well-known affirmation of Keats, "I am certain of nothing but of the holiness of the heart's affection, and the truth of the Imagina-tion".[4]

The Victorian Age may be characterized as an age of constant doubt and collapse of belief in religious matters. Yet the rationalists and agnostics had their own faith, which formed the basis for a varying moral code, often as strict, narrow or prudish as that of their Christian contemporaries. Essentially, agnostic faith empha-sised those aspects of Christian ethics suggested by the command to 'love thy neighbour', while scrupulously rejecting all superhuman sanctions, Their teaching was that man should try

to do as well as possible what we can do best; to work for the improve-ment of the social organisation; to seek earnestly after truth and only to accept provisionally opinions one has not enquired into; to regard men as comrades in work and their freedom as a sacred thing: in fact to recog-nise the enormous and fearful difference between truth and falsehood, right and wrong, and how truth and right are to be got by free enquiry and the love of our comrades for their own sake and nobody else.[5]

Humanism thus expresses itself in a passionate search for truth, which may be found through the medium of human intercourse and human love.

That which distinguished the great Victorian agnostics from the doubters who attempted to create new systems, or objects, of faith to replace the old was their acceptance of uncertainty in religious matters. This acceptance enabled them to live confidently without a clear revelation and without an inclusive knowledge or solution to

---

[4] For an elaboration of the two traditions see: H. A. Smith, "Forster's Human-ism and the Nineteenth Century", *Forster. A Collection of Critical Essays*, pp. 110-114; For Forster's possible debt to Romanticism see: Ernest Beaumont, "Mr. Forster's Strange Mystics", *Dublin Review*, CCXXV (1951), p. 48; J. B. Beer, *The Achievement of E. M. Forster*, pp. 14-15.

[5] Statement by the Victorian geometer, W. K. Clifford, quoted in, Noel Annan, "Strands of Unbelief", *Ideas and Beliefs of the Victorians* (New York, 1949), p. 156. For a more detailed discussion of English agnostic thought in the nine-teenth century see: A. O. J. Cockshutt, *The Unbelievers* (London, 1964).

the problems upon which their doubts had originally grown.[6] Forster does not add new perspectives to the nineteenth century pattern, rather he is typical of it. A pious childhood is followed in early manhood by an unspectacular loss of faith. In his presidential address to the Cambridge Humanists in 1959, Forster discusses this development. He begins with an account of late Victorian family churchgoing and morning prayers. Forster states that he was a pious child and quotes a letter home from his preparatory school, dated Good Friday 1891, to support this statement.[7] He admits that it was Cambridge that finally put an end to a faith that had already dwindled somewhat during his public school days, and describes himself at eigtheen with devastating sincerity, "I went on to Cambridge (King's), immature, uninteresting and unphilosophic".[8] At Cambridge, there seem to have been two factors at work to effect the disappearance of Forster's religious beliefs: "my friendship with Hugh Meredith" and "the general spirit of questioning that is associated with the name of G. E. Moore".[9] Forster goes on to describe the disputes in King's which arose over the College Mission. The dispute soon led to a split in the Christian ranks, lampooned with zest by their opponents. It was this gay liveliness on the part of the disbelievers which seems to have attracted Forster finally, for, as he explains, this gaiety "connected disbelief with daily life".[10] Here we have an indication of the criterion which always comes into play when Forster has to consider the validity of a principle, ideal or question of belief. That which is important is the relevance of the ideal to life as Forster has experienced it. Moreover, the above remark is indicative of his whole attitude to religion, authority, and power: in so far as these are not connected with, but attempting to act upon and dictate, "daily life", Forster rejects them.[11]

[6] C.f. H. J. Blackham, *Humanism* (Harmondsworth, 1968), p. 125.
[7] "A Presidential Address", p. 3.
[8] *Ibid.*
[9] "A Presidential Address", p. 4.
[10] "A Presidential Address", p. 5.
[11] C.f. "I dread them (religions) all, without exception, as soon as they become powerful. All power corrupts. Absolute power which believes itself the instrument of absolute truth corrupts absolutely". – "A Letter", *Twentieth Century*, CLVII (February 1955), p. 100.

From his undergraduate days on, Forster remains a self-styled free-thinker,[12] continually challenging established religion, and questioning, gently, sincerely, yet pertinaciously, those aspects of the Christian religion which he finds unacceptable. This tendency is particularly noticeable in his writings on Church history in his history of Alexandria and in some of the essays collected in *Pharos and Pharillon*.[13]

Forster concludes his Presidential Address by discussing his attitude to biblical Christianity and the figure of Christ. "I am", he writes of the Gospel presentation of Christ, "unsympathetic towards it".[14] This somewhat naive statement becomes, however, of extreme importance, since, as Forster argues, believing as he does in the importance of personal relations, personal contact with an uncongenial person is difficult for him to conceive of: "I don't desire to meet Christ personally, and, since personal relations mean everything to me, this has helped me to cool off from Christianity."[15] This is, admittedly, a disappointing statement, an anti-climax, like so many of Forster's pronouncements on questions of belief. Yet it is no less sincerely meant than the weightier utterances of many of the critics, and demands attention as a personal conviction just because it is so naively expressed. It is the statement of a confident agnostic whose religious doubts and antipathies do not disturb him. For Forster, as too for the orthodox Protestant Christian, belief in Christ and in biblical Christianity implies a surrender of will and personal initiative – a renunciation which is clearly uncongenial to him. Therefore, Forster states his own particular form of alternative:

What I would like to do is to improve myself and to improve others in the delicate sense that has to be attached to the word improvement, and to be aware of the delicacy of others while they are improving me.

---

[12] C.f. Forster's letter, "On Remaining an Agnostic", *Listener*, 31.10.1957, p. 701. It is important to remember that, like many of the Victorian humanists, Forster was an agnostic rather than an atheist. C.f. "The existence of a divine order, though it cannot be tested, has never been disputed". – "Art for Art's Sake", *Two Cheers for Democracy*, p. 101.

[13] In his essay "Clement of Alexandria", Forster dismisses early Christianity as "unphilosophical and anti-social". – *Pharos and Pharillon* (1923) (London, 1967), p. 38.

[14] "A Presidential Address", p. 6.

[15] "A Presidential Address", p. 7.

Improve! – such a dull word but it includes more sensitiveness, more realisation of variety, and more capacity for adventure. He who is enamoured of improvement will never want to rest in the Lord.[16]

We have quoted at such length from Forster's address because it forms the most direct piece of information we have from Forster himself on his attitude to Christianity, with which we may measure the worth of the critics who have commented on Forster and religion.

Whether, with Lacotte, one sees Forster as merely rejecting the Victorian Anglican conscience,[17] or agrees with Crews in stating that he rejects Christianity itself,[18] it is clear that Forster, having spent many years in working out his own position, may hardly be accused of "spiritual muddledom".[19] What does appear astonishing, however, is Waggoner's assertion that Forster has a religious view of life.[20] One feels here the necessity of redefining 'religious' so that it may be made to bear a totally non-dogmatic, non-ecclesiastical and non-theological meaning. Such a view is clearly based upon those aspects of Forster's fiction – his over-imaginative fantasies and his interest in mysticism – which could suggest a concern for eternity or the suprahuman. Forster's writings may be said to exhibit traces of religion in the orthodox sense, only in so far as remnants of an evangelical vocabulary, biblical phrases, and an occasional Anglican intonation may be detected.[21]

---

[16] "A Presidential Address", p. 8. One can note here an echo of Arnold's belief in human perfectibility (*Culture and Anarchy*, pp. 45-49), although Forster and Arnold would not have agreed on questions of religious belief.

[17] Lacotte, "Études récentes sur E. M. Forster", p. 428.

[18] Crews, *E. M. Forster. The Perils of Humanism*, p. 16. Crews suggests that the rejection is based on the fact that Forster cannot accept Christianity as a moral system.

[19] "It may well be that the state of 'spiritual muddledom' attributed to Mrs Moore is a projection into a created character of a state of which the author is aware in himself" (Beaumont, "Mr E. M. Forster's Strange Mystics", p. 50).

[20] Forster's novels "suggest an essentially religious view of life. They suggest the seed of perspectives that will carry us beyond convention, beyond personal and individual instincts, desires, and ideas, beyond worldliness and subjectivity" (Hyatt Howe Waggoner, "Notes on the use of Coincidence in the Novels of E. M. Forster", *Forster. A Collection of Critical Essays*, p. 81); c.f. Crews, p. 14.

[21] Christian critics have tended to try to see Forster as one who is much nearer to orthodox belief than he is willing to admit. C.f. Ault, "Aspects of E. M. Forster", p. 113. The Christian irritation caused by Forster's failure to admit

What in fact takes the place of revelation, salvationism and other aspects of Christian teaching in Forster's thought and writing is a concentration on the Christian virtue of brotherly love, or the liberal belief in man's goodness, coupled with Moore's elevation of personal relations to the position of a good in itself.[22] Translated into active terms, this becomes for Forster, as too for the Victorian humanists, a concern for the "humanization of man in society".[23]

2

Humanism as an alternative to Christianity and as an expression of agnosticism has often run the danger of being vague and difficult to define. This need not be the case with Forster, whose humanism rests on his almost unshakeable belief in the individual and his potentialities. Humanism has been defined as resting upon "an assumption that man is on his own and this life is all and an assumption of responsibility for one's own life and for the life of mankind".[24] Blackham denies the possibility that anyone calling himself a humanist can accept less than these basic assumptions. We have already seen that Forster's humanism developed out of his rejection of any concepts of divine aid or communion with God. Man for him is, indeed, on his own. Yet, in many ways, one could say that there is an element of egoism in the humanism that Forster stands for; the same sort of egoism which Moore found inherent in Mill's Utilitarianism.[25] Nevertheless Forster makes it

original sin is clearly expressed in the following: "What he will not admit is that the source of... evil may be in man himself... For to admit the doctrine of the Fall of Man would be the beginning of admitting the rest of the claims of the Christian faith" (J. D. C. Pellow, "The Beliefs of Mr Forster", *Theology*, XL [April 1940], p. 281).

[22] C.f. "Forster has detached the Christian teaching from the circumference of the churches and concentrated it into the nucleus of the personal relationship" (Stephen Spender, *The Creative Element* [New York, 1954], p. 86).

[23] Blackham, *Humanism*, p. 127.

[24] *Humanism*, p. 13.

[25] C.f. "The aim of the liberal humanist is not service of party or creed, but self-fulfilment. He inclines to the belief that man is innately good, and that in a proper form of society he should be allowed to express his true nature without restriction" (Cox, *The Free Spirit*, p. 7).

clear that the fates of individual and community are, for him, inextricably bound together: "We are here on earth not to save ourselves and not to save the community, but to try to save both".[26]

In his essay on André Gide and Stefan George, Forster enumerates the characteristic qualities of the humanist: "curiosity, a free mind, belief in good taste, and belief in the human race".[27] Curiosity in Forster, or in anyone else, is not a quality the existence of which one can set out to prove; one assumes that a novelist possesses it as a condition *sine qua non* of his craft. Forster's love of freedom and the implied good taste of anyone who accepts Moore's ideals need not be questioned further. There remains the belief in humanity. In 1915, in a short article in which he pays homage to the work of the Quakers in the war-torn areas of France, Forster notes their belief in civilization and humanity. His agreement with this belief is at least implicit when he writes of the Quaker, "He believes that though civilization may slide, the power of which civilization is only a partial expression stands firm, being rooted in humanity."[28] More explicit is Forster's remark at the end of a series of four articles that he wrote for *Time and Tide* in 1934. The series is marked by warnings of approaching disaster, and by outspoken attacks on military ceremony, chemical warfare, and Fascism. In spite of having noted all these signs of humanity's weaknesses and propensity to destroy itself, Forster writes:

I am all for the human race, and think "Plus que je vois les hommes plus j'aime les chiens" one of the most hopeless and ignoble maxims ever uttered. The human race must be served first.[29]

It is a matter for some wonder that someone with so firm a belief in the human race was not completely shaken out of it by the experience of a second World War. But in 1948, Forster notes that mankind is beginning to forget what it is capable of; that it *is* capable of much that is good is not questioned.

We, today – we are inventive and adaptable, we are stoical and learning

---

26 "The Ivory Tower", p. 58.

27 "Gide and George", *Two Cheers for Democracy*, p. 233.

28 "Reconstruction on the Marne and the Meuse", *Westminster Gazette*, 30.8.1915, p. 2.

29 "Notes on the Way", *Time and Tide*, 23.6.1934, pp. 796-7.

to bear things, our young men have acquired what may be termed the "returning warrior" attitude, and that is all very well. But we are losing the sense of wonder. We are forgetting what human nature can do, and upon what a vast stage it is set.[30]

Statements on unqualified belief in humanity may often be understood as vague and ineffectual calls for love and brotherhood. Such a view implies a criticism that the believer is either unwilling or unable to act. D. H. Lawrence, who criticised Forster on these grounds,[31] did not realise how eminently more practical Forster was than himself, and that his own ideas of Rananim were based far more on egoism than any genuine belief in individual or community.

Forster is a liberal humanist who is continually aware of the weakness and difficulties of his position.[32] This is implicit in the hesitancy with which Forster applies the term 'humanist' to himself.

How indeed do I define myself? If I say I am an atheist the obvious retort is "That sounds rather crude"; if I say I am an agnostic the retort is "That sounds rather feeble"; If I say I am a liberal the answer is "You can't be; only Socialists and Tories", and if I say I am a humanist there is apt to be a bored withdrawal. On the whole humanist is the best word, though. It expresses more nearly what I feel about myself.[33]

The apparently elusive quality of Forster's humanism – seldom directly expressed, often only to be deduced from remarks in other contexts – has made it difficult for the critics to more than hint at its characteristics. Contrary to Lawrence's strictures there is more evidence of Forster's humanism in his public attitudes than in his fiction.

In the attempt to apprehend the nature of Forster's humanism, we may take a remark he makes in his biography of Lowes Dickinson as a starting point.

[30] "Mahatma Ghandi", *E. M. Forster: A Tribute*, p. 80.
[31] C.f. Lawrence's letter to Bertrand Russell of 12.2.1915: "Forster knows, as every thinking man now knows, that all his thinking and his passion for humanity amounts to no more than trying to soothe with poetry a man raging with pain which can be cured" (*The Collected Letters of D. H. Lawrence*, ed. Harry T. Moore [London, 1962], pp. 317-318).
[32] C.f. Malcolm Bradbury, "Introduction", *Forster. A Collection of Critical Essays*, p. 4.
[33] "A Letter", p. 99.

It is difficult for most of us to realise both the importance and unimportance of reason. But it is a difficulty which the profounder humanists have managed to solve.[34]

It is Forster's distinction that he is able to achieve such a balance between the rational and the irrational.[35] Two quotations from Forster may serve to partially uphold this view. The first comes from a discussion of saints, more particularly, of Joan of Arc: "They too, must enter the kingdom of reason. They may alter it by entering, but they must enter... In the long run there can only be one sort of wisdom, which neither saint nor worldling will monopolise".[36] The second is from Forster's thoughts on getting old, written over thirty years later: "I connect [wisdom] with length of years, and I distinguish it from intuition which may occur at any age... The possession of it arises from human relationships, rightly entertained over a long period."[37] From these two extracts, it may be seen that just as reason must control the saint, so too reason itself becomes subservient to human affection. One returns, as one inevitably does with Forster, to the question of human relationships; only with a slight difference: the qualification that Forster himself makes, they must be "rightly entertained". Here is where reason plays its part.

The impression one gains of Forster's humanism is that it is more effective the more there are specific individuals to be helped, befriended or campaigned for. Human relations, as Forster visualises them, take place between individuals and not between groups or nations.[38] This does not ignore the work Forster did for groups and organisations, but rather clarifies his motives. The part he played in the National Council for Civil Liberties,[39] or in international P.E.N. conferences, together with his many pleas for the freedom of the artist, is well known.[40] Other such public activities have received

34 *Goldsworthy Lowes Dickinson*, p. 120.
35 C.f. McDowell, *E. M. Forster*, p. 24.
36 "The True Joan of Arc. Shaw's or France's", *New Leader*, 19.6.1925, p. 10.
37 "De Senectute", *London Magazine*, IV (Nov. 1957), p. 17. There is a parallel here to the close of W. K. Clifford's statement quoted on p. 47 above.
38 C.f. Lacotte, "Études récentes sur E. M. Forster", p. 427.
39 C.f. Letters to *Time and Tide*, 28.6.1941, p. 540; 5.7.1941, p. 561; "Ronald Kidd", *Two Cheers for Democracy*, pp. 59-61, et al.
40 C.f. "International Congress of Writers", *New Statesman and Nation*,

less notice, or have not been so well documented, namely his membership of the Freedom Defence Committee[41] and the Council for Abolishing Nuclear Tests.[42] However, although Forster's humanism can engage itself in work for society and be recruited to protest against abuses, it "regards this as unfulfilled unless it is led on to a point where it can see humanity... neither statistically nor sentimentally, but with passion".[43]

Although we have noted the elusive quality of Forster's humanism as a theory, the multiple instances of it as a way of life can leave no doubt as to its power to generate action. Moreover, we must insist that for Forster humanism presents a very clear alternative to Christianity, to organised, powerful religion of any kind. Never is his writing more forceful that when asserting this:[44] as in a short letter, written at the age of eighty-five to the editor of the *Cambridge News*:

Sir, – In your issue of February 19 you print an entry headed, "Humanism without God is not Enough." May I further suggest that God without Humanism is not enough, and was responsible for much of the bloodthirstiness in the Old Testament?[45]

Forster's stand for liberal humanist values, traditional as it may

---

6.7.1935, p. 9; Foreword to Alec Craig, *The Banned Books of England* (London, 1937); "The New Disorder", *Writers in Freedom*, ed. Herman Ould (London, 1942); "The Hollywood Ten", *Author*, LXI (1951), pp. 87-8.

[41] See letter to *Socialist Leader*, signed jointly by Benjamin Britten, E. M. Forster, Augustus John, George Orwell, Herbert Read and Osbert Sitwell, 18.9.1948. Reprinted in George Orwell, *Collected Essays, Journalism and Letters*, ed. S. Orwell and I. Angus (London, 1968), Vol. IV, pp. 446-7.

[42] Forster mentions this in his contribution to the symposium, *The Fearful Choice*, ed. Philip Toynbee (London, 1958), p. 83.

[43] Beer, *The Achievement of E. M. Forster*, p. 74; see too: René Cazes' description of Forster as a militant humanist in his review of *Two Cheers for Democracy* in *Études Anglaises*, V (1952), p. 266.

[44] C.f. "I asert there is an alternative... in Humanism" ("A Letter", p. 101).

[45] *Cambridge News*, 22.2.1964, p. 4. One may here compare Forster's attitude to that of another distinguished humanist: "Although I think, with most humanists, that Christianity, by teaching the fatherhood of God, may make a great contribution to establishing the brotherhood of man, I also think that those who undermine man's faith in reason are unlikely to contribute much to this end" (K. R. Popper, *The Open Society and its Enemies*, Vol. 2 [London, 1966], p. 258).

be, is still undeniably an attitude with a strongly personal bias. For over fifty years Forster proclaimed a faith in man and in man's ability to save himself. Given the evidence of man's activity in that period (1910-1970), many would assert, as many have done, that humanism and liberalism have failed. One can, however, prefer to side with those who insist that Forster himself is an argument to the contrary.[46] In his stand for humanism one is reminded of the way in which Fielding, in *A Passage to India*, describes himself to Aziz: "I'm a holy man minus the holiness".[47] Although Fielding is made to use this remark with reference to his unencumbered mode of living, taken quite literally the remark could serve well as an epitaph for its author.

[46] C.f. "People sometimes say liberal-humanist values are soft, have become discredited and inadequate. That view would be easier to argue if it were not for the sustained convictions of Russell and Forster, which suggest that the ideas have discredited us, not the other way round" (Gransden, "E. M. Forster at Eighty", p. 77).

[47] *Passage to India*, p. 118; c.f. "For Forster... there is a serenity in skepticism" (Martin Price, "EMF and DHL", *Yale Review*, IV [1965-1966], p. 598).

4

THE SEARCH FOR REALITY

"Real"is at the service of all schools of thought.

E. M. Forster[1]

We have already noted that Forster's choice of a life lived in and with the world resulted in the divorce of his original ideal from the reality of experience.[2] This inevitably leads him into a constant attempt to adapt ideal to reality. This concern implies a moral preoccupation, and, in fact, one of the common labels for Forster since Zabel first used it in 1938 has been that of 'moral realist'.[3] What this term implies is suggested by Lionel Trilling when he ranks Forster with Nathaniel Hawthorne:

Forster stands with him [Hawthorne] in his unremitting concern with moral realism... which is not the awareness of morality itself but of the contradictions, paradoxes and dangers of living the moral life.[4]

Trilling's use of the term "the moral life" in itself tends to beg the question; but it is, perhaps, sufficient for the moment to see a relation between the moral life, or the search for the truth, and an adequate vision of reality which eventually harmonises with the ideals, moral, ethical or aesthetic, which Forster espoused.

In a letter of 1928 Lowes Dickinson writes to Forster:

Your constant preoccupation to bring realistic life into contact with the

---

[1] "India Again", *Two Cheers for Democracy*, p. 328.
[2] C.f., p. 40 above.
[3] C.f. Morton Dauwen Zabel, "E. M. Forster", *Nation* (New York), 22. Oct. 1938, p. 412; V. S. Pritchett, "Mr Forster's New Year", *New Statesman and Nation*, 27. Dec. 1958, p. 912; Cox, *The Free Spirit*, pp. 74-5.
[4] Lionel Trilling, *E. M. Forster*, p. 12.

background of values (or whatever it is) is very difficult to bring off, and I am apt to feel the cleft.[5]

This is the nature of the problem which we shall be investigating through the course of the following chapters; a problem which, as we shall see, resulted in Forster's abandonment of fiction for direct statement by means of the written or the spoken word.

The search for reality begins to play an important role early in Forster's career. In his 1960 introduction to the World's Classics edition of *The Longest Journey*, he tells us that the Cambridge he portrayed there, the Cambridge of his own student days, was "the fearless uninfluential Cambridge that sought for reality and cared for truth".[6] There, then, are the twin props of the 'moral life': reality and a passionate concern for the truth. It is the search for this elusive reality that marks Forster's works and, as Rose Macaulay has pointed out, gives them their unity.[7]

The study of this search and the attempt to limit and define the object of the quest has been commented on, if not carried out, by other critics; Norman Kelvin has claimed it as a legitimate approach and at the same time suggested that the quest is for moral realism which, for him, means the search for "a relation between life and artistic form in which the first is not weakened or made to play a perfunctory role".[8] Morton Zabel comes closer, to my mind, to the exact nature of Forster's concerns, which are certainly more centrally human than the reconciliation of artistic form and life, when he writes:

He made his object the search for the *wholeness* of truth; the synthesis of matter and essence, of civilization with its inhibitions and nature with its blind energy, of the fragments and denials on which life is commonly founded and the total vision of reality that man's sloth or cowardice forbids him to unveil.[9]

If Zabel errs, it is on the side of making Forster appear too heroic, too isolated an intellectual adventurer. However, it is the almost

---

[5] *Goldsworthy Lowes Dickinson*, p. 216. The letter is dated 19.4.1928 and the above extract refers directly to Forster's short stories.
[6] *The Longest Journey*, World's Classics edition (London, 1960), p. xi.
[7] Rose Macaulay, *The Writings of E. M. Forster*, p. 10.
[8] Norman Kelvin, *E. M. Forster* (Carbondale and Edwardsville, 1967), p. 14.
[9] Zabel, "E. M. Forster", *Nation* (N.Y.), 22.10.1938, p. 413.

biblical, or perhaps Lawrencean, tone of the word "wholeness" that puts the observation in its true perspective. Given the ideals which Forster himself adopted, it is not surprising that anything less than wholeness, anything less than Arnoldian 'perfection' is unacceptable. Once again Forster is revealed as a true inheritor of the Liberal tradition. It is Lionel Trilling, who, in a voice similar to Forster's own, supplies the gentle corrective to Zabel's over-enthusiastic proclamation. Trilling sees Forster's quest as being not so much for truth as for reality, for, he writes: "reality is a more exact concept than truth and simple people are more interested in it than in truth; reality is the word used for what can be relied on, felt, pushed against. It is what is thick and lasts."[10] Once again we are made aware of the practicalness of Forster's 'philosophy'; it is the desire to find something which will stand the test of time and experience which motivates so much of his writing and musing. Reality for Forster, as too for his mentor and friend Lowes Dickinson, is not a matter of eternal verities, or the life beyond the grave: "Dickinson was not a mystic. He had a strain of mysticism in him, but he didn't think reality lay in some other existence. The time to work for humanity is now, the place here..."[11]

In this here and now, the search for reality takes on the appearance and nature of a hard inner struggle. Writing at the beginning of the second World War Forster notes,

Besides our war against totalitarianism, we have also an inner war, a struggle for truer values, a struggle of the individual towards *the dark, secret place where he may find reality*.[12]

This deep concern for "truer values", the attempt to reach the "secret place", has the effect of changing the perspective of many other moral questions. That is, the concern for reality places it in the supreme position in the normal scale of moral values, supplanting the more rational questions of the moralist concerning good and evil. The result becomes a shifting of emphasis within the whole scale.[13]

---

[10] Trilling, *E. M. Forster*, p. 68.
[11] "Lowes Dickinson", *Listener*, 19. Oct. 1932, p. 572.
[12] "The Individual and his God", *Listener*, 5.12.1940, p. 802 (my italics).
[13] C.f. von Einsiedel, p. 637; Bradbury, "Two Passages to India", p. 128.

The whole question of 'reality' in relation to E. M. Forster's works is complicated, however, by the consideration that in this discussion we are dealing, in fact, with two realities. There is, first of all, the ideal which is being aimed for; what we might call a metaphysical and ethical *summum bonum*, the essence of the good life. Secondly, there is the more down to earth reality of every day; that which we might paraphrase as 'experience of the world', 'life as it is observably lived', and so on. The essential conflict in Forster's thought, and more particularly in his fiction, is between these two realities, between the ideal and, practically, all that is less than the ideal.[14]

Referring this problem specifically to the task of the writer, in the important years between *Howards End* and *A Passage to India*, Forster gives a perfectly clear account of the "reality outside his ordinary self", in which his own experience is implicit:

If the author started with a plan it is all forgotten and faded, just as our anticipations about a new place or person fade as soon as we have had the experience of seeing that place or person. The reality has swallowed it up. It is *a reality outside his ordinary self.*[15]

We now, clearly, have two concepts, both Forster's, with which we may operate in our further examination of his writings: 1) the dark secret place where he may find reality, and 2) a reality outside his ordinary self. In the case of the first of these two, the reality is ideal and maybe even hypothetical, not yet experienced, and, the suggestion is, individual. In the case of the second, the reality is actual and experienced, and, we may infer, not so much reserved for the individual as opposed to him. That which remains to be discovered is the extent to which these two concepts are mutually exclusive. Shusterman suggests that the attempt to reconcile ideal and actual has been "Forster's abiding interest throughout his adult life",[16]

[14] Herbert Howarth sees this contrast resulting not merely in a realization of the situation but in an active participation in the conflict: "He (Forster) evidently told himself that the ideal is problem-beset, and an honest writer can only approach it faltering; and meanwhile the real strikes and strikes again, and the real is evil-beset, and an honest writer must approach it belligerently". – Herbert Howarth, "E. M. Forster and the Contrite Establishment", *Journal of General Education*, October 1965, p. 201.

[15] "Inspiration", *Author*, XXII (1912), p. 281 (my italics).

[16] Shusterman, *The Quest for Certitude...*, p. 102.

and certainly it is this very easily documented interest which will largely direct our approach to his novels.

At this stage we may go so far as to note the progress within Forster's novel writing from moral questions to those of existence, from, that is, mere presentations of various forms of behaviour or attitudes to life, to the discussion of attitudes in terms of the life they reveal.[17] The suggestion being that Forster's viewpoint underwent a significant change, or rather, the emphasis was altered. Whereas in the first two novels inherited liberal humanist values are the yardstick by which behaviour is measured, the vision of reality and the conflict with experienced reality bring about the state of affairs that reaches its climax in *Passage*, where liberalism itself is now that which is being measured; what the yardstick is remains to be shown. We may for now postulate that the process we shall observe may be seen in terms of an interchangeable, mutually critical relationship between the two realities, in which experience is analysed and judged in terms of the ideal, and the ideal is modified and revised in terms dictated by experience.

After *Howards End* the antagonistic reality – the reality of experience – becomes more and more identifiable with such concepts as 'the modern world', and Forster shows a tendency to wish to withdraw altogether from it. What this could have meant in terms of fiction is suggested by the remarks appended to that part of his unfinished novel, *Arctic Summer*, which Forster read at the Aldeburgh Festival in 1951, where he characterises one of the novel's protagonists as "the hero straying into the modern world which does not want him and which he does not understand".[18] The full significance of this remark can, perhaps, first be grasped when one realises that the fragment of *Arctic Summer* is dated Spring 1914.

The development of Forster's fictional search for reality may be further documented by noting the remarks of two of Forster's ablest critics, Crews and Trilling; the one, discussing the antecedents of *Howards End*, notes a contrast between reality and myth in the early novels in which reality is bad,[19] and the other suggests that

[17] Crews, *E. M. Forster. The Perils of Humanism*, p. 178.
[18] "Arctic Summer", *Tribute to Benjamin Britten*, ed. Anthony Gishford (London, 1963), p. 54.
[19] Trilling, p. 99.

the more experienced reality comes to the fore, the more isolated Forster's humanism becomes, "until finally in *A Passage to India* we find ourselves peering uncertainly into the dark itself".[20] In his biography of his great-aunt, Forster writes: "She felt (as some of us do) the ground slipping beneath her."[21] The parenthesis indicates that he identifies himself with this feeling.

Although Forster may have been opposed to the world of reality as experience (in so far as it was the uncongenial 'modern world'), far from contenting himself, in later life, with escape, he appears to regret his inability to share the more easily apprehended reality of the world around him. Faced with such ambivalence, one can certainly agree with Crews in noting Forster's "posture of standing ready to alter his interpretations of reality at a moment's notice",[22] which implies, and is coupled with, his ability to compromise. The characterisation of the *Times Literary Supplement*'s ninetieth birthday tribute is appropriate here: "Forster-the-realist, the man who has been able to accept what could not be altered, and do it with dignity."[23] Yet even here the implications of "accept" and "with dignity" suggest at the same time the ideas of loss and defeat. What Forster was forced to lose or to give up, what renunciations were made in the cause of tolerance and compromise, will be a further object of our examinations of his writing. Yet, cost what it may, reality in the sense of a close relation to life as lived, a view of the real as being that which is ideal and that which may be put into practice, is at the heart of what Forster is attempting. This task is, in its dimensions, almost heroic, and echoes the underlying message of so much of Forster's fiction, "only connect", in this case the connection being between the seen and the unseen, to use Forster's own terminology.[24]

[20] Crews, p. 123.
[21] *Marianne Thornton* (London, 1956), p. 231.
[22] Crews, p. 164.
[23] "E. M. Forster at Ninety", *Times Literary Supplement*, 2.1.1969, p. 812.
[24] C.f. "As for the life of the spirit... Mr Forster disallows it if it involves a rejection of the life of the body. Furthermore, it is not genuine if it is based on any retreat from reality". – Howard N. Doughty, "The Novels of E. M. Forster", *Bookman* (New York), October, 1932, p. 544. It is a measure of Forster's achievement that he has never been with any illusions as to the nature of the reality that Doughty was thinking of.

In one of his lesser imaginative ventures, published, apparently with some editorial misgivings in 1912,[25] and republished in 1956 in the Cambridge satirical review, *Granta*, Forster introduces reality into a pastoral dialogue between a punt and a canoe on the river Cam, in the form of a traction engine. The dialogue continues:

CANOE: Who's that?

TRACTION ENGINE: Humph! What have we here? Everyone happy? This'll never do.

PUNT: It's a traction engine. It's reality, it's the hard facts of life. Oh what a lucky chance that they happened to be passing.

TRACTION ENGINE: I shall pass often enough in the future... I see much amiss here...[26]

When the punt suggests that the traction engine's aims are splendid, this latter replies, "I am not splendid... I am the squalor of experience", a phrase which at this stage in our investigation is significant, having been written in a period between the vague positive values of Mrs Wilcox and the resigned pessimism of Mrs Moore.[27]

Forster, then, may be seen both as the idealist who searches for truer values and the nature of ultimate reality, and as the realist who seeks to discover the true value of experience. Our task will be twofold: to trace the fictional portrayal of both searches, and to follow the modification of the ideal by experience, to see what remains that can still have relevance for the world of men.

---

[25] "An Allegory (?)", *Basileon H*, June 1912, p. 6, editorial note.

[26] "An Allegory (?)", pp. 6-7.

[27] It is doubtful, whether one can go all the way with the opinion that Forster's "view of reality is ultimately more tragic than anything else" (Shusterman, p. 108). Like so many of Shusterman's pronouncements, this is too much of a simplification to be of any great value.

5

ENGLAND AND ITALY

Italy is the school as well as the playground of the world.

E. M. Forster[1]

1

Where Angels Fear to Tread is the first of a five part fictional investigation of the potentialities of love as an ideal, in the sense in which that word has been used in earlier chapters. This fictional investigation will take us from the optimism of, "human love and love of truth conquer where love of beauty fails" (*Angels*, p. 62), by way of the calm climax: "Love is the best, and the more she let herself love him, the more chance was there that he would set his soul in order" (*Howards End*, p. 205), to the final disillusion of: 'I no longer want love', he said ... 'No more do I. My experiences here have cured me...' (*Passage*, p. 256).[2] That is, in *Angels* we are at the beginning, with the young Forster still filled with the enthusiastic optimism of Cambridge, still convinced that ideals such as those of G. E. Moore will work in the world of the reality of experience. Yet the novel shows experienced reality, in this case the Sawston world of the Herritons, in antagonism to the ideal; but Sawstonian reality is on the losing side, and the forces of dark-

---

[1] *Where Angels Fear to Tread*, Penguin edition (Harmondsworth, 1959), p. 9. All further page references are to this edition. See too: "(Italy's) austere beauty was an image of the millenium towards which all good citizens are co-operating" ("Arctic Summer", p. 53).

[2] This development reminds one of a much later remark of Forster's: "The true history of the human race is the history of human affection" ("De Senectute", p. 18).

ness – authority, powerful religion, and the cramping of intellectual freedom – are routed. However, the contact with them taints and modifies the ideal of the 'good life'.

Forster begins his career, as he was to continue it, writing of a community, of a social order, familiar to him, and of which, with the exception of Anglo-India, he was a part.[3] From this position, he sets out in *Angels* to criticise, by gently mocking, that society's weaknesses as viewed from the heights of the Cambridge ideal,[4] with an effectiveness that was not missed by its first readers.[5] However, Forster's main concern is not to be seen only in terms of class or community, but rather in the effects of various groupings upon a central ideal – in this case the bridging of a racial gap (the largest gap possible between communities) by love – and the using of love, or passion, as a means of measuring human worth. Within this context, the setting of one set of social values against another could well have, as Mark Goldman suggests, a certain "symbolic intention which solidifies the social structure while it intensifies the underlying poetry".[6]

The English social groupings are clearly indicated in the opening scene of *Angels*, where the entire cast of English characters are gathered at Charing Cross Station. Philip Herriton, the sensitive but theoretical practioner of personal relations, calls to his sister-in-law, "Love and understand the Italians, for the people are more marvellous than the land" (p. 5). This is typical of Philip's theoret-

---

[3] Stone's suggestion that the world of Sawston, the middle-class society of the Herritons, is Forster's "own world, and he is at home in it", is born out by the remarks of the original reviewers of the novel: "he has undoubtedly caught the essential tone of the modern English mind" (Stone, *The Cave and the Mountain*, p. 162); review of *Angels* in *The Speaker*, 28.10.1905, p. 90. But note that *The Spectator's* reviewer, although commenting that the lessons of the novel are a "confirmation of orthodox views", does so out of a complete misunderstanding of the novel, for the lessons of *Angels* according to him are "the dangers of international marriages... and the futility of ill-considered rebellion against convention" (*Spectator*, 23.12.1905, p. 1090). This view at least pays tribute to the success of Forster's portrayal of the Sawston milieu.
[4] C.f. Laurence Brander, *E. M. Forster. A Critical Study* (London, 1968), pp. 90-91.
[5] *Speaker*, 28.10.1905, p. 90.
[6] Mark Goldman, "Virginia Woolf and E. M. Forster: A Critical Dialogue", *Texas Studies in Literature and Language*, VII (1966), p. 389.

ical knowledge of reality which the more emotional characters, in this case Caroline and Lilia, will experience, and which he can only see as a hypothetical situation. Mrs Herriton remains a spectator, unable and unwilling to involve herself with others ("Mrs Herriton, who was standing pensively a little out of the hubbub", p. 6); and Harriet, the only one of the middle-class constellation who is given no redeeming feature, is characterised here by the most typical of middle-class concerns: that for property. "'Handkerchiefs and collars,' screamed Harriet, 'in my inlaid box! I've lent you my inlaid box.'"(p. 6).[7] Lilia herself, the centre of the excitement is character-ised by her gaity and lack of concern with propriety. Caroline Ab-bott, who is to emerge as the leading character in the last half of the novel, remains silent but is briefly described as "Tall, grave, rather nice-looking", and as behaving "in a more decorous manner" (p. 6). Thus she is allied, for now, in her silence and decorum, with Mrs Herriton as a guardian of Sawstonian reserve and good manners.

Towards the end of this farewell scene, Lilia calls from the carriage window: "Caroline, my Caroline! Jump in, or your chap-erone will go off without you" (p. 6). Yet the role of "chaperone" is assigned shortly after to Caroline;[8] and when the scandal of Lilia's marriage to Gino breaks, the responsibility is partly laid at Miss Abbott's door for having failed in her duties as companion and chaperone. Lilia's remark is not, however, to be seen as merely another way of expressing the difference in age between the two women; far more it is an indication of the role that Lilia plays with-in the terms of the theme of love in the book and is an indication of the initiation into love that Caroline Abbott is to receive indirectly through Lilia in the later part of the book. Lilia is to be the chap-erone of the inexperienced and as yet emotionally undeveloped Caroline in their journey to Italy where emotion rules behaviour.

After the close of the brief first chapter, Italy takes over from

[7] C.f. "Possessions... are the most wearisome forms of wealth... and the man who is entangled by them always develops heaviness of outlook and sluggishness of movement" ("The Terrible Tolstoy", *New Leader*, 4.9.1925, p. 12). See too: "My Wood", *Abinger Harvest*, p. 35; "Notes on the Way", *Time and Tide*, 2.6.1934, p. 696.
[8] "It is mortifying to think that a widow of thirty-three requires a girl ten years younger to look after her" (p. 8).

England for the remainder of the novel apart from chapter 5, to which we shall return shortly. The first Italian venture, although vital for the development of the plot, is of lesser interest to us than the second and it will be sufficient to note a few incidents. On Philip's arrival in Monteriano, he is met by Miss Abbott and during the conversation which occupies their ride from station to town, Philip is confronted by the revelation of Gino's identity and station in life. Miss Abbott is not concerned with social differences and reveals already that side of her nature, as yet theory rather than experience, which is to dominate later in the book, when she announces in passing, "But I feel that you, and at all events your mother – so really good in every sense, so really unworldly – after all, love – marriages are made in heaven" (p. 25). It is significant that sandwiched between the platitudes and commonplaces the little unfinished phrase "after all, love" should be slipped in. For as we have already stated, that which will be one of our chief interests in this examination will be the way in which Caroline Abbott's apprehension of love develops throughout the novel to become a dominant experience in her life.

During this conversation, Philip's chief experience is the shock to his weakly based ideals of the sudden confrontation with reality: "He shuddered all over, and edged away from his companion. A dentist! A dentist at Monteriano. A dentist in fairy-land!... He thought of Lilia no longer. He was anxious for himself: he feared that Romance might die." To which Forster adds the auctorial comment which makes quite clear that Philip has not marched far on the way to reconciling the two realities we discussed in the last chapter:

Romance only dies with life... But there is a spurious sentiment which cannot resist the unexpected and the incongruous and the grotesque. A touch will loosen it, and the sooner it goes from us the better. It was going from Philip now... (p. 25)

That is, we may see Philip's first visit to Monteriano as having the function of purging away much that up till now has been merely theoretical idealism. The test of his character will be in what he finds to put in the place of the "spurious sentiment". [9]

[9] It would however be a gross simplification to see this contrast as being the

On his first attempt to bring Sawston standards and manners to bear upon Italian emotion, freedom, and equality, Philip learns nothing more. But Caroline, faced with the triumph of love in the marriage of Gino and Lilia,[10] feels her Sawstonian reserve breaking down; what other explanation could there be for her cry at the end of chapter two: "I can't stop here... I daren't stop here" (p. 35)? We shall note later that at each confrontation with love the emotional jar becomes greater, until she reaches the crisis after the kidnapping and the death of the baby, and is able to translate emotion into action by caressing and embracing the momentarily collapsed Gino.

The next two chapters centre on the later married life of Gino and Lilia, and would appear to have as their function the establishment of the weaknesses of the 'all for love' attitude with which Lilia entered upon the liaison. Certainly Lilia as a character develops little or not at all; it is Gino who gradually dominates the story of their brief marriage. For him life with Lilia is marked by his arrival at maturity, in the sense of a growing awareness of what society expects of him as a grown-up, married man.[11] At the same time, maturity only increases the awareness of difference and the establishment of national barriers between the two; national barriers which at the same time have the function of emphasising the nature of the conflict involved in the novel. A great deal in *Angels* depends on the way in which people react to each other, and Gino, in this context, is used as the measure by which the various protagonists are accepted or found wanting. The crisis in the marriage of Lilia and Gino is not to be seen in the incidents of the plot (Gino's infidelities or Lilia's attempts to assert her independence), but in the cool realization of each other's worth that they arrive at. For Lilia he becomes "a cruel, worthless, hypocritical, dissolute upstart" (p. 57), an estimate which is so exaggerated as to

---

theme of the whole novel. C.f. Phyllis Bentley, "The Novels of E. M. Forster", *College English*, IX (1948), p. 351.

[10] Lilia, in her apology for her marriage, concludes with the statement, "I can stand up against the world now, for I've found Gino, and this time I marry for love" (p. 33).

[11] C.f. "And all the time the boy was watching her, and growing up" (p. 39).

serve as an indication of the extent to which after her brief adventure she has reverted to type; and indeed her outburst comes after a period of acute homesickness for the regular pattern of Sawston life (p. 55). Gino, on the other hand, is able to arrive at a more down to earth estimate of his wife: "his wife was a very ordinary woman, and why should her ideas differ from his own?" (p. 58). Any love which he may have had for Lilia is at once transferred to his as yet unborn son, the desire for fatherhood and an heir becoming "the first great passion of his life" (p. 60).

One detail remains to be noted from these two chapters. In the discussion about men and women between Gino and his friend Spiridione, they are talking about the quality of sympathy, and establish that men are "simpatico" in that they can "pour forth every thought and wish, not only in speech but in silence" (p. 46), but women do not share this quality. At which point, Gino makes a statement that has some bearing on the later events of the book: "One I have seen who may be so. She spoke very little, but she was a young lady – different to most. She, too, was English, the companion of my wife here" (p. 46). The revelation that the feelings that Caroline Abbott later entertains for Gino may well have been reciprocated only goes to support the idea that Gino is the test-case for the judgement of the ability to enter into personal relationships.[12]

Chapter five brings us back to the world of Sawston which we are now able to view more critically after the possibilities of contrast with another world have been given. It is clearly Forster's intention that the two worlds should now be set off against each other and that the English characters should be allowed to emerge more clearly defined than before. That the chapter begins with an account of Philip's intellectual development and that the events of the chapter centre round his conversation with Miss Abbott on the

---

[12] One may here note Forster's own estimate of Gino in a letter he wrote on the occasion of the first performance of the stage version of the novel in 1963. Speaking of the actor who played Gino, Forster writes:
"He brought to his part the charm, coarseness, tenderness, and explosive power that it requires... without the addition of Mr Baxter's strength I do not see how the play could have existed, any more than the novel could have existed without a Gino." – *Times*, 12.7.1963, p. 11.

train to London indicate a shift of interest in the novel which will involve a regrouping of the characters. Philip's ideals, or his illusions, have suffered a notable reverse after his first Italian intervention, and he has settled down to a passive existence: "he concluded that nothing could happen" (p. 62). His attitudes to people have become fixed, particularly his estimation of Gino – "the betrayer of his life's ideal" (p. 62).[13] In this respect he appears to have become reconciled to his mother's outlook on life, that is he has returned to Sawston, to the ranks of the damned.[14]

During the conversation in the train, Caroline Abbott reveals that she was, much more than the Herritons ever suspected, indirectly responsible for Lilia's 'unfortunate' marriage: " 'Do you love this man?' I asked. 'Yes or no'? She said 'Yes.' and I said, 'Why don't you marry him if you think you'll be happy?'" (p. 66). For Miss Abbott, then, love has been the test for human relations. Furthermore, Caroline reveals that in the conflict between Italy and Sawston, Italy had gained the upper hand, not only because she feels that she "might have got influence" over Gino but because before the start of the journey she already hated Sawston (p. 67). She quite clearly saw that Lilia's power to enjoy herself and to accept life freely and fully, taken together with Gino's youthful splendour and strength, should be allowed the chance of marriage (p. 68). The crux of the conversation is, however, contained in her estimate of reality, seen as the greater world of experience, contrasted with the restrictions which society places upon the individual. She summarises the whole experience in Monteriano with Lilia, as having made her unhappy since she has failed in adequately responding to the real life:

"its the only time I've ever gone into what my father calls "real life" – and look what I've made of it!... I wanted to fight against the things I hated – mediocrity and dullness and spitefulness and society. I actually

[13] That is, within the context of the characters being measured by their attitude to Gino, Philip sees him as the reality of experience opposed to the ideal, whereas Caroline will later see him as revealing the ultimate reality which confirms the ideal.

[14] C.f. " 'We cannot judge a country by anything but its men.' 'That's quite true,' he said sadly" (p. 64). An ironic state of affairs when one compares it to his advice shouted to Lilia on her departure (c.f. p. 65 above).

hated society for a day or two at Monteriano. I didn't see that all these things are invincible, and that if we go against them they will break us to pieces" (p. 69).

Caroline's outburst serves to re-awaken Philip from his passive reacceptance of Sawston morality, and leads to the establishment of friendly relations between him and Miss Abbott. But, we should notice, this relationship is still based on theoretical untried ideals.

"Society *is* invincible – to a certain degree." [Philip replies] "But your real life is your own and nothing can touch it. There is no power on earth that can prevent you... retreating into splendour and beauty – into the thoughts and beliefs that make the real life – the real you" (p. 69).

It is because Philip visualises the real life as being an interior condition, because he talks of retreating into this mental existence,[15] that he is doomed to failure when confronted with the other reality, the reality of experience. Moreover it is because Caroline Abbott can say "I and my life" (p. 69) that she can cope better with experience and is able to turn her mission of duty to Gino into an acceptance of beauty and love in the scene where she washes the baby (chapter 7).

This conversation leads us directly to the second mission to Monteriano and the central chapter 7 of that visit. Miss Abbott's all important experience is preluded, the night before, by indications of what must happen. Forster makes it clear that Miss Abbott is, of the three English people present in town, the most likely to respond rightly when the chance is given her. Back in her hotel bedroom after the performance of *Lucia di Lammermoor*, she looks out on the warm Italian evening and is filled with a happiness reminiscent of "a night in March, the night when Gino and Lilia had told her of their love" (p. 108). Once again love is the dominant note in her memories, and, although she reminds herself that "She was here to champion morality and purity, and the holy life of an English home" (p. 108), she falls asleep to dream of "a joyless, straggling place, *full of people who pretended*. When she woke up she knew that it had been Sawston" (p. 108, my italics). Thus we see that before the all important events of the following chapter, Miss

---

[15] C.f. page 59 above.

Abbott is presented to us as being filled with the memories of love and the concern for reality, the two chief themes of the novel. We are therefore prepared for her receptiveness to the sort of appeal that is presented by the combination of parental love and natural beauty in the pages to come.

Forster leaves us in no doubt as to the outcome of Miss Abbott's mission. Even before Gino and Caroline meet, he introduces the symbolic smoke ring from Gino's cigar which floats out from the room where he is with the baby and in at the door of the mausoleum-like reception room where the woman is waiting: "The ring had extended its pale blue coils towards her. She lost self-control. It enveloped her. As if it was a breath from the pit, she screamed" (p. 112). Thus the involvement with Gino and his child, with the world of love, is prepared. Both her horror and her final fascination are contained in the introductory scream. From then on the twin themes of love and reality develop and interwine rapidly. The key passage is the confrontation with the baby, the contrast between ideal and reality: "The real thing, lying asleep on a dirty rug, disconcerted her" (p. 113). Miss Abbott's conversion is completed in a moment as she summons to mind all the concepts that the baby has been in the past and contrasts Sawston plans with Italian flesh and blood: "She had a great disposition... to exert no more influence than there may be in a kiss or in the vaguest of the heart-felt prayers. But she had practised self-discipline, and her thoughts and actions were not yet to correspond" (p. 113). Here again the unifying element between hypothesis and reality is, in Caroline Abbott's mind, love and affection, but the stultifying Sawstonian element of self-discipline is still present. The influence of this element is to be broken only by the actual experience of love rather than its mere postulation. So it is not surprising that the conversation between Gino and Miss Abbott proceeds by way of a discussion about his second marriage which centers on the question of love again (p. 116), to the discovery that Gino loves his son.

She was silent. This cruel, vicious fellow knew of strange refinements. The horrible truth, that wicked people are capable of love, stood naked before her, and her moral being was abashed. It was her duty to rescue the baby, to save it from contagion, and she still meant to do her duty.

But the comfortable sense of virtue left her. *She was in the presence of something greater than right or wrong* (p. 118, my italics).

Here that which is greater than moral distinctions is surely reality as ideal become experience.

The closing tableau of the chapter, reminding Philip of a Renaissance painting, is in itself a confrontation with love although none of the members of the group are aware of the full implications nor of the true extent of the love which is as yet merely seen as that of Gino for his child. Here, however, are the seeds of Caroline's love for Gino, Philip's for Caroline and the masculine affection of the two men. Somehow, yet, the relationships deteriorate rather than improve from this moment on, the vision of reality is not accepted, the opportunity is passed by; Caroline returns to Sawston, Philip is unable to get nearer to her than promises of confidences and friendliness and the two men remain unaltered, just good friends. The baby, at the end of chapter seven the source of potential love, is itself overcome by Sawston in the shape of Harriet.

Although the revelation of love has turned into experience of love for Caroline, for Forster, perhaps, the significant experience is that of Philip. He too reaches the point where love is more than a mere ideal, and we learn that he loved Caroline very much (p. 153) although even this discovery is qualified by the suggestion that he has loved her for her thoughts and qualities rather than for her beauties. But the realisation of love brings him no closer to her. Love is, ultimately, for Philip ineffectual. He remains that which he has been throughout the novel, the spectator rather than the participant. The only knowledge that he has gained seems, in the light of the vision that has been granted, small: "Life was greater than he had supposed, but it was even less complete. He had seen the need for strenuous work and for righteousness. And now he saw what a very little way those things would go" (p. 155). If one considers that Forster sees in Philip one of those characters which to some extent represent himself,[16] one gets some idea of the dilemma of the young

---

[16] C.f. P. N. Furbank and F. J. Haskell, "The Art of Fiction, I: E. M. Forster", *Paris Review*, I (1953), p. 38. And certain episodes in this novel are close to Forster's own experience. The accident at the close of the second Italian episode is based on an event of his childhood; Forster gives an account of a very similar

Forster – sensitive, educated, refined – in the face of certain cruder realities of the experience of everyday. Faced with his own lack of first-hand knowledge of the life of the world, he falls back upon an analysis of his companions' experience.[17] This solution seems, however, a poor way out, and that Forster must have realised too. Although he portrays the same type again (Rickie in *The Longest Journey* is a notable example), one of the strains in his fiction is, as we shall observe, the slow widening of the range of experience of such characters, until one meets the older, wiser, and more sceptical Mr Fielding of the last novel.[18]

To return to *Angels*; the last moments on the journey home through Italy are devoted to a final conversation between Caroline and Philip (who always seem to be most intimate when least connected with the world around them, that is, on train journeys, in transit). The essence of the conversation, beyond the mere exigencies of the plot, is a final observation on Philip's character: "You're without passion; you look on life as a spectacle; you don't enter it; you only find it funny or beautiful" (p. 158). Philip is thus shown to be still in the ranks of the typical public school Englishman of the undeveloped heart.[19] More important, however, are the revelations Caroline makes about herself: first of her unashamed love for Gino (p. 158) and more important of her own nature:

Get over supposing I'm refined. That's what puzzles you. Get over that... I say again, don't be charitable. If he had asked me, I might have given myself body and soul. That would have been the end of my rescue party. But all through he took me for a superior being – a goddess. I who was

---

calamity in "The Charm and Strength of Mrs Gaskell", *Sunday Times*, 7.4.1957, p. 10. Similarly Forster recounts that he saw the opera *Lucia di Lammermoor* with the then unknown soprano, Tetrazzini, in Italy as a young man and "I put her and her opera into a novel of mine" ("My first opera", *Opera*, XIV [June 1963], p. 374).

[17] C.f. Gransden, "E. M. Forster at Eighty", p. 78.

[18] The connection between Philip and Fielding, first novel and last, is maintained by Robert Langbaum: "Forster has written two masterpieces – his last novel and his first" ("A New Look at E. M. Forster", *Southern Review*, NS IV [1968], p. 34). C.f. Elizabeth Bowen's suggestion that *Angels* "contained in embryo all the other books". – "Abinger Harvest" (Review of Forster's book of the same title) *Spectator*, 20.3.1936, p. 521.

[19] C.f. "Notes on the English Character", *Abinger Harvest*, p. 13.

worshipping every inch of him, and every word he spoke. And that saved me (p. 160).

Here we learn that love was faced with misapprehensions about reality, and love withdrew. Withdrawal, as of the vision, is the result, not defeat or collapse. Thus the concluding note of *Where Angels Fear to Tread* is a note of sadness, but it is the note of the sadness that goes with an increase of wisdom, a wisdom gained by experience. And for Forster, wisdom springs from contact with other human beings rather than from rational exercise.[20]

The close of the novel and its 'message' have not always been sympathetically received by the critics. Barbara Hardy feels that the ending is glib and suggests that the solution Forster proposes may well have been clear, ideologically, in his mind but is not substantiated in the novel itself.[21] Here one need only counter that it does not seem that Forster is proposing *any* solution, but rather recording certain findings and theories with regard to the nature of love, its potentialities and its relation, as ideal, to the toughness of reality as experience.[22]

2

It is not my preferred novel... but
it may fairly be called the nicest.

E. M. Forster[23]

There can be little denial of Forster's own estimate of *A Room with a View* as "nice", in the sense of light, pleasant, amusing and, above all, optimistic. We should, however, remember that this love story with a happy end does not represent a reversal of the sadness and resignation that concluded *Where Angels Fear to Tread*. The first half of *Room* was, in Forster's own words, "almost the first piece of

[20] C.f. "De Senectute", p. 17.
[21] Barbara Hardy, *The Appropriate Form* (London, 1964), pp. 74-5.
[22] C.f. Trilling, *E. M. Forster*, p. 66, and, more particularly, Alan Wilde, *Art and Order. A Study of E. M. Forster* (New York, 1964), pp. 26-7.
[23] "A View without a Room", *Observer*, 27.7.1958, p. 15.

fiction I attempted",[24] which would place it between *Albergo Empedocle* and the early short stories, and *Angels*. In other words, this apparent re-assertion of the triumph of love over muddle and convention is properly in the first stage in the progress of Forster's developing attitude to love as an ideal. As in *Angels* there is a concern to bring out the contrast between real and pretended feeling,[25] where the varying attitudes to love and passion are used as the touchstone to the individual worth of the characters concerned.[26]

The social contrast, noticeable in *Angels*, is much more in the background in *Room*; here the concern is with individuals rather than with social groupings.[27] The main concern is a sort of *éducation sentimentale*, with Lucy Honeychurch, perhaps the most easily likeable of Forster's heroines, in the central rôle. During the awkward discussion about changing rooms with the Emersons we learn:

She had an odd feeling that whenever these ill-bred tourists spoke the contest widened and deepened till it dealt, not with rooms and views, but with – well, with something quite different, whose existence she had not realised before.[28]

Like Caroline Abbott, Lucy has as yet had no experience of love and little of reality, and it is these concepts whose existence is strange and new to her. In Lucy's case, it is not Italy that brings the revelations; Italy is used in this novel as a charming background, a possible catalyst, but little more. Rather it is the direct encounter with the unconventional, and certainly somewhat unlikely Emersons[29] that brings Lucy to self-knowledge.

The first real meeting, in the church of Santa Croce, precipitates the development of the novel. George describes his father: "He is kind to people because he loves them; and they find him out, and

---

[24] Ibid.; c.f. Furbank and Haskell, "The Art of Fiction, I: E. M. Forster", p. 36.
[25] C.f. Rose Macaulay, *The Writings of E. M. Forster*, p. 123.
[26] C.f. Crews, *E. M. Forster, The Perils of Humanism*, p. 72.
[27] For a different view see, James Hall, "Forster's Family Reunions", *ELH*, XXV (1958), p. 61.
[28] *Room with a View*, Penguin edition (Harmondsworth, 1964), p. 9. All further page references are to this edition.
[29] C.f. "Mr Emerson might be taken to be an idealized portrait of Forster's own humanist position" (Cox, *The Free Spirit*, p. 75).

are offended, or frightened" (p. 30). Here Forster already hints that reactions to the discovery of love and being loved are going to be a measure of the value of the characters confronted by the phenomenon. Old Mr Emerson reveals to Lucy, and to the reader, that through love, affection, and the attempt to understand another human being, one may hope to find one's own salvation: "By understanding George you may learn to understand yourself. It will be good for both of you" (p. 32). Moreover, it becomes clear that Mr Emerson's function within the novel is that of revealing the truth about herself to Lucy. His analysis of her condition at this early stage introduces a theme which will run not only through this book but through later novels as well: "You are inclined to get muddled... Let yourself go" (p. 32). For Forster, muddle is a negative concept resulting in, if not disaster, at least mistaken and wrong action: "When an Englishman has been led into a course of wrong action, he has nearly always begun by muddling himself."[30] That Lucy is in a muddle will be repeated at significant moments in the story, namely, shortly before she leaves for Rome after the first of George's kisses (p. 87), and during her last interview with Mr Emerson, which leads up to her acceptance of and marriage to George (p. 214).[31]

— Another of Lucy's problematical traits is her inability to connect theory and practice, or, in later Forsterian terminology, "prose and passion".[32] This is presented to us, in symbolic form, in her piano playing, about which Mr Beebe remarks: "If Miss Honeychurch ever takes to live as she plays, it will be very exciting – both for us and for her." To which Lucy replies by repeating a remark her mother had made on hearing a similar comment: "she trusted I should never live a duet" (p. 36). Lucy's problem is the same as Caroline Abbott's: the attempt to find a means of reconciling ideal and everyday life.

The first meaningful experience that Lucy has is of the murder of the Italian stranger in the Piazza Signoria. This is structurally im-

---

[30] "Notes on the English Character", p. 20.
[31] For later references to muddle see *Howards End*, pp. 66, 287 & 315; *A Passage to India*, pp. 68, 203 & 256.
[32] C.f. *Howards End*, p. 174.

portant since it brings George and Lucy together in an emotionally charged atmosphere, and reveals, too, the distance Lucy will have to travel to rid herself of inhibiting conventions in order to accept reality and learn its true value. When George announces his intention to try to cope with the experience they have just had – "something tremendous has happened; I must face it without getting muddled" (p. 50) – Lucy immediately tries to head the conversation into another direction. Thus we see that although she behaves conventionally, with her requests that George should not relate what has happened or how she behaved, she has sufficient insight and potential sensitivity to grasp immediately what he means. That she has not, however, seen the necessity to integrate experience, to connect the prose and the passion, becomes clear at the end of chapter 4: "'Well thank you so much,' she repeated. 'How quickly these accidents do happen, and then one returns to the old life!'" (p. 51). That an association with George Emerson will involve a negation of this attitude is implicit in his reply: "I shall probably want to live" (p. 51).

It is only natural that Forster should have chosen as the climax to the Italian section of the book the first kiss between George and Lucy. Yet this leads to a wrong action – Lucy's rejection of George – since the event has taken place under the influence of a threefold muddle: the confusion of Mr Eager's arrangements for the excursion (p. 65); then the muddle over the behaviour of the driver and his girl friend (pp. 68-70); and finally, the third muddle arising out of Lucy's clumsy use of Italian (pp. 73-5), which precipitates the encounter with the younger Emerson. The second of these incidents is commented on by Mr Emerson with the significant statement:

Do you suppose there's any difference between spring in nature and spring in man? But there we go, praising one and condemning the other as improper, ashamed that the same laws work eternally through both. (p. 71)

Mr Emerson's attempt to force his companions to see the connection between man's acceptance of a romantic ideal of nature, and the acting out of the ideal in terms of human experience, underlines his function as "guardian of reality both as ideal *and* as experience",[33] and, furthermore, the introduction of "spring" with its con-

[33] A function which no doubt accounts for his otherworldliness and leads

ventional associations suggests that Mr Emerson insists on the physical as well as emotional aspects of love.[34] As far as the scene between George and Lucy among the violets is concerned, it is sufficient to note that its importance within the context of Forster's five novels is made clear if one compares Lucy's experience, and her reaction, to those of Adela Quested in the Marabar Caves in Forster's last novel. The difference is implicit, surely, in the intruding figure of Miss Bartlett who breaks the "silence of life" to stand "brown against the view" (p. 75). The implications of the incident within *Room with a View* are carried over into the chapter which follows. Shortly before Lucy comes on George, the driver of the carriage calls after her, "Courage and love" (p. 75); whereas during the drive back to Florence in the thunderstorm, Mr Eager comforts the frightened Lucy with the words, "Courage and faith" (p. 77). Here is a further justification, surely, for insisting on the centrality of the belief in love as a truer value than conventional Christian belief.

With the return to England, in Part 2, the novel takes on a new tone; the passion and adventure of Italy gives way to the gentler charm of Summer Street.[35] The introduction of Cecil Vyse into the novel is a weakness where sacrifices have been made to the plot, even though we are led to believe that Vyse has something of Forster in his make up.[36] He is, however, an uninteresting character.

Gransden to refer to him at the end of the book as a saint. C.f. Gransden, *E. M. Forster*, Writers and Critics series (London, 1962), p. 36. It might, however, be simpler to suggest that Mr Emerson is one of Forster's failures in so far as he is unconvincing as a human being. For a more positive view see, Brander, *E. M. Forster. A Critical Study*, p. 107.

[34] C.f. "love is of the body; not the body, but of the body" (p. 216); c.f. Alan Friedman, *The Turn of the Novel* (New York, 1966), p. 109. Trilling goes a step further and suggests that *Room* "deals with the physical reality upon which all the other realities rest". A view which it is difficult to accept since it demands a further definition of "reality", which would go beyond the scope of the present study, c.f. Trilling, p. 86.

[35] This is the most successfully drawn of Forster's English communities, suggesting the middle class life of a Surrey village such as the author's own Abinger Hammer. The success is due to the fact that of the English communities that Forster describes, the rural village with its middle-class, capitalist patronage must have been the one he knew best, and whose gradual disintegration after 1918 certainly gave him cause to mourn.

[36] C.f. Furbank and Haskell, p. 38.

Even so, his engagement to Lucy produces a revealing comment on the part of the author:

The spirit of the generations had smiled through them [the relations who congratulate the couple], rejoicing in the engagement of Cecil and Lucy because it promised the continuance of life on earth. To Cecil and Lucy it promised something quite different – personal love (p. 104).

This remark, indicating the hypothesis upon which Lucy enters into her engagement, shows that she, like Caroline Abbott before her, has failed to accept the vision of spontaneous passion offered in Italy. It is, however, a measure of the difference between *Room* and *Angels*, that this time a second vision is to be offered and then again, a third.

Chapter 10, the chapter which is to reveal Cecil as continuing to further the plot by bringing the Emersons to Summer Street, opens with a passage which serves as a summary of the state of affairs to date; more particularly as an analysis of the state of Lucy's emotional development, and, as such, is also a prelude to the events of the last part of the novel.

A radical out and out, she learnt to speak with horror of Suburbia. Life so far as she troubled to conceive it, was a circle of rich, pleasant people, with identical interests and identical foes. In this circle one thought, married, and died. Outside it were poverty and vulgarity, for ever trying to enter (pp. 117-8).

That is Lucy's state before she went to Italy, indicating a naive misconception of reality (experience) and the typical, privileged middle class suppositions.

But in Italy... this conception of life vanished. Her senses expanded; she felt that there was no-one whom she might not get to like, that social barriers were irremovable, doubtless, but not particularly high... She returned with new eyes (p. 118).

Thus does Forster prepare the reader for the re-assumption of relations between Lucy and George Emerson, who is socially not of the same class. It is significant that Forster uses the phrase "her senses expanded". That which Italy has accomplished, and we may substitute 'reality as experience' for Italy, is to have awakened her emotionally to appreciate the worth of individuals rather than of groups, and to trust more to her intuitive evaluation of people rather than to measure them by the code of convention and class.

There would seem to be no discrepancy between the new Lucy and the hypothesis upon which she and Cecil are prepared to enter upon marriage. However, whereas Lucy sees 'personal love' in contrast to the demands of a social convention which has lost its meaning, Cecil sees the social conventions of the rural middle classes invalidated by his pose as an urbane intellectual. This is emphasised when, listing those aspects of the new Lucy which Cecil has not been able to understand, Forster writes,

Nor did he realise a more important point – that if she was too great for this society, she was too great for all society, and had reached the stage where personal intercourse would alone satisfy her (p. 118).

When Lucy and George do finally meet again after church on Sunday, Lucy is all the more prepared for the experience by being out of harmony with Cecil because of the sneering tone of his remarks when the churchgoers set out, leaving him, at his own wish, behind. The meeting itself has distinct similarities with the confrontation between Gino and Caroline Abbott in *Angels*. Caroline had first been drawn to Gino by the spectacle of his love for his child; in *Room*, that which Lucy first remarks is the love of George for his father. As George puts his arm round his father's neck, "The kindness that Mr Beebe and Lucy had always known to exist in him came out suddenly... She remembered that in all his perversities he had never spoken against affection" (p. 162). Furthermore, the realisation that George is shy and awkward in the presence of Miss Bartlett destroys the possible illusion about the superiority of men which Lucy owed to her class and their conventions: "Perhaps anything that he did would have pleased Lucy, but his awkwardness went straight to her heart: men were not Gods after all, but as human and clumsy as girls; even men might suffer from unexplained desires, and need help" (p. 163). Once again Forster suggests a potential sensitivity and understanding in Lucy that is able to penetrate to the true meaning, in this case, of George's hesitancy, and name it: "unexplained desires".

Having begun so propitiously, the chapter ends with revelation and once again Lucy fails to accept the vision that is offered. Faced with the experienced reality that it is George and not Cecil who loves her, class decorum and propriety dictate to her a refusal. Lucy is still unable to distinguish between real and pretended. As Forster writes, a page later, at the beginning of Chapter 16 which will end with the dismissal of Cecil:

The contest lay not between love and duty. Perhaps there never is such a contest. It lay between the real and the pretended, and Lucy's first aim was to defeat herself (p. 172).

Her aim is temporarily reached and Lucy is for the moment beyond salvation, since she is unable to take decisions which have either a rational or an emotional basis. She dismisses Cecil with the statement that there is no one else whom she loves, and she denies to George that she could love him. Lucy has therefore reached roughly the same position that Caroline Abbott reached at the end of *Angels*. She is saved by the intervention of the first of Forster's wise elderly people, who are wise because, being elderly, they have had the chance of gaining considerable experience, and are now granted the leisure to meditate upon it and to gain wisdom from their encounters with other individuals. Mr Emerson precedes Mr Failing, Mrs Wilcox, and Mrs Moore in the ranks of what E. K. Brown has called Forster's "contemplatives".[37]

In the closing interview between Mr Emerson and Lucy in Mr Beebe's study (the acceptance of salvation takes place, symbolically, under the physical aegis of the church), the old man begins his argument by uniting love and reality: "I taught him... to trust in love. I said: 'When love comes, that is reality'" (p. 209). For some time Lucy cannot, or will not, understand and announces that she is leaving Summer Street for Greece, and so will be out of the way, giving as her reason her broken engagement. Mr Emerson counters this with what amounts to a sermon on the consequences of muddle and muddled thinking, reaching a climax with the bald statement that she does in fact love George. He concludes, "You can transmute love, ignore it, muddle it, but you can never pull it out of you" (p. 215). A call, that is, for the acknowledgement of reality as the ideal. The chapter ends with the transformation of Mr Emerson

C.f. E. K. Brown, "E. M. Forster and the Contemplative Novel", *University of Toronto Quarterly*, III (1933-4), p. 354.

into a sort of virtue-giving, holy man, which can be seen as a sign that Forster, at this stage, still believes that his ideal, even when divorced from reality as experience, can work.

He gave her a sense of deities reconciled, a feeling that, in gaining the man she loved, she would gain something for the whole world... he had shown her the holiness of direct desire... It was as if he had made her see the whole of everything at once (p. 218).

With the conclusion of *Room with a View*, Forster appears to be offering a means of relieving the human condition, but is, in fact, evading the very realities which later were to occupy him so much.[38] The suggestion that love can be followed and can reconcile the vision with the everyday has a tone of wishful optimism which Forster was never again to recapture.

[38] C.f. Langbaum, "A New Look at E. M. Forster", p. 38; see too the charge that Forster's "personal ethics drift too easily into sentimentality" (C. M. Bowra, "Beauty in Bloomsbury", *Yale Review*, XLIV [1954-5], p. 463).

6

A CONTACT WITH REALITY:
THE LONGEST JOURNEY

> In it I have managed to get nearer
> than elsewhere towards what was in
> my mind – or rather towards that
> junction of mind with heart where
> the creative impulse sparks.

E. M. Forster[1]

This novel stands apart from the two Italian books as being more intensely autobiographical both as regards detail and facts, and as regards mental or spiritual development.[2] In the *Paris Review* interview, in answer to the question as to which characters in the novels represent himself, Forster replied, "Rickie more than any".[3] Fur-

[1] Introduction to World's Classics edition of *Longest Journey*, p. ix.

[2] C.f. "There is a chasm... between *The Journey* and the other books". – Letter from T. E. Lawrence to Forster, 8.9.1927, *The Letters of T. E. Lawrence*, ed. David Garnett (London, 1938), p. 538; "*The Longest Journey* can... be considered more intensely Forsterian than any other novel". – Frederick P. W. McDowell, "Forster's Many-faceted Universe: Idea and Paradox in *The Longest Journey*", *Critique*, IV (Fall-Winter 1960-61), p. 44.

[3] Furbank and Haskell, p. 38. That the Cambridge chapters of the book in particular have an autobiographical basis is supported by further details. At the beginning of Chapter 2, Forster gives us a description of the dell along the Madingley Road: "when Rickie was up, it chanced to be the brief season of its romance, a season as brief for a chalk-pit as a man" (*The Longest Journey*, Penguin edition [Harmondsworth, 1960], p. 23. All further page references are to this edition). In one of Forster's earliest pieces of published writing, the essay "On Grinds", written when he was an undergraduate at Cambridge, we find during a reference to a walk along the Madingley Road: "a happy few find the little chalk pit this side of the village where they may wander among the firs and undergrowth, folded off from the outer world" (*Cambridge Review*, 1.2.1900, p. 185); we may note, too, the similarity between the description in *Journey* of Rickie's efforts as an undergraduate to entertain his visitors to Cambridge (e.g.

ther, he has told, in his introduction to the *World's Classics* edition
of the novel, how many of the themes which are to be found in *The
Longest Journey* were added to the original idea of 1904 about "a
man who discovers that he has an illegitimate brother".[4] These
additional themes Forster notes as being "the metaphysical idea
of Reality... the ethical idea of reality... the idea of the British
Public School... the title, exhorting us... not to love one person only,
there was Cambridge, there was Wiltshire".[5] The majority of critics
have overlooked one item in Forster's list: the ethical aspect of
reality. Shusterman, Trilling, and Wilde all concentrate on the
conflict between appearance and reality, or on the nature of reality
itself.[6] Another group of critics shift the emphasis somewhat and
concentrate on the conflict between ideal and reality, the reality of
experience.[7]

What in fact does emerge from an examination of *The Longest
Journey* is that, in contrast to the two novels already considered, we
are now dealing with a much more complex work. It will be our
suggestion that Forster is concerned with three central ideas: love,
reality, and morality. He investigates the effects of conventional
moral thinking and reality, seen as experience, upon love and human
affection, and at the same time investigates the limitations of love
within this context. The conflict centres upon the spiritual life of
the novel's protagonist Rickie Elliot, where the struggle is played
out between Ansell and Stephen on the side of reality and straight
thinking, and the Pembrokes, brother and sister, on the side of

---

pp. 73-5) and Forster's unsigned article, "A Long Day", *Basileona*, Nr. 1.,
1.6.1900, p. 13.
[4] P. ix.
[5] Pp. ix-x.
[6] Shusterman, *The Quest for Certitude...*, p. 87; Trilling, *E. M. Forster*, p. 67;
Wilde, *Art and Order*, p. 30.
[7] C.f. "Rickie's struggle to live by the truth of the wine while being immersed
in knowledge of the world" (Leavis, *The Common Pursuit*, p. 266); c.f. Phyllis
Bentley, "The Novels of E. M. Forster", p. 351. Crews discusses this aspect too,
but points to the connection with *Howards End* by suggesting that the central
problem in *The Longest Journey* is also 'only connect' (Crews, *E. M. Forster.
The Perils of Humanism*, p. 66). Yet another element is introduced by Gransden's
comment that the novel "emerges as a meditation on the dangers and attractions
of romanticism" (Gransden, *E. M. Forster*, p. 50).

convention, morality, and middle class prejudice. Ansell represents the Cambridge of G. E. Moore, the speculative formulation of ideals and philosophic position,[8] whereas Stephen in questions of morality is clearly a Mill-Utilitarian,[9] and in other respects personifies the life of the body as a further development of Gino Carella. It would be easiest to describe Stephen as the artistic development of the combination of Gino and the Emersons.

In the three structural divisions of *Journey*, with the corresponding change of scene, we may notice the way in which Forster makes use of the 'spirit of place'. The link between locality and theme was tentatively formed in the role of Italy in the two Italian novels; later we have the symbolic role of the English countryside as the embodiment of tradition and irrationality in *Howards End*, and the overwhelming centrality of India as locale in *Passage*. In *Journey* the three divisions of the book correspond to the tripartite theme we have delineated above; Cambridge provides an ideal which has both metaphysical and ethical implications and is also based to a large extent on personal affection; Sawston, with its insistence on the school as the microcosm, presents one vision of the great world and fills out the vision with conventional patterns of morality and behaviour; it is Wiltshire which provides the decisive, the truer, vision, Rickie's rejection of which precipitates disaster.[10]

The opening chapter presents the main characters in typical poses: Ansell the theoretician, Rickie in a muddle, Agnes majestic, and Herbert Pembroke insensitively conventional. It is Ansell, however, who dominates, both with his views on perception (where Miss Pembroke comes off second best to the cow) and, more particularly, with his drawing of circles and squares.

[8] There is a similarity between the discussion which opens *The Longest Journey* and the account of G. E. Moore's lecture "The Nature and Reality of Objects of Perception", contained in Lytton Strachey's letter of January 1906, quoted in Watt, "G. E. Moore and the Bloomsbury Group", p. 121.

[9] C.f. conversation between Stephen and Rickie in the train on the way to Cadover, where, referring to bodily temptations, and in particular to 'women', Stephen says: "But that's absolutely different. That would be harming someone else.", and in reply to Rickie's query whether this belief is the only guide to morality he possesses, Stephen says, "What else should?" (p. 264).

[10] It can be no mere chance that the all-important, yet often problematical, Chapter 28 precedes the final intrusion of Wiltshire to rout Sawston.

he sat on the edge of the table and watched his clever friend draw within the square a circle, and within the circle a square, and inside that another circle, and inside that another square.
"Why will you do that?"
No answer.
"Are they real?"
"The inside one is – the one in the middle of everything, that there's never room enough to draw" (p. 23).

Although at this moment in the novel, Ansell's diagram is merely a representation of the philosophical problem which fascinates him (and which he cannot turn into an acceptable dissertation),[11] but later in the novel we are to be reminded of the drawing by the description of Cadbury Rings: "A bank of grass enclosed a ring of turnips, which enclosed a second bank of grass, which enclosed more turnips, and in the middle of the pattern grew one small tree" (pp. 102-3). These Rings become central to the Wiltshire episodes of the story; it is here that Rickie will have the vision offered to him and where he will reject it (pp. 134-7). Further, it is at the Rings where Rickie says he will meet Stephen when they return to Cadover (p. 263) and where he finally realises they shall never meet (p. 280). Here then we have both a symbol of the alliance between Ansell and Stephen, the union of contemplation[12] and action, and, too, a symbol of the search for reality as ideal, but, by association, an ideal that has been reconciled to experience.

Ansell it is, too, who dominates the scene in the dell in the first part of Chapter 2. He shows up the weaknesses in Rickie's ideal of personal intercourse: "You want to love every one equally, and that's worse than impossible – it's wrong" (p. 25). He also, in passing, reinforces his judgement on Agnes as non-existent, when he reminds Tilliard: "The other night we had been discussing a long time, and suddenly the light was turned on!" (p. 25).[13] Ansell's use

---

[11] When we meet Ansell writing his second dissertation, he is drawing circles and squares on the manuscript (p. 182).

[12] C.f. E. K. Brown, "E. M. Forster and the Contemplative Novel", p. 354. Brown places Ansell among the "true contemplatives".

[13] In the previous chapter, we read of Agnes' arrival in Rickie's room: " 'Wicked, intolerable boy !' She turned on the electric light. The philosophers were revealed..." (p. 10).

of the passive is shown to be as incisively critical as his ignoring of
Agnes earlier. The important moment in the conversation in the
dell is, however, when Ansell suggests to Rickie that he hates more
people than he pretends. Rickie, full of the unreflected optimism
of this period of his life, says boldly, "I hate no one" (p. 26). The
full weight of this remark is first felt near the end of the book when
Rickie is paying his final visit to Mrs Failing at Cadover: "She
could not annoy him now, and he was not vindictive. In the dell
near Madingley he had cried, 'I hate no one', in his ignorance.
Now, with full knowledge, he hated no one again" (p. 260). Here,
then, is the measure of Rickie's ability to assimilate experience, and
incidentally an indication of Forster's valuation of such a process:
it does not matter whether you advance from a belief or an ideal to
another or not, as long as the final position is supported by and
based on reality seen as experience. In other words from the conversation in the dell to the end of the book we shall be tracing this
process of emotional and spiritual education in Rickie.

Forster interrupts the narration of Rickie's childhood only once
to give the remarks of his hearer, Widdrington. Rickie is remembering how, at the age of twelve, he came to the realisation that he
would never have a brother. "'No loss', interrupted Widdrington.
'But I shall never have one, and so I quite want one, even now'"
(p. 30).[14] This underlining of Rickie's realisation ("never have a
brother"), coupled with his wish to have one, turns the discovery of
Stephen's identity and Rickie's subsequent behaviour into a further
measure of his spiritual and emotional state, or, in other words, a
measure of the gap between Cambridge and Sawston.

With the brief introduction to, and parting from, Gerald Dawes
the plot of *The Longest Journey* is launched on its next phase. Gerald
is the fictional precursor of Charles Wilcox in *Howards End*, as the
conventional, clean-living, good sort. His determined denigration
of the intellectual ("I know nothing about the 'Varsity'", p. 42) and
his strict separation of the classes ("I can't stand talking to serv-
ants", p. 44) are precursors of the sort of attitude that at first fascinates and then repulses Helen Schlegel.[15] Gerald, however, is, in

[14] A wish that is repeated again, implicitly, on p. 72.
[15] C.f. *Howards End*, pp. 6-7 and 179.

himself of no importance whatsoever, he is merely the man Agnes loves[16] and as such enables Rickie to have his first vision: his own secondhand experience of love. Like Caroline Abbott in *Angels*, Rickie's first contact with love is with the love of two other people, but it is no less an encounter with the ideal. His perception of the true significance of his accidental view of Gerald and Agnes embracing is, in spite of the purple patch style of Forster's writing, ultimately non-romantic: "Was Love a column of fire? Was he a torrent of song? Was he greater than either – the touch of a man on a woman? It was the merest accident that Rickie had not been disgusted. But this he could not know" (p. 46). It is the realisation that love is a human and personal concern and, as such, greater than images of love that is Rickie's most precious perception in the first part of the book,[17] and which he is to guard carefully. Later when the second vision is offered, the revelation of Stephen's identity, Rickie remarks afterwards: "Once before a symbol was offered to me – I shall not tell you how; but I did accept it, and cherished it, through much anxiety and repulsion" (p. 142). The danger with Rickie is that in these early days, he allows his suddenly won perception to run away with his fantasy and so finds himself, certainly in the view of others, if not as yet in his own estimation, in a muddle,[18] which leads him to such misunderstood actions as the offering of money to Gerald. More important is the view that this vision gives Rickie of Agnes. Forster writes of Rickie's idea of her as "a kindly Medea" and that "she had more reality than any other woman in the world" (p. 53). How deeply muddled Rickie is may be divined from the later description of Agnes by Mr Jackson, one of the 'right-headed' characters of the novel, as "Medusa in Arcady" (p. 182). Thus Rickie's estimates of reality are seen to be far from the ideal which Forster proposes. Agnes herself is much more clearseeing and, excusing Rickie to Gerald at the end of Chapter 4, makes, in another way, a statement about Rickie's relation to reality: "He

---

[16] C.f. "Her own splendid lover" (p. 12).
[17] C.f. Frederick P. W. McDowell, "The newest elucidations of Forster", *English Literature in Transition* V (1962), p. 51.
[18] C.f. Beer, *The Achievement of E. M. Forster*, p. 78.

muddles all day with poetry and old dead people, and then tries to bring it into life. It's too funny for words" (p. 55).

Rickie's return to Cambridge is marked by the rapid increase in his state of muddledom. The first step in Rickie's progress away from the vision and the adoption of an ideal is marked by a concern to clarify the possible divisions of his world, which finds its climax in the distinction Rickie attempts to make between the great world and Cambridge. This is, however, preceded by a sudden revelation about human existence:

> He knew once for all that we are all of us bubbles on an extremely rough sea. Into this sea humanity has built, as it were, some little breakwaters – scientific knowledge, civilized restraint – so that the bubbles do not break so frequently or so soon. But the sea has not altered... (p. 62).

This, almost haphazard, view of life reveals that Rickie is already moving into the dangerous position of failing to see his ideal, love and affection, as divorced from the central problems of life and existence. For him the breakwaters are thought to be intellectual or conventional, but certainly not emotional. Forster hints at what such a division may lead to at the beginning of Chapter 7. Describing Rickie and his friends, he writes: "They are full of the wine of life. But they have not tasted the cup – let us call it the teacup – of experience, which has made men of Mr Pembroke's type what they are" (p. 66). The suggestion here being that while the assimilation of experience by reality so as to modify the ideal is desirable, the accentuation of the value of experience which involves the mocking of the ideal leads to damnation.[19]

Once again it is Ansell who dominates the central discussion of this closing Cambridge period, the argument about the great world.[20] He argues that the only valid distinction to be made is between good and bad societies, that is, he applies the principles of

---

[19] The somewhat sneering tone that Forster adopts towards Mr Pembroke here will become the somewhat sad acceptance of the value of even such men in *Howards End*, where the world of Herritons, Honeychurches, and Pembrokes combine in the Wilcoxes.

[20] C.f. "The Cambridge chapters are still... crucial for me, and I still endorse Ansell's denunciation of the Great World." – Introduction to the *World's Classics* edition, p. xi.

the ethics of reality, and in doing so destroys much of the cant to be later associated with Sawston.[21]

Cambridge makes its last appearance in *The Longest Journey* as the setting of Rickie's own experience of love. Although we learn (p. 71) that he is already in love with Agnes, this emotion makes him afraid to meet her. The fear is not, however, due to shyness but because Rickie still fears to destroy the immensity of that earlier vision of love. Here we must insist that there can be no doubt that Rickie, like the early Forster, has established love as an ideal, but Forster has reached the point where he can already survey the dangers of too complete a trust in ideals untried as yet by experience. So Rickie enters into love without any consideration that it has human aspects and human consequences; as he says to Agnes within the dell, "I prayed you might not be a woman" (p. 79). The combination of Mr Failing's essay on 'Gaps' (where Seclusion, who lives in a similar dell, finally makes a gap in the wall and the Profane invade, but in the intervals between their invasions "the heart of Nature is revealed to him" (p. 213)), the combination of this tale and the earlier comment on Rickie's undergraduate attitude to the place[22] emphasise the symbolic necessity of choosing this setting for the revelation of love for Agnes. Although Rickie as yet does not realise it, Agnes belongs to the vulgar,[23] and as such will slowly draw Rickie away from the possibilities of further perceptions. Ansell does realise this and therefore his aggressive strictures on their engagement: "She is happy because she has conquered; he is happy because he has at last hung all the world's beauty on to a

---

[21] C.f. Mr Pembroke's beginning of term speech on p. 161: "school is the world in miniature". Over 160 years earlier Henry Fielding had introduced such a view into *Joseph Andrews*, where the hero quotes Sir Thomas Booby as saying, "great schools are little societies, where a boy of any observation may see in epitome what he will afterwards find in the world at large" (Everyman edition [London, 1970], p. 179). Later in life Forster was to write, "School was the unhappiest time of my life, and the worst trick it played me was to pretend that it was the world in miniature" ("Breaking Up", *Spectator*, 28.7.1933, p. 119).

[22] C.f. "He did not love the vulgar herd, but he knew that his own vulgarity would be greater if he forbade it ingress, and that it was not by preciosity that he would attain to the intimate spirit of the dell" (p. 24).

[23] C.f. Mr Failing's distinction between coarseness and vulgarity: "coarseness revealing something; vulgarity concealing something" (p. 211).

single peg" (p. 86). It is Ansell, too, who in his letter to Rickie first introduces Shelley's poem which gave the novel its title into the book,[24] and warns him that such a course of action may lead to disaster. Ansell, that is, although inexperienced in the Pembroke sense of the word, is, by virtue of his detachment and of his carefully adopted ideals, the one character in the book who has the true insight into the catastrophes and disasters which courses of conduct will inevitably lead to.[25]

The Cambridge section of the book is infiltrated by Wiltshire before it ends, in fact the last third of this section belongs to the Wiltshire world, thus making the section of the book which began with a discussion of reality end with the presentation of the force of reality. Rickie's first trip to Cadover is overhung from the beginning by disaster and presentiments of disaster. Stephen breaks the news that the train which brought Agnes and Rickie to Cadover was responsible for the death of a child. "'A child' – said Rickie. 'I can't believe that the train killed a child.' He thought of their journey. They were alone in the carriage. As the train slackened speed he had caught her for a moment in his arms..." (p. 100). For Rickie

---

[24] Shelley's *Epipsychidion* (strangely enough addressed to "Emily"). The main burden of the poem centres round the concept of marriage or companionship for life, which involves, in the acceptance of one person, the rejection of the many. It is the view, that is, of the unencumbered man, and may be largely identified with Forster's own. One need only think of the way in which he draws his most clear representative of this school of thought, Cyril Fielding. The poem points out that the view of the necessity to establish oneself with one companion is the majority view, the view of convention, and so, in the novel, of middle-class Sawston. The association made here between the romantic concept – love – and the moral one – marriage – is one that Forster himself makes explicitly later in the novel, when Stephen tells Rickie of his own plans concerning marriage. Forster writes: "Romantic love is also the code of modern morals, and, for this reason, popular. Eternal union, eternal ownership – these are tempting baits for the average man" (p. 271). Finally, Shelley's reference to the "one sad friend, perhaps a jealous foe" echoes not only the development of Rickie's marriage to Agnes, but also the marriages of other characters in the book, namely, his own parents and Mr and Mrs Failing.

The entire poem is read by Rickie just before the relevation of Stephen's identity, and may thus be seen as an appeal to him to widen the confines of his love. The third mention of the poem is just before Rickie makes the decision to leave Agnes and go with Stephen, thus making the mistake of again trusting to one loved person alone.

[25] C.f. Trilling, p. 75; Wilde, *Art and Order*, p. 31.

the train has existed, understandably enough, as the background for his attempts to recreate his first vision of love for himself. That the train may also have been an instrument of death is impossible for him. Rickie cannot accept the idea that disaster and love could have existed simultaneously. That is, he is in danger of insisting on the necessary remoteness of the ideal (love) from reality as experience (the death of the child). Stephen's insistence, "You've got to believe it", is the first indication that he, like Ansell, but in a different manner, has reached a more satisfactory position in relation to the problem of reality and experience. It is Stephen, too, who concludes the discussion: "There wants a bridge... A bridge instead of all this rotten talk and the level-crossing... Then the child's soul, as you call it – well, nothing would have happened to the child at all" (p. 101). Stephen is the practical realist with the insight that perceives that which is of importance and that which is not. He is, in this sense, the precursor of the Schlegel insistence on 'proportion' in *Howards End*.

The remainder of the visit to Cadover prepares for, and leads up to, the final revelation among the Rings. Even the ride to Salisbury, which on the whole serves the plot more than the development of themes, contains hints of the future and reaches even beyond the events of this visit. In particular Rickie's analysis of Stephen's somewhat pugnacious character is to be echoed with stronger repercussions later in the book. Rickie is reminded of Gerald ("the Gerald of history, not the Gerald of romance", p. 112) as Agnes later is going to be physically reminded of him at the critical last encounter of the book (pp. 255-259).[26] The discussion that Rickie and Agnes have after his return from the abortive ride is both a further measure of Rickie's disintegration and of his isolation. When he admits the divorce between ideal and human affection, he shows that in Forsterian terms he has broken faith with the original ideal:

[26] In the discussion of marriage Rickie's mental separation of Agnes from the general line of well-beloved figures emphasises his own withdrawal from reality. C.f. "He loved Agnes, not only for herself, but because she was lighting up the human world" (p. 114). Rickie is in danger, here, of substituting a symbol for a person – Agnes as "the human world" in miniature, rather than as the girl he loved.

Don't you think there are two great things in life that we ought to aim at – truth and kindness? Let's have both if we can, but let's be sure of having one or the other (pp. 127-8).

Moreover Rickie admits that he has arrived at the realization that there are a lot of people in the world who are not important to him. A statement that on its own seems reasonable and honest, but Forster makes the wry comment, "There was only one gate to the kingdom of heaven now" (p. 128), namely Agnes. It is after the conversation which forms the context for these remarks that Rickie goes out for a walk and reads Shelley's poem. The poem sets the mental condition in which he arrives with Mrs Failing, Agnes and Stephen at the Rings where the second and more important vision awaits him. [27]

On arrival at the Rings, Forster emphasises the visitor's careful progress from ring to ring to the central tree, and Mrs Failing's account of the devil leaning against the tree in the centre. Here we are clearly meant to see the parallel, first to Ansell's circles and squares diagram, in which the centre is marked by reality, and secondly the biblical parallel to the tree of knowledge watched over by the snake, the devil. Thus for Rickie reality is inevitably to be bound up with the revelation of new knowledge, and in fact, Mrs Failing makes the fatal statement about his half-brother as they approach the tree (p. 136). The circle image is concluded, after his outburst that the news is all a lie:

But he heard her no longer. He was gazing at the past, which he had praised so recently, which gaped ever wider, like an unhallowed grave. Turn where he would, it encircled him. It took visible form: it was this double entrenchment of the Rings (p. 136).

The vision has been granted, and although at first unwilling to accept that which is revealed, Rickie does not yet totally reject it. It is Agnes who prevents any possible acceptance on Rickie's part. He, in fact goes so far as to see the connection with reality, [28] and it is he who defines the nature of the vision:

[27] We may note here a parallel in technique to the way in which Miss Quested is mentally 'conditioned', before she enters the fateful cave in *Passage*.
[28] C.f. "it's a real thing" (p. 142).

It seems to me that here and there in life we meet with a person or incident that is symbolical. It's nothing in itself, yet for the moment it stands
for some eternal principle. We accept it, at whatever cost, and we have
accepted life. But if we are frightened and reject it, the moment, so to
speak, passes; the symbol is never offered again (p. 142).

That Rickie, acknowledging this, still allows Agnes to talk him out
of telling Stephen the truth is an indication of the catastrophe and
disintegration to come.[29] Agnes is able to dominate Rickie by a
combination of conventional morality ("doing right is its own
reward", p. 142)[30] and strategy (getting rid of Stephen and barring
Rickie's view of him from the window, p. 143). The final blow in
Agnes's campaign is when she persuades Rickie not to tell Ansell
anything about the incident (p. 144). From this moment Rickie, like
Lucy Honeychurch, but more irrevocably, goes into the dark.

Before entering on the vulgarising process of becoming a teacher
at Sawston school, Rickie has one last attempt to make his way as
an author and is given the advice, "See life, Mr Elliott, and then
send us another story" (p. 150). Rickie is already too far gone to be
able to accept or to evaluate the remark that the editor of the *Holborn* has made. Part One of *The Longest Journey* ends on a significant note:

He loved, he was loved, he had seen death and other things; but the heart
of all things was hidden. There as a password and he could not learn it,
nor could the kind editor of the *Holborn* teach him. He sighed and then
sighed more piteously. For he had known the password once – known it
and forgotten it already? (p. 150).

That Rickie's situation is truly hopeless is indicated by the word
"But" at the beginning of the next sentence, indicating a finality and
a change in approach. Away now from speculation and fancy, and

[29] C.f. "a careful study of an impassioned idealist who is forced, by dint of
time and circumstance, to shed most of his ideals... or perhaps, rather, to
witness their gradual disintegration" (Review of *Journey*, *Athenaeum*, 18.5.1907,
p. 600).
[30] McDowell suggests that Rickie's denial of this maxim and the replacing of
it by the suggestion that "doing right is simply doing right" (p. 143) is the key
to "Forster's humanistic ethic" (*Critique*, p. 53). As we shall see later, Forster's
ethic is perhaps more nearly defined in terms of the principle of "good-and-evil"
than by Rickie's statement here.

to work in the great world: "But at this point his fortunes become intimately connected with those of Mr Pembroke" (p. 150).

The tone of the first three chapters of Part Two of *The Longest Journey* is set by the remark near the end of chapter 16: "He (Rickie) did not aspire to beauty or wisdom, but he prayed to be delivered from the shadow of unreality that had begun to darken the world" (p. 156), and we read again at the end of chapter 19, before the interval with Ansell in the British Museum:

> The same routine, the same diplomacies, the same old sense of only half knowing boys or men – he returned to it all; and all that changed was the cloud of unreality, which ever brooded a little more densely than before (p. 180).

The fact that Rickie sees Sawston as existing under the "cloud of unreality" indicates the role that his period as a schoolmaster is to play. Sawston, intermingled as it is with the public school ethos that Forster so deplored and overlaid with middle-class convention, is unreal in the sense that its very air of solid anti-intellectualism,[31] its insistence on being a microcosm of the great world and the value it would appear to place on experience, make it the apotheosis of sham, the pretended preferred to the real. Sawston is unreal for it is far-removed from the reality represented by the ideal. Moreover, within the context of Rickie's experience, Sawston is a form of existence whose value can only be measured by comparison with the other forms known to him: "He would compare Cambridge with Sawston, and either with a third type of existence, to which, for want of a better name, he gave the name of 'Wiltshire'" (p. 159). Looking ahead this comment prepares for the final evaluation of the experience of reality that Rickie has, namely, that Wiltshire becomes a more important touchstone than Cambridge. Or, in more general terms, life reveals what theory could only hint at.

The first part of Rickie's Sawston existence is dominated by the split between Mr Jackson and his group and the Dunwood House set of the Pembrokes. In this struggle, Rickie while revealing that he is still the vague unpractical Rickie of the Madingley dell, who wanted to love everyone equally (p. 25), goes under to the more

---

[31] C.f. Mr Pembroke's earlier advice to Rickie: "I wish you could move among schoolboys, and see their healthy contempt for all they cannot touch" (p. 52).

powerful demands of loyalty, duty, and convention. His defeat is due to his inability to make fixed moral pronouncements based on an absolute scale of values. "For Rickie suffered from the Primal Curse, which is not – as the Authorised Version suggests – the knowledge of good and evil, but the knowledge of good-and-evil" (p. 175). Forster's concern with absolute values in questions of ethics and morality is to persist throughout his life.[32] At this stage he is dubious about the ability to distinguish moral absolutes of this sort and clearly sympathises with Rickie. At the same time, however, Forster is aware of the weakness and dangers of such a position to which he opposes, on the one hand, the clearer thinking of Ansell, and, on the other hand, the sentiment and non-thinking of the Pembrokes. In fiction this position with reference to right and wrong, good and evil, will end in the complete merger of the two opposites as twin aspects of Professor Godbole's Lord.[33] For Rickie Elliott, this subtlety of mind in questions of moral value has the effect of rendering him unable to sort out the human value of the people around him;[34] it leads him, that is, into the muddle where Sawston standards are good, Ansell and Cambridge irrelevant, and Stephen Wonham unwholesome and tainted.

The brief interval of Chapter 20 serves as a means of distancing the reader from the events at Sawston, and to review them once again through the eyes and ideals of the philosopher, Ansell. The chapter opens with a clear statement of Ansell's position in regard to the search for reality.

It was worth while to grow old and dusty seeking for truth though truth is unattainable, restating questions that have been stated at the beginning of the world. Failure would await him, but not disillusionment (p. 180).

Here we note that which most consistently characterises Ansell: a

---

[32] C.f. "It is childish to simplify, either in the favour of Heaven or of Hell; both tricks have been tried and neither works" ("The Book of the Age?", *New Leader*, 12.3.1926, p. 14); c.f. "Notes on the Way", 2.6.1934, p. 696. The concept of 'good-and-evil' is also implicit in the views of morality in *Howards End*, both in the principle 'only connect' (p. 287) and with reference to Helen Schlegel (p. 290).

[33] *Passage to India*, p. 175.

[34] C.f. Frederick P. W. McDowell, "E. M. Forster: Romancer or Realist?", *English Literature in Transition*, XI (1968), p. 104.

calm certainty, even if it is a certainty of failure, which gives him, like Stephen, a certain heroic dimension, and certainly endows him with strength. Ansell's view of the situation is at this stage passive and suggests that his philosophic position lacks affection: "We don't go to see people because they are happy or unhappy. We go when we can talk to them" (p. 184). A lack which is later revealed as simply repression for practical reasons.

The second part of Rickie's Sawstonian existence, leading up to the collapse resulting from Ansell's visit and the disclosure that Stephen is the son of Rickie's mother, speeds up Rickie's spiritual ruin.[35] Forster makes it clear that this ruin is the result of the failure to reveal to Stephen his true identity. The rejection of the vision once offered has embittered the lives of the Elliotts. Rickie himself realises this but cannot fight against it: "The lie we acted has ruined our lives" (p. 195). When Rickie later rebukes Agnes for attempting to turn Mrs Failing against Stephen, we become aware of this lie behind the first signs of the collapse of Rickie's marriage.

Against this background Ansell's visit to Sawston is set. A visit which Ansell has undertaken "to assure himself of his friend's grave. With quiet eyes he had intended to view the sods, with unfaltering fingers to inscribe the epitaph. Love remained. But in high matters he was practical. He knew it would be useless to reveal it" (p. 210). Ansell has to all intents and purposes given up his old friend as irretrievably lost, yet love for him remains, a love which Ansell will not reveal since it would only muddle and confuse his task. Ansell, is able to discipline his love to be subservient to his vision of the ideal. This is a new attitude to love in Forster's works and seems to represent the development away from emotion and passion, which were still seen as the desirable ideal in *Angels* and *Room with a View*, towards the belief in the greater, more enduring powers of a more wary affection. Love is still the highest ideal, but Forster is beginning to realise that contacts with experience may well lead to modifications so great as to weaken Love as the ultimate reality.

Ansell's mission is given a new turn by a further "contact with

35 C.f. "Henceforward he deteriorates... He remained conscientious and decent, but the spiritual part of him proceeded towards ruin" (p. 197).

reality"[36] in the shape of Stephen Wonham.[37] Before Stephen tells
Ansell the story of his break with Cadover and Mrs Failing, Forster
gives us a further insight into Ansell's make-up which reveals the
belief which qualifies Ansell for the philosophic task he has set
himself: the search for reality and truth.

He had a great many facts to learn, and before he died he learnt a suitable
quantity. But he never forgot that *the holiness of the heart's imagination*
can alone classify these facts – can alone decide which is an exception,
which an example (p. 212, my italics).[38]

Here Forster reveals the relation between ideal and reality seen as
experience: that is he reveals the means whereby the gap between the
two realities may be bridged: by making experience subservient yet
necessary to love and affection. Love, too, is at the centre of the
declaration that Ansell makes to Rickie in front of the assembled
members of Dunwood House; love that will be able to see Stephen
for what he is, and still love (p. 229). Again Rickie rejects the
message with the result that "he was withered up at last" (p. 229)
and with no spiritual reserves left he is unable to cope with the final
revelation that the disgrace of adultery and illegitimacy are his
mother's and not his father's. Rickie's bankruptcy is complete.

At this point in the novel, before Part Three, where Rickie will
have the last redemptive chance offered him, Forster inserts the
oft-discussed chapter 28.

The soul has her own currency. She mints her spiritual coinage and stamps
it with the image of some beloved face. With it she pays her debts, with
it she reckons, saying, "This man has worth, this man is worthless."
And in time she forgets its origin; it seems to her be a thing unalterable,
divine. But the soul can also have her bankruptcies.

Perhaps she will be the richer in the end. In her agony she learns to
reckon clearly. Fair as the coin may have been, it was not accurate; and
though she knew it not, there were treasures that it could not buy. The
face, however beloved, was mortal, and as liable as the soul herself to err.
We do but shift responsibility by making a standard of the dead (p. 230).

In the context of the events of the novels to date, Forster is doing

[36] Ansell's own words, albeit somewhat ironic, for his meeting with Stephen
(p. 226).
[37] C.f. Robert Fricker, *Der moderne englische Roman* (Göttingen, 1958), p. 82.
[38] C.f. The comment on Forster and romantic humanism, p. 47 above.

little more than symbolising the mistake that Rickie has made in trusting so exclusively in his own memory of his mother as a personification of the good. However, Forster is also symbolising what we have all along recognised: namely, the insistence on the ideal which has been tempered and modified by an understanding contact with the reality of experience.[39] The chapter ends:

There is indeed, another coinage that bears on it not man's image but God's. It is incorruptible, and the soul may trust it safely; it will serve her beyond the stars. But it cannot give us friends, or the embrace of a lover, or the touch of children, for with our fellow-mortals it has no concern. It cannot even give the joys we call trivial – fine weather, the pleasure of meat and drink, bathing and the hot sand afterwards, running, dreamless sleep. Have we learnt the true discipline of a bankruptcy if we turn to such coinage as this? Will it really profit us so much if we save our souls and lose the whole world? (p. 230).

This paragraph is a final statement of position, a humanist outcry against the escape from reality to religion. In the context of the novel it shows up again the mean narrowness of the world of Sawstonian morality and makes Herbert Pembroke's taking holy orders a just conclusion to his career. Forster establishes with a symbolic finality the conflict he feels to exist between the unimpeded free search for truth and reality on the one hand, and the demands of religion and trust in God on the other. From now on *The Longest Journey* builds up to a climax which will assert the "costly but unmistakably plain" victory of humanism.[40]

Part Three, Wiltshire, centres around two crises: Rickie's final acceptance of Stephen on the latter's return to Sawston, and the return of both to Cadover culminating in Rickie's death. The first crisis is in the nature of a repetition of the vision, the second marks Rickie's inability to accept that which is offered. Throughout the whole section, Rickie's failure is characterised by his inability to accept people and events for what they are and his propensity to see them as symbols, as personifications of an ideal.

There is no doubt that the Rickie who finally welcomes Stephen

---

[39] C.f. "[Rickie] has lost his soul precisely because he has lost his sense of the material world" (McDowell, "Recent Books on Forster and Bloomsbury", p. 135.
[40] Crews, p. 64.

back to Sawston has already changed sides again, has begun "a new life" (p. 248), although he is still associated with Herbert Pembroke as they carry Stephen upstairs: "They carried the drunken mass into the spare room. A mass of scandal it seemed to one of them, a symbol of redemption to the other. Neither acknowledged it a man..." (p. 248). But Rickie's redemption does seem very near, both in his analysis of past situations as muddles (p. 249) and in his remark to Mr Pembroke: "I never did belong to that great sect whose doctrine is that each one should select – at least, I'm not going to belong to it any longer" (p. 249). That is, Rickie now sides with Ansell and is once again, as in the early pages of the Cambridge section, quoting him without being able to remember what comes next.[41] He has got as far as seeing Agnes and the Pembrokes as the enemy, he has been able to see that his marriage was wrong in the sense that it isolated him from other possible relationships, and he can get as far as deciding to start again, but he still makes the mistake of choosing a single companion, Stephen, for the last stage of his longest journey. In terms of the coinage image of Chapter 28, the coinage in his mother's image and that in the image of Agnes have brought bankruptcy and out of this he does not learn the whole lesson and chooses another corruptible currency. It is left to Stephen to show Rickie where he has gone wrong in the matter of human relationships, but Rickie still cannot respond correctly: "'Last Sunday week,' interrupted Stephen, his voice suddenly rising, 'I came to call on you. Not as this or that's son. Not to fall on your neck. Nor to live here... I simply came as I was, and I haven't altered since'" (p. 253). Instead of accepting the truth here presented – Stephen is real, not because he represents an ideal but because he does not, because he is able to be himself – Rickie responds by once again approaching Stephen in terms of an idea, this time the idea of sharing the same mother, and Stephen responds with a gesture worthy of Ansell, by tearing up their mother's photograph.

Now Rickie collapses, as he had collapsed in the face of Mrs Failing's revelations up at the Rings. By a slight detail Forster makes us realise that for all Rickie's correct perceptions at this moment, once again the vision has retreated.

41 C.f. *Journey*, p. 21.

He did not love him, even as he had never hated him. In either passion he had degraded him to be a symbol for the vanished past.[42] The man was right, and *would have been lovable* (p. 255 my italics).

The tense of the verb in the italicised passage makes it clear that the moment for love has passed.

Nevertheless with the collapse of Agnes, attracted by physical association to Stephen (p. 255-6 see also p. 259),[43] Rickie is freed from the muddle and in a last impetuous moment leaves with Stephen, and yet it is wrong; had Agnes not broken down, Rickie would not have gone, but now he needs the one companion; it is also wrong for Rickie once more follows Stephen not as Stephen, not as a man, but as an echo of his own mother: "Habits and sex may change with the new generation, features may alter with the play of a private passion, but a voice is apart from these... it can, at all events, over-leap one grave" (p. 257).

The close of the novel, the final visit to Cadover, is prefaced by a last symbolic moment. The incident of the flames on the stream, when Stephen and Rickie throw burning balls of paper on the water and watch them disappear, gives us the last hint at the future. The significance of the fact that Rickie loses sight of the last ball of paper before Stephen is clear; he is still bound by the same arguments with which the book opened, the question of reality, of the cow. Rickie can only conceive of reality either as that which is tangible or that which is a mental concept, Stephen, on the other hand, represents the newer Forsterian ideal where reality as ideal and reality as experience are brought closer to one another by imagination, by belief in that which one can only pretend.[44] This is the same sort of attitude that Forster expressed thirty years later in the essay "What I believe":

The people I respect most behave as if they were immortal and as if society was eternal. Both assumptions are false: both of them must be accepted as true if we are to go on eating and working and loving...[45]

---

[42] C.f. Caroline Abbott's response to the sight of Gino's baby in *Angels*, p. 113.
[43] Again there is a clear parallel to Miss Abbott and Gino.
[44] C.f. "Those elms were Dryads – so Rickie believed or pretended, and the line between the two is subtler than we admit" (p. 8).
[45] *Two Cheers for Democracy*, p. 81.

From the moment when, symbolically, the potential difference between Rickie and Stephen has been established, the gap between them widens until the close of the novel is almost a conflict between the two. This conflict is complicated by the part that Mrs Failing herself plays in undermining Rickie's newly found though momentary confidence. Forster uses her, in Chapter 34, as a vehicle for the middle-class's final attempt to reassert its dominance over Rickie. We are presented with her as the personification of muddle ("in the end her private view of false and true was obscured, and she misled herself", p. 276), and thus the Wiltshire representative of the cloud of unreality which has hung over Rickie for so long. In this function she makes the appeal of conventionality to him:

We are conventional people, and conventions – if you will but see it – are majestic in their way, and will claim us in the end. We do not live for great passions or for great memories or for anything great."
He threw up his head. "We do" (p. 274).

Yet as the above passage shows, Mrs Failing has her perceptions of truth also. In the insistence on little things and her rejection of great passions, she is setting things in proportion for Rickie. He is still lost hopelessly in a sort of romantic idealism, he sees Stephen as a heroic figure (p. 278) and so is once again doomed. He is still not content to accept Stephen for what he is, but attaches to him significances which Stephen cannot bear. Thus once again Rickie places his fragile untempered love at the mercy of the reality of experience. So that when Stephen is discovered drunk again, Rickie collapses: "Gone bankrupt, Leighton, for the second time. Pretended again that people were real. May God have mercy on me!" (p. 280). Here in a brief utterance, all that is at fault in Rickie is revealed: his total confusion on matters of reality as they affect personal relations and his weakness in face of experience, when in the last cry he turns his hopes to the divine coinage of Chapter 28, and so turns his back on the possibility of attaining love and affection of his fellow-mortals. Rickie's dying words at Cadover, affirming that Mrs Failing was right, are a further revelation, for to say that Mrs Failing was right implies accepting the superiority of artificiality over the natural (p. 273), the rejection of the intellect (p. 274), and the acceptance of the position 'people are not important at all' (p. 274).

Any account of *The Longest Journey* would be incomplete without, however, an evaluation of the closing scenes. Rickie is finished with, and we are left with Stephen and Herbert Pembroke. Stephen has become the bearer of the positive themes of the book which Forster now needs to clarify. To some extent one could bring the same critical arguments to bear here as have been brought against the closing scene of *Howards End*, namely that the ending is too vaguely expressed for one to gain much positive value from it. This would however be unjust. Forster uses the last encounter between the established Pembroke and the farmer Stephen to reaffirm the paucity of Pembroke's spiritual and intellectual position, to assert, let it be said, the true reality. Stephen takes hold of Pembroke and shows him the view from the window:

Look even at that ... that's the world, and there's no miniature world. There's one world, Pembroke, and you can't tidy men out of it (p. 285).

The acceptance that reality is here and now and around us is the final 'message' that Forster would seem to be giving. At the close of the book Stephen is presented to us with his little daughter whose touch awakens in him, as a sign of the marvel of life, thoughts of Rickie who comes to his mind too as associated with the Rings, which Stephen thinks he can see through the half-light. Rickie has saved him, not merely physically but, the suggestion is, spiritually, emotionally as well. Saved him because now he (Stephen) can see the continuity of life. He looks for something to do in return and kisses his child. At the end of *The Longest Journey* love and affection remain triumphant. But they are a love and an affection which do not exist as theories or as ideals but as a present reality won by experience, by the experience of other human beings. Thus, the novel is a reaffirmation of Forster's humanism, a restating of the belief in the individual's ability to find a form of truth through affection and personal relations.

7

LOVE AND MONEY: *HOWARDS END*

> It is dangerous, very dangerous, to
> pretend that money does not exist.
>
> E. M. Forster[1]

1

Ever since Trilling's comment that *"Howards End* is a novel about England's fate. It is a story of the class war"*,[2] critics have tended to emphasise its national, social, and economic aspects. This had led to a number of generalisations and over-simplifications which always will result in interpretations based on a preconceived theory. The general tendency of these critics, as with those who discuss, more particularly, the social aspects of the novel, has been to confuse a setting with a theme. Whereas in the three preceding novels Forster was concerned with relating and reconciling ideal and reality in terms of a conflict with conventions of *morality* and *conduct*, his concern in *Howards End* is to replace these conventions with other typical characteristics of the middle class – money, property, and social relationships. As the Marxist critic D. S. Savage has observed, in *Howards End* Forster replaces the drama of personal relationships by "the drama of social relationships".[3] In

---

[1] "The Legacy of Samuel Butler", *Listener*, 12.6.1952, p. 956.
[2] Trilling, *E. M. Forster*, p. 102.
[3] D. S. Savage, *The Withered Branch* (London, 1950), p. 58; c.f. "however disinterestedly (Forster) reminds us of our dependence on society, his novel ends by crushing society on the altar of the private life" (Crews, *E. M. Forster. The Perils of Humanism*, p. 122).

so doing, money and property, or rather attitudes to these, become a focal point in the novel, but unsympathetic critics see in it more than was ever there when they declare the novel to be a "justification of economic privilege".[4] The second part of Trilling's comment, "the class war", has led to just as much misunderstanding and ambiguity as that remark contains. The conflict is within one and the same class and implies a recognition that civilization will be judged according to the standards and values of that class.[5] As far as one may admit a social theme in the novel, and surely it is *a* theme if not *the* theme, then one must cast Forster in the role of a critic of his own class values.[6] In fact, the conflict in *Howards End* is not to be seen as between class and class, but as between culture and materialism within the middle class,[7] resulting in a realisation that, since there is no culture whithout security,[8] the two elements are complementary to each other.[9] In this connection, to see the theme as "the struggle of the modern intelligentsia to define its alliance"[10] is to be close to the position, which in relation to this *aspect* of the novel is no doubt very relevant, of one of Forster's earliest critics,

---

[4] Savage, p. 122. C.f. for related views, "In the novel money and freedom are proclaimed enemies" (Gransden, *E. M. Forster*, p. 55); "the focal point of *Howards End* is the psychic life of property" (Howarth, "E. M. Forster and the Contrite Establishment", p. 202). Both these views overemphasise an important element of the novel by magnifying it beyond its context.

[5] C.f. Frederick Grubb, "Homage to E. M. Forster", *Contemporary Review*, CXCV (Jan. 1959), p. 21; Müllenbrock, "Gesellschaftliche Thematik in E. M. Forsters Roman *Howards End*", p. 377.

[6] C.f. "*Howards End*, by its far sighted criticism of middle class ideas, is a book that says most effectively those very things that the intelligent minority feel, but rarely arrive at formulating." – Review of *Howards End* by Edward Garnett, *Nation*, 12.11.1910, p. 282. Although anonymously published, authorship of the review is given in Carolyn G. Heilbrun, *The Garnett Family* (London, 1961), p. 139. Miss Heilbrun also prints a letter from Forster saying that Garnett's criticisms were the only fair ones he read. See for contrast, Arnold Bennett, *Books and Persons* (London, 1917), p. 292.

[7] C.f. Review of *Howards End*, *Spectator*, 5.11.1910, p. 757.

[8] C.f. N. M. Lunan, "The Novels of E. M. Forster", *Durham University Journal*, XXXVII (1945), p. 55.

[9] C.f. Hans A. Hammelmann, "Der Romancier E. M. Forster", *Die neue Rundschau*, 1958, p. 545; William Plomer, "An Introduction to E. M. Forster", *Penguin New Writing*, XX (1944), p. 138.

[10] Malcolm Bradbury, Introduction to *Forster. A Collection of Critical Essays*, p. 4.

who maintains that in *Howards End* he "has given in essence the history of prewar 'reform'".[11]

Within a wider context, other critics have related *Howards End* to Forster's position both as a humanist and as a liberal. For some the novel is a typical product of humanism, concerned with questions of good and evil, civilization, and man's position.[12] It has also been noted that the humanism of the novel consists in its insistence on solutions to spiritual problems in terms of this life rather than in terms of a belief in higher existence or life after death.[13] The discussion of *Howards End* in terms of liberalism in general and Forster's liberalism in particular ranges from the view that it is "one of the last statements of the liberal enlightenment",[14] "the one novel in Forster's career that projects a reasonable hope for the survival of liberalism",[15] to the criticism that the weaknesses in the novel all spring from Forster's "insufficient awareness of the limitations of liberalism".[16] All three comments are complementary and correct, or, rather, would be if Forster's novel were really that much concerned with liberalism and its survival. It is certainly true that much of *Howards End*, in particular the conversations of Helen and Margaret and their circle, is reminiscent of late nineteenth century Liberal opinion. We may, too, agree that *Howards End* suggests a possibly optimistic view of the future of certain values which are

[11] Doughty, "The Novels of E. M. Forster", p. 547.

[12] C.f. Bradbury, "Howards End" (1962), *Forster*, p. 136; Austin Warren, *Rage for Order* (Chicago, 1948), p. 123.

[13] C.f. George H. Thomson, "Theme and Symbol in *Howards End*", *Modern Fiction Studies*, VII (1961), p. 242; Ault, "Aspects of E. M. Forster", p. 119.

[14] Gransden, *E. M. Forster*, p. 79.

[15] Crews, p. 105. The anomaly of this view rests on the possibility that 1910 could well have been a period of particular urgency for Liberals (though not political) like Forster. C.f. "The year 1910... is actually a landmark in English history, which stands out against a peculiar background of flame. For it was in 1910 that fires long smouldering in the English spirit suddenly flared up, so that by the end of 1913 Liberal England was reduced to ashes... the true pre-war Liberal – supported, as it still was in 1910, by Free Trade, a majority in Parliament, the ten commandments and the illusion of Progress – can never return." – George Dangerfield, *The Strange Death of Liberal England* (1935) (London, 1966), pp. 13-14.

[16] Donald Hannah, "The Limitations of Liberalism in E. M. Forster's Work", *English Miscellany*, XIII (1962), pp. 177-8.

held in high repute in the novel. Even the critical diagnosis of the novel's weaknesses may be accepted as showing something symptomatic in Forster's position in 1910, but all these remarks are on the fringe of the central theme we have already outlined.

There is, in fact, a much closer connection between *Howards End* and the earlier novels than would seem apparent from many of the critical statements we have quoted.[17] Seen in terms of the conflict between ideal and reality, *Howards End* marks a crisis in the possible acceptance of love as the ideal. Personal relationships are raised to a high plane in the novel, but in replacing love by comradeship and affection, Forster so modifies his ideal as to make it practically inadequate for the tasks still left for it to complete.[18] Several critics have also noted Forster's preoccupation with experience and reality in *Howards End*. Whereas Hoy sees a conflict of metaphysical opposites leading up to the "overwhelming question: wherein lies the reality of experience?",[19] Bradbury places the emphasis upon the other reality, the ultimate truth, when he sees one of the themes of the novel as being the question about "the way in which reality may be known".[20] The balance between the two views, leading on to the consideration that Hoy emphasises of the true value of experience in relation to reality, is put somewhat cryptically by Herbert Howarth:

In *Howards End* Forster goes on to tell his readers that since the world is

[17] It is, however, only fair to note instances of critical awareness of a relationship to the other novels. C.f. "*Howards End* is undoubtedly Forster's masterpiece; it develops to the full the themes and attitudes of the early books.... It justifies these attitudes by connecting them with a more mature sense of responsibility" (Trilling, p. 99); "The promise of *Where Angels fear to Tread* was renewed, but not fulfilled, in *Howards End*" (Leonard Woolf, "Arch Beyond Arch" [Review of *Passage*], *Nation and Athenaeum*, 14.6.1924, p. 354). E. K. Brown sees *Howards End* as "the re-doing of *The Longest Journey*", a view supported by Crews, who notes a similarity between the problems of Margaret and Rickie. C.f. E. K. Brown, "The Revival of E. M. Forster" (1944), *Forms of Modern Fiction*, ed. William Van O'Connor (Bloomington, 1964), pp. 165-6; Crews, p. 138.

[18] C.f. Cyrus Hoy, "Forster's Metaphysical Novel", *PMLA*, LXXV (1960), p. 135; Dorothy Hoare, *Some Studies in the Modern Novel* (London, 1938), p. 91; Crews, p. 113; Macaulay, *The Writings of E. M. Forster*, pp. 123-4.

[19] Hoy, p. 126.

[20] Bradbury, "*Howards End*", p. 130.

real and comes first (not necessarily last, but first), they must honour the fact of basic living. [21]

2

The first three chapters of *Howards End* deal with one sort of love, and go far to defining the nature of the reality of experience with which it will be tried and by which it is measured. The fascination which the Wilcoxes have for Helen and her response both to the family and to Paul are certainly not far removed from Lilia's reaction to Monteriano and Gino in *Where Angels Fear to Tread*, although Helen is a Lilia who is tempered in her vulgarity by the sensibility of a Caroline Abbott or a Lucy Honeychurch. Yet it is clear that this sort of love – a releasing of the emotions, untouched by reason – is not, as that of the earlier heroines, to be viewed in a positive light. Forster's ideal in this novel is, as Helen is made to realise later, a modification of love "where man and woman, having lost themselves in sex, desire to lose sex itself in comradeship". [22] For this reason the contrast is built up between affection and passion (p. 10), between poetry and prose (p. 163). Since in each case the milder, more prosaic quality is associated with Margaret, the final heroine of the book, they may be understood as those qualities which the author himself endorses. [23] Love is also to be shown as opposed to three further factors: reality (p. 240), truth (p. 215), and property and propriety (p. 165), yet Forster's ultimate hope (hope rather than belief) will be that love, albeit in a modified form, will still remain a workable ideal:

London was but a foretaste of this nomadic civilization which is altering human nature so profoundly, and throws upon personal relations a stress greater than they have ever borne before. Under cosmopolitanism, if it comes, we shall receive no help from the earth. Trees and meadows and

[21] Howarth, p. 199; c.f. James Hall, "Forster's Family Reunions", p. 62; Frederick J. Hoffmann, "*Howards End* and the Bogey of Progress", *Modern Fiction Studies*, VII (1961), p. 251.
[22] *Howards End*, Penguin edition (Harmondsworth, 1953), p. 290. All further page references are to this edition.
[23] See, too, Forster's letter to T. E. Lawrence quoted on p. 43 above.

mountains will only be a spectacle, and the binding force that they once exercised on character must be entrusted to Love alone. May Love be equal to the task (p. 243).[24]

As for reality (in the sense of the ultimate reality), though not explicitly such a central theme as in *The Longest Journey* it is continually implied as that which is to be attained by the principle of "only connect". Early in the novel we are made aware that the reality of experience is closely related to money and to culture; Leonard Bast emerges from "beneath the superstructures of wealth and art" (p. 44) as a hint that all is not for the best in the best of all possible worlds. This reality is seen as a test and as an opponent; it will be a test of the loves of the novel, and it will be a measure of Margaret's ability to maintain the validity of the ideal in practice – "To have no illusions and yet to love – what stronger surety can a woman find?" (p. 240).[25] The confrontation with reality as the truth rather than as muddle will finally expose the weakness of the materialist-middle-class standpoint.[26]

Margaret differs from the earlier Forsterian heroines in that she needs no vision to awaken her responses, no appeals are made to a latent sensitivity – it is there from the very first crisis between Helen and Paul Wilcox. Forster describes her as neither particularly beautiful nor remarkably clever but as having "something best described as a profound vivacity, a continual and sincere response to all that she encountered in her path through life" (p. 11). That is, unlike Stephen Wonham or even Rickie at his best, there is nothing 'heroic' about her, yet neither is she ordinary, in the sense that Lucy Honeychurch was, she is the individual capable of living out the best possible ideal in the everyday life of society.[27]

---

[24] C.f. Hoy, p. 135. For similar views on the future of civilization being opposed to nature and 'the earth' see: *Howards End*, p. 102; *Pharos and Pharillon*, p. 85; "Recollections of Nassenheide", *Listener*, 1.1.1959, p. 14; "Pylons on the March" (Letter), *Times*, 5.9.1964, p. 9.

[25] C.f. "Love and Truth – their warfare seems eternal" (p. 215).

[26] In the last chapter Margaret says of Henry Wilcox: "He has worked very hard all his life, and noticed nothing. Those are the people who collapse when they do notice a thing" (p. 313).

[27] Associating Margaret with Aziz in *Passage*, Elaine Johnson points out that they both "live rather than exemplify"; this is certainly true of Margaret, although the comparison with Aziz is unfortunate. C.f. Elaine H. Johnson,

Mrs Munt's reflections as she travels on her mission to Howards End give Forster the opportunity for filling out the background of the Schlegel sisters, with references to the twin poles of their existence: money and culture (pp. 14-15).[28] In their belief in culture, the Schlegel sisters are typical representatives of the privileged members of their class; the position is put clearly, in the form of Margaret's meditation on Leonard Bast:

Culture had worked in her own case, but during the last few weeks she had doubted whether it humanised the majority, so wide and so widening is the gulf that stretches between the natural and the philosophic man, so many the good chaps who are wrecked in trying to cross it (p. 109).

Nowhere is Forster himself more typically a member of his own class as in this remark with its, to our ears at least, patronising references to "the good chaps". The comment is, however, revealing of Forster's general position at the time of writing *Howards End*. The Liberal belief in culture is already weakening under the impact of the reality of experience and in spite of a faith in culture or the combination of culture and tradition, which he was to continue to proclaim,[29] Forster is already nearer the less hopeful position of a later remark:

Art is not enough, any more than love is enough, and thought isn't stronger than artillery parks now... But art, love and thought can all do something.[30]

Of the Schlegels, at this stage in the novel, we can do little further than echo former critics of the novel and note them as typical of the liberal uneasiness about the vulnerability of their position to criticism on grounds of their freedom from economic cares,[31] as representative of the best of their class,[32] as typical new liberal intellectuals of the twentieth century.[33]

"The Intelligent Mr E. M. Forster", *Personalist*, Jan. 1954, p. 56; C.f., too, John Edward Hardy, *Man in the Modern Novel* (Seattle, 1964), p. 42.

[28] Walter Allen talks of the Schlegels belonging to the "*rentier* class" in this connection. C.f. Allen, "Reassessments – *Howards End*", *New Statesman and Nation*, 19.3.1955, p. 408.

[29] C.f. "Notes on the Way", *Time and Tide*, 16.11.1935, pp. 1657-8.

[30] "Notes on the Way", 9.6.1934, p. 723.

[31] C.f. Cox, *The Free Spirit*, p. 9.

[32] C.f. Traversi, "The Novels of E. M. Forster", p. 29.

[33] C.f. C. K. Stead, *The New Poetic* (London, 1964), p. 85.

It is with these qualities largely established that the first confrontation with another world, another social grouping, takes place, and even during the essentially comic argument between Charles Wilcox and Mrs Munt, Forster makes us aware of the pressures which are to be brought to bear upon love in this novel: "So they played the game of Capping Families, a round of which is always played when love would unite two members of our race" (p. 21). In this sentence Forster, by the introduction of the words "love" and "unite" in combination, both underlines the irony which Mrs Wilcox is to reveal in her last remark of the chapter[34] and pinpoints that function of love which is to be the theme of the novel: it connects. Yet against this connection are set social conventions, here in a mildly humourous form, later in greater earnest.

The introductory presentation of Mrs Wilcox which follows has been commented on so often that one hesitates to add anything more. However, one aspect of the description introduces a concept that appears here for the first time in Forster's writings: the concept of the past. We read: "One knew that she worshipped the past, and that the instinctive wisdom the past can alone bestow had descended upon her", and Forster goes on to suggest that it is this wisdom that helps her to see people as human beings, as individuals (p. 22).[35] Later in the novel this concept is caught up again – when Helen and Margaret are alone in the house Howards End – in the phrase "the past sanctifying the present" (p. 278). Forster was later to return to this theme more than once, and in doing so he clarifies it for us. In the article "Recollectionism", for example, Forster sees the value of the past in the terms of personal memory, "Memory gives mental balance", particularly in times of crisis, by restoring perspective and, that which is to figure large in *Howards End*, a sense of proportion.[36] Furthermore the past, as in the case of Mrs Wilcox, may be used to interpret the present.[37] However, as with so many of

---

[34] "They have broken off the engagement.... They do not love any longer, if you prefer it put that way" (p. 23.)

[35] C.f. Gransden, *E. M. Forster*, pp. 68-9.

[36] "Recollectionism", *New Statesman and Nation*, 13.3.1937, p. 405.

[37] C.f. "It strengthens our outlook occasionally to glance into the past, and to lift our eyes from the wave that threatens to drown us – to the great horizons of the sea of history, where personal safety no longer signifies" ("Edward Gibbon",

the earlier, and often longest-held, beliefs, the pressure of time and circumstance was to leave Forster in doubt, if not disillusioned.[38] By virtue of being rooted in the past (or in the earth),[39] Mrs Wilcox herself tends to belong to the past, to a disappearing world. Nevertheless she emerges as one who instinctively puts into operation the principle of proportion which Margaret will preach to her later (p. 70) and it is her attitude to her own past and the past of her ancestors represented by the house, Howards End, that enables her to live so.

Chapter four brings the introductory stage of *Howards End* to a close with a theoretical confrontation of the two families. The first two pages of the chapter deal with Helen Schlegel and serve to delineate her unstable emotional nature; this is indicated by such phrases as: "she had been stunned" (23), "her responsive mind" (23), "the supreme joy of life" (24), "that abandonment of personality" (24) and by the account of her willingness to be shown that her ideals were nonsense. Paul's flirtatious kiss was for Helen the climax of her visit, but, at the same time, the reader must surely feel let down to learn, "her life was to bring nothing more intense than the embrace of this boy who played no part in it" (25).

Paul Wilcox's reaction the next morning is used by Forster to introduce the theme of reality into the novel. But his treatment of this theme in *Howards End* marks a departure from the three earlier novels: reality is now those inner reserves which can cope with experience, and in its turn, experience is that which tests the validity of an attitude to life. The ideals which are set up before us in this novel are, on the one hand, the belief in personal relations, love, affection, in a word, the 'inner life'; and, on the other hand, material success, conventional moral strength, the masculine world of business and activity: the "great outer life" (p. 27). The theme is introduced, significantly enough, by Margaret herself: "This outer

Talking to India, ed. George Orwell [London, 1943], pp. 11-12); c.f. "Freedom for What?", *Listener*, 1.6.1939, p. 1177.
[38] Writing of the possibilities of nuclear war, Forster admits that the world, society, has changed so much that "the past is no longer much use as a guide" ("The Fearful Choice", p. 82).
[39] C.f. Rickie and Mrs Failing in *Journey*, p. 273.

life, though obviously horrid, often seems the real one – there's grit in it. It does breed character. Do personal relations lead to sloppiness in the end?" (p. 27). In posing the question Margaret not only indicates the direction in which Forster's own thoughts may be leading him, but clearly separates herself from Helen, whose reply[40] clearly indicates her unwillingness to compromise, a trait which will mark her throughout the book. The world of personal relations is related to the search for the truer life, the ultimate reality: "It is private life that holds out the mirror to infinity; personal intercourse, and that alone, that ever hints at a personality beyond our daily vision" (p. 77).[41] Later Margaret is to realise that the function of the outer life is to be practical action which makes the inner life effective in the public world (p. 98) and she writes to Helen: "Don't brood too much... on the superiority of the unseen to the seen. It's true, but to brood on it is medieval. Our business is not to contrast the two, but to reconcile them" (p. 98).

Chapter four ends, after an account of the childhood of the Schlegels and their romantic but totally unreal father, by bringing the two sisters into focus. We are shown Margaret reaching similar conclusions as the passage quoted above about the function of the private life: "Her conclusion was, that any human being lies nearer to the unseen than any organisation, and from this she never varied" (p. 30). It is this unwavering devotion to an ideal that characterises Margaret but does not prevent her from making compromises, nor is itself affected directly by such compromise. Although Helen shares the ideal, we are told she was more irresponsible, another trait which will emerge later, particularly in her dealings with the Basts. The chapter ends:

The sisters were alike as little girls, but at the time of the Wilcox episode their methods were beginning to diverge; the younger was apt to entice people, and, in enticing them, to be herself enticed; the elder went straight ahead, and accepted an occasional failure as part of the game (p. 30).

[40] "I know that personal relations are the real life, for ever and ever" (p. 27); Margaret's response ("Amen") should, surely, not be understood as unqualified agreement, but far more as an expression of hope that this may be so.
[41] Forster returns to this theme of the two lives and the need for connection between them in later articles and broadcasts. C.f., for example, "Notes on the Way", *Time and Tide*, 2.11.1935, p. 1571; 23.11.1935, p. 1704; "Here's Wishing", *Listener*, 5.1.1939, p. 18.

Here then is the revelation of what our main concerns should be in investigating the novel: the split between Helen and Margaret and the contrast between their various approaches to life. This involves an examination of the abilities of the established Forsterian heroine of the first three novels (Helen) to cope with yet another form of experience as yet not presented, and an evaluation of the new Forsterian heroine (Margaret) who embodies the experiment: how much can one, of necessity, compromise an ideal without destroying it.[42] One conclusion that the novel will reach in this context is that Helen's unwillingness and inability to compromise means that she will never be able to relate her idealism to the reality of experience, and it is just there that Margaret succeeds.[43]

Chapter 7,[44] which precedes the friendship of Mrs Wilcox and Margaret, introduces the all important theme of money into the novel. This theme arises in a conversation between Mrs Munt and Margaret about the Wilcox family. Mrs Munt, having heard of the imminent arrival of the Wilcoxes in the flat across the road, is concerned about the risks of contact. To which Margaret replies: "I hope to risk things all my life", and she then goes on in answer to her aunt's expostulation: "There's never any great risk as long as you have money" (p. 58). There follows on Margaret's part a clearly realised account of her own economic position and an acceptance of its face value: "I stand each year upon six hundred pounds, and Helen upon the same, and Tibby will stand upon eight, and as fast as our pounds crumble away into the sea they are re-newed... And all our thoughts are the thoughts of six-hundred pounders and all our speeches" (p. 59). The relation of all three Schlegels to money is discussed in the course of the novel; whereas

---

[42] C.f. Beer, *The Achievement of E. M. Forster*, p. 114; Hall, "Forster's Family Reunions". p. 63; H. J. Oliver, *The Art of E. M. Forster* (Melbourne, 1960), p. 43.

[43] C.f. Hoy, "Forster's Metaphysical Novel", p. 133.

[44] The intervening chapters serve to introduce two yardsticks by which Helen and Margaret may further be measured – Beethoven's symphony and the encounter with Leonard Bast. Helen, we are told, sees "heroes and shipwrecks" in the music, whereas Margaret "can only see the music" (p. 31); a detail which merely underlines that which we have observed of the two sisters so far. In the encounter with Leonard Bast, Margaret talks to him as to an equal, but Helen never notices him as a human being and merely chatters about the umbrella (pp. 38-41).

Margaret is simply glad to have it (p. 103), Tibby lacks her humanity and sees money as his own right thus becoming economically a
snob (p. 289), and Helen, remaining true to her ideal, points out
to the starving Leonard that money is not everything (p. 222). For
Margaret money is not an end in itself but is a very useful and
civilising means to a civilized end. In the lunchtime debate in which
the sisters and their circle discuss the disposal of money in relation
to the poor and underprivileged, Margaret insists that "money's
educational" and goes on to put the matter in perspective: "So few
of us think clearly about our own private incomes, and admit that
independent thoughts are in nine cases out of ten the result of independent means" (p. 120).[45] Yet, after the discussion about money
with Aunt Juley, Margaret, now firmly ensconced in her safe world
of private incomes, fails to obtain a satisfactory housemaid at the
registry office (p. 60) and thus enters on her first contact with the
Wilcoxes marked as someone who, although economically on the
same ground, if not the same level, is, in practical matters, hopelessly lost in comparison with their abilities to deal with the outer life.

The first interview with Margaret reveals Mrs Wilcox as a
vaguer version of Mrs Honeychurch in *Room with a View*; she is not
particularly out of the ordinary, she is the typical middle class
mother of grown up children, inclined to bore others with accounts
of their doings (p. 69). The only thing that sets her off against her
predecessors (one may include Mrs Herriton in this line) is her
sensitivity to place, to the country. Otherwise Mrs Wilcox is a
colourless personality, and within the context of the plot of *Howards End* would hardly justify the critics' interest in her. That which
is notable about Mrs Wilcox, however, is her relation to the over-all
theme. Mrs Wilcox cannot be associated with the great ideal, love,

---

[45] C.f. "The sinews of art and literature, like those of war, are money"; "People
oppose money to culture, and imply that if a man has spent his time in making
money he will not be cultivated. Fallacy of fallacies! As though there could be
a greater aid to culture than the having earned an honourable independence"
(Samuel Butler, *The Notebooks*, ed. Geoffrey Keynes and Brian Hill [London,
1951], pp. 160 & 309). Forster has acknowledged the great influence Butler had
on him, and notes that one of Butler's most important lessons was "It is a good
thing to get clear about one's economic position". – The Legacy of Samuel
Butler", p. 955; Crews, p. 95.

although she herself is lovable (p. 73), rather she represents a more acceptable aspect of everyday reality than the great world of her menfolk. Nor can she be associated, with the world of the Schlegels, for "Her tastes were simple, her knowledge of culture slight" (p. 70) and her life is bound up with her family (p. 71). Yet "she could give the idea of greatness" (p. 73). This greatness of Mrs Wilcox seems to lie in her way of standing apart from daily life, in her ability to remain detached, a quality often associated with Forster himself.[46] Her function at this stage in the development of the novel is quite clearly to make Margaret see the unreality of some aspects of her London existence,[47] and to pave the way towards the remainder of the family: "I sometimes think that it is wiser to leave action and discussion to men" (p. 74). The brief friendship between Margaret and Mrs Wilcox has the value of being just that: friendship – a quality upon which great value is placed in this novel. The climax of this particular relationship is Mrs Wilcox's invitation to visit Howards End: "She discerned that Mrs Wilcox, though a loving wife and mother, had only one passion in life – her house – and that the moment was solemn when she invited a friend to share this passion with her" (p. 81). It is the family who prevent the excursion from taking place and the chapter ends with friend and house being subordinated to the family's needs. Mrs Wilcox disappears from the scene an unsatisfactory creation, who seems to have done nothing, to have accomplished nothing. It is only much later in the novel that Forster suggests her true worth and her function; Margaret comments to Helen when they are alone at Howards End: "I feel that you and I and Henry are only fragments of that woman's mind. She knows everything... She knew about realities. She knew when people were in love" (p. 292). Although an ephemeral and somewhat disappointing figure when seen within the context of the plot and story of the novel, seen in terms of the theme of ideal and reality, Mrs Wilcox occupies a crucial position in *Howards End*. Not only does she represent an acceptable aspect of everyday reality, but, as Margaret suggests, she also takes on aspects of the ultimate reality

---

[46] C.f. Lord David Cecil, *Poets and Storytellers* (London, 1949), pp. 181-2; Cox, p. 7; Crews, p. 16.
[47] C.f. p. 74.

too. This would seem to be born out by her detachment from the immediate concerns of the world of experience, and by Forster's insistence on her relation to the past. Thus, by extension, reality as the fulfilment of the ideal is shown to be elusive and difficult to relate to reality seen as the experience of every day.[48]

One further incident in the history of this friendship remains to be discussed: Margaret's introduction into the first conversation of her idea of proportion and Mrs Wilcox's acceptance of it.

Life's very difficult and full of surprises. At all events I've got as far as that. To be humble and kind, to go straight ahead, to love people rather than pity them, to remember the submerged – well one can't do all these things at once, worse luck, because they're so contradictory. It's then that proportion comes in – to live by proportion (p. 70).

Here is, not only the measure of Margaret's ability to cope with reality and to compromise on the ideal, but here, too, is the theme of the novel set out in its relation to the plot. Being humble is what Margaret has to learn when submitting to her husband;[49] kindness is involved in her relations with Mrs Wilcox; going straight ahead characterises her unswerving devotion to the ideal; love is at the centre of the novel itself; remembering the submerged introduces the theme of Leonard Bast and his wife. The principle of proportion involves seeing the value that the Wilcox life may have (p. 98), it is behind the necessity to connect inner and outer life, prose and passion (pp. 98, 135 & 174), it is implied in the demands to see life steadily and see life whole (pp. 152 & 250), and it is discussed in relation to love (p. 173) and money (p. 169). It is proportion, too, that is invoked in the final search for truth:

truth, being alive, was not half-way between anything. It was only to be found by continuous excursions into either realm, and though proportion is the final secret, to espouse it at the outset is to ensure sterility (p. 182).

Moreover it is Margaret's whole effort to keep proportion that calls forth Helen's admiring comment: "You mean to keep propor-

---

[48] C.f. E. K. Brown, "E. M. Forster and the Contemplative Novel", pp. 356-7 and 361.
[49] Humility is a virtue for which, in later life, Forster had only limited admiration. C.f. *Aspects of the Novel*, p. 117.

tion, and that's heroic" (p. 181). It is, however, this decision on Margaret's part that finally separates her from her sister.

The sudden, though not unexpected (p. 86) death of Mrs Wilcox[50] brings her once more into focus and at the same time serves as the reader's first introduction to the Wilcox family, and to Henry Wilcox in particular. In his description of Mr Wilcox Forster includes a number of details which are relevant to the novel as a whole. We are told (p. 86) that he "was in appearance a steady man", where the word "appearance" suggests a discrepancy between that which is seen and the truth. A hint supported a few lines later by the sentence, "But there was no external hint of weakness", where "external" presupposes "internal" and so, the inner life of reality. Finally the close of the same paragraph, describing his forehead: "it had the effect of a bastion that protected his head from the world. At times it had the effect of a blank wall. He had dwelt behind it, intact and happy, for fifty years."[51] There is altogether a peculiar aptitude in presenting the Wilcoxes at this moment of family crisis, since Forster can thus reveal their inadequacies in the face of a reality which is foreign to them: "they avoided the personal note in life. All Wilcoxes did. It did not seem to them of supreme importance. Or it may be, as Helen supposed, they realised its importance, but were afraid of it" (p. 88).[52]

The second crisis, brought about by Mrs Wilcox's note leaving Howards End to Margaret, is important, not because it reveals the Wilcoxes in an unpleasant light but because it has the significance that the more obvious visions in the earlier novels had: "The desire for a more inward light had found expression at last, the unseen had impacted on the seen, and all they could say was 'Treachery'"

---

[50] C.f. Henry Wilcox's recollections after her death, when he remembers his wife's revelation of her knowledge of her fatal illness: "He had been told of the horror by a strange doctor, whom she had consulted during his absence from town" (p. 86). The invitation to Margaret to visit Howards End was thus extended under the shadow of the knowledge of approaching death.

[51] C.f. Gransden's description of Henry as "late-Victorian humbug", *E. M. Forster*, p. 72; McDowell characterises him further in relation to the Victorian tradition. C.f. "'The Mild Intellectual Light': Idea and Theme in *Howards End*", p. 457.

[52] To which we may contrast Helen's ability to relate her ideal to the same reality, the reality of death, c.f. p. 128 below.

(p. 94). It is the Wilcox's failure to understand the import of Mrs Wilcox' message, and in particular Henry's inability to even recognise the vision for what it is, that shows that he is in need of the sort of salvation that Margaret will finally be able to bring. In every respect they are shown as failing to comprehend the values which were attached to Mrs Wilcox; both her love for her house ("To them Howards End was a house", p. 94) and her attachment to the past ("Mother believed so in ancestors – it isn't like her to leave anything to an outsider", p. 95). Such attitudes serve to highlight the true significance of Mrs Wilcox, and a subsidiary symbolic theme of the novel, that to Mrs Wilcox the house "had been a spirit, for which she sought a spiritual heir" (p. 94).

The first section of *Howards End*, separated by a gap of two years from the next, closes on the note of spiritual stocktaking that often occurs in Forster's novels. Margaret is given the chance to review the events of the past months which centre largely around the Wilcoxes; she is grateful for the offer of a memento of her dead friend and expresses admiration for Mr Wilcox's work (p. 101). She concludes with a reverie centering on the nature of the reality of every day:

Margaret realized the chaotic nature of our daily life, and its difference from the orderly sequence that has been fabricated by historians. Actual life is full of false clues and signposts that lead nowhere... Life is indeed dangerous, but not in the way morality would have us believe. It is indeed unmanageable, but the essence of it is not a battle. It is unmanageable because it is a romance, and its essence is romantic beauty.
Margaret hoped that for the future she would be less cautious, not more cautious, than she had been in the past (pp. 101-2).

Leonard Bast's attempted walk into the sunrise is a gesture in recognition of this ideal of life as romance, but behind the view must be heard the reminder that Margaret speaks from an unrealistic position in the sense that she speaks from the safety of an independent income. Thus her rebuke to Bast about struggling against "life's daily greyness" (p. 135). This view of life is connected, too, with Margaret's view of human variety at the end of the novel (p. 314); a view that insists that the variety and contradictory

differences in the human race are, too, a means of fighting against
this greyness, or sameness.[53] More important, however, for Margaret, after the experience of Mrs Wilcox and her family, is her
distinction between reality and pretence, and her willingness, in
spite of all, to be less inhibited than before. Her resolution here
may be seen as the willingness to give the heart supremacy over the
head, but it is still to a great extent an intellectual resolution based
on experience. Thus is she distinguished yet again from Helen.

Chapters 13 and 14, with their reintroduction of Leonard Bast
into the Schlegels' lives, begin, however, with a marked step on
Margaret's part towards reconciling her position with that of the
Wilcoxes. She begins to see the need for such values as industry and
labour and having a fixed purpose in life (p. 104); the desire for
work is valued as good and the Wilcoxes are apostrophised as "the
right sort" (p. 105). In terms of preparation for the return of Leonard Bast, this suggests that Margaret is developing a perception
which may have relevance for his problems, and in the context of
her own development, it indicates her continual willingness to learn
and to redefine her position. Whereas in the earlier novels Forster
demanded a clear-sighted but firm adherence to the ideal, here he
acknowledges that the search for reality, which must involve some
form of personal intercourse, demands resoluteness of purpose and
strength of will which the idealist himself may not possess. This new
point of view goes far to redefining the reality sought for: the indications become clearer that it is most definitely of this life and, of
necessity, must be so.

The Basts re-enter the novel at this point as a means of insisting
on the nature of everyday reality within which the ideal may have
to try to flourish, or at least against which it must protect itself.
Margaret herself sees imminent danger, in so far as she is being
confronted with a life that is neither sharply defined as negative, nor
as positive, and is thus an unknown, an unexperienced form of

---

[53] To which we may contrast, "Most of life is so dull that there is nothing to be
said about it" (*Passage to India*, p. 132); a statement that in itself measures
something of the gap between the two novels. Later, Forster comes to see that
an ability to recognise the variety of life can be a safeguard against mass-instinct
and dictatorship. C.f. "Efficiency and Liberty – Great Britain", p. 498.

reality which she has to encounter and test. "Mrs Lanoline had risen out of the abyss, like a faint smell, a goblin footfall, telling of a life where love and hatred had both decayed" (p. 108). Helen is quite unmoved by Mrs Bast's visit, since she is less able than Margaret to assimilate such people *as* people. In fact, when Leonard visits them the next day and sends up his card, Helen still reacts as though the whole matter were an entertainment and not another chance for personal relations (p. 109). For Margaret this visit is the occasion, in her musings over Leonard's appearance, to formulate her doubts about the universal humanizing influence of culture which we have already quoted (p. 111 above).

Leonard himself is used as a further illustration of the collapse of an insufficient ideal in the face of the reality of experience, and although his view of the dawn was not wonderful (p. 113), he is still unable to assimilate experience to the extent of modifying his ideal. He formulates his own beliefs in a way that indicates so much of the problem of the novel: "There one goes on day after day, same old game, same up and down to town, until you forget there is any other game. You ought to see once in a way what's going on outside, if it's only nothing particular after all" (p. 113). Here in a naïve form is the expression of the longing to embark on the search for reality which looks forward to *A Passage to India*, a novel in which the phrase ("if it's nothing particular after all") will take on almost sinister overtones. As a part of the social background of the plot, Leonard emerges in this and later chapters not only as representing a section of the middle-class of which Forster at this stage in his career knows comparatively little,[54] more particularly Mr Bast widens the scope of the social and economic realities which will ultimately both test and be tested in relation to the ideal of love and personal relations as the novel develops.[55]

[54] C.f. Furbank and Haskell, "The Art of Fiction, I: E. M. Forster", p. 33. Forster insists fairly consistently on individuals rather than classes, social groupings or such concepts as 'the people', an attitude which does not demand wide sociological knowledge of the class strata of England. C.f. "Our only hope of education lies in ourselves, whatever our class, in the individual, in decent personal talk" (Foreword to Alec Craig, *The Banned Books of England*, p. 11).
[55] In this context it is irrelevant whether Leonard is a working class symbol or not. C.f. Oliver, *The Art of E. M. Forster*, p. 48. Lacotte, in commenting on

The transition from Leonard to the Schlegels and Wilcoxes is accomplished by means of a discussion of that element they all have in common: money. A discussion we have already examined in its relation to the money/property theme in general. Afterwards Margaret and Helen discuss Mr Bast further and whether they will act or not. In the course of this talk, Margaret again reveals that she is approaching the Wilcox ethos via Mrs Wilcox. Helen asks what it is that complements money in strengthening one's existence and view of the world: "Now that we have to leave Wickham Place, I begin to think it's that. For Mrs Wilcox it was certainly Howards End" (p. 123). Margaret's cryptic reply is not to be understood as referring to property but to the past, to tradition, even to the life of the spirit, the inner life. This becomes clear if we recall the nature of Mrs Wilcox's attachment to her house. Furthermore in the ensuing chance conversation with Mr Wilcox, Forster indicates, again using the house as yardstick, how far Henry and Margaret have to move before they can meet on common ground. Henry dismisses Howards End as not being practical (it doesn't "really do", p. 128; "it is neither one thing nor the other", p. 129). In their attitudes to houses the essence of the development of the relationship between Henry and Margaret is indicated. They are continually defined in their relation to values, objects, and people around them, so that, for example, Howards End and Helen become means of testing each other, and the chances their emotions and attitudes have of survival.[56]

In chapter 16 a number of the various themes and ideas are brought together, as too are the three major groupings of the characters. Central to the chapter is the breakdown in communication between the Schlegels and Leonard Bast over the question of money. This failure is due to lack of experience on the one side and a failure to connect, or rather to see connections, on the other. In many ways the chapter is an illustration of the theoretical position at which

Oliver's description and largely agreeing with it, uses a formulation which is certainly more apposite, in seeing Leonard as appropriate to the period (transition to democracy). C.f. Lacotte, "Études récentes sur E. M. Forster", p. 426.
[56] C.f., for a roughly similar view, Alice R. Bensen, "E. M. Forster's Dialectic: *Howards End*", *Modern Fiction Studies*, I (Nov. 1955), p. 18.

both Margaret and Helen have arrived in relation to the link between culture and materialism, between romance and money.

These were women with a theory, who held that reticence about money matters is absurd and that life would be truer if each would state the exact size of the golden island upon which he stands, the exact stretch or warp over which he throws the woof that is not money (p. 133).

The Schlegels' failure is rooted in the same error that hindered the progress of the protagonists in the earlier novels from establishing relations with others; like Caroline Abbott and the baby, like Philip Herriton and Italy, like Rickie and Stephen, so too the Schlegels have made a symbol out of Leonard. Margaret and Helen treat him first as a vehicle for their theories and only secondly as a human being.

Into the ensuing muddle comes Mr Wilcox and immediately establishes a new standard by which the sisters will have a chance of measuring and being measured. Rightly he rebukes them for having assumed too much about Leonard and having judged him according to theory rather than on his own individual merits.

That's where we practical fellows... are more tolerant than you intellectuals. We live and let live, and assume that things are jogging on fairly well elsewhere, and that the ordinary plain man may be trusted to look after his own affairs (p. 137).[57]

This speech reveals both the strengths and the weaknesses of Henry's position;[58] on the one hand as a "practical fellow" he is not bound by a theory and so can afford the generosity of attitude he calls here "tolerance", on the other hand Henry manifests the unreal aspects of the *laissez-faire* attitude which is as divorced from reality as the Schlegels'. It is to be revealed later as an attitude that brings its own destruction with it in the sudden nemesis of the Basts' intervention at Evie's wedding. In terms of the social aspect of the novel we can see in it the seeds of the downfall of upper-middle class delusions of

[57] C.f. "In his moral and sociological ideas, Henry combines the *laissez-faire* tenets of Manchester economics and of utilitarian ethics with the struggle and survival pattern of social Darwinism" (McDowell, "'The Mild Intellectual Light'...", p. 457).

[58] It seems more consistent with the facts to talk of Henry's position throughout rather than the Wilcox position, since the ideas expressed are nearly always only spoken by Henry and the younger generation of the family are, on the whole, background figures.

security, which are slowly being undermined by a class of whom they profess ignorance, and of whom they maintain that all is well. The chapter ends with two hints at later events. When Margaret, apologising to Mr Wilcox and Evie for Leonard, justifies him with the words: "He's vulgar and hysterical and bookish, but don't think that sums him up. There's manhood in him as well. Yes, that's what I'm trying to say. He's a real man" (p. 138-9), she realises that she has touched off an emotion in Mr Wilcox which is discovered to be jealousy. A revelation is given of the grounds on which Mr Wilcox can accept love into his scheme of things: on the level of possessiveness, property instinct, and sex. When Margaret goes to bring Helen back to the company, Helen, in her brief remarks about Leonard ("Such a muddle of man, and yet so worth pulling through. I like him extraordinarily", p. 140), reveals another approach to love, via pity, which is going to lead her into as great a muddle as Henry. The fault of both Henry and Helen, and still to some extent of Margaret, as revealed in this chapter, is that which Forster notes, a few years later, in connection with the emotionalist. To him Forster gives the following advice, which, in essence, is the lesson that Margaret is going to learn in this novel:

When he is interested in people and things for their own sake, the hour of his deliverance has approached, and while stretching out his hand for some other purpose, he will discover – quite simply! – that he can feel.[59]

It is property that finally brings Henry and Margaret together, property in the form of house hunting. We are made to realise that Henry's affection for Margaret is stimulated by the realisation that on matters of money and property they are on safe ground where they can meet without disagreement:

"I'm glad you don't despise the goods of this world."
"Heavens, no! Only idiots and prigs do that."
"I'm glad, very glad," he repeated, suddenly softening and turning to her, as if the remark pleased him (p. 152).

It is the note of quiet understanding struck here that sets the tone for Henry's proposal and Margaret's acceptance; they are both, as

[59] "To Simply Feel", *New Weekly*, 8.8.1914, p. 246.

James Hall has pointed out, "managers of life and the emotions rather than followers of them".[60] Furthermore, Margaret it is who manages the whole scene; she realises in advance what Mr Wilcox wants to say, she understands too what nature of response he expects and yet the experience is an intense one for her: "Never before had her personality been touched" (p. 155). Love is now presented, unlike the earlier novels, as an experience involving the whole man, and not merely "the facts of sex... mere yearnings for the masculine" (p. 155). And yet, of course, there is, from the point of view of the plot, an element of the ridiculous and of the unbelieveable in this relationship. It is not, however, unrealistic within Forster's chosen theme,[61] since the ideal, love and affection, is now to be set off against the very values, economic and social, which Mr Wilcox incorporates.

Helen's breakdown in the face of Margaret's engagement is prefaced by a remark she makes to her cousin which reveals how ill prepared she is to assimilate the change in events because of a blind faith in an unstable ideal: "Helen shook her head. 'The Great Wilcox Peril will never return. If I'm certain of anything it's of that'" (p. 160). Margaret, however, has arrived at that point, so near to personal salvation, of maintaining an emotional position although being aware of the realities which could influence it:

The real point is that there is the widest gulf between my lovemaking and yours. Yours was romance; mine will be prose. I'm not running it down – a very good kind of prose, but well-considered, well thought out... I know all Mr Wilcox's faults. He's afraid of emotion. He cares too much about success, too little about the past. His sympathy lacks poetry, so isn't sympathy really. I'd even say... that, spiritually, he's not as honest as I am (p. 163).

Two important points emerge from this statement: first the difference between the sisters is established on the basis of their approaches to love, the central ideal; secondly, Margaret is allied with the

---

[60] Hall, p. 69.
[61] A point which Leavis and David Craig fail to grasp, because they confuse plot and theme, and, in Craig's case, there is clearly a political bias against the union. C.f. Leavis, *The Common Pursuit*, p. 269; David Craig, "Fiction and the Rising Industrial Classes", *Essays in Criticism*, XVII (1967), p. 72.

first Mrs Wilcox, in an emphasis on the values of the past. Margaret goes on to develop a variation on the theme of connection, by insisting on the value of people like the Wilcoxes to the "literary people" and refusing to play the double game of judging the Wilcox type adversely and yet accepting that which is of personal value from them: "More and more do I refuse to draw my income and sneer at those who guarantee it" (p. 164). Thus, once again, the three themes of property, love, and culture are joined and brought into relation with each other.

Once Margaret has gone so far as to express a potential willingness to compromise in order to build up a workable relationship with Henry, Forster develops a concept of love, through the remainder of the book, that will be equal to, and at the same time the product of, such a modification. Love is shown in relation to property, death, reality and truth, and although the end and result may seem but a shadow of the romantic, intuitive love of Lucy Honeychurch and George Emerson, it is seen to have greater revelance to the more detailed and complex world of *Howards End*. For Margaret, at the outset of her engagement, love is seen as having the task to "confirm an old relation rather than reveal a new one" (p. 166); that is, love must be in the position to absorb the experience of the past and still see clearly for the future, still to love. Further she realises that should she wish to transform Henry in any way, she can only do so by first loving him: "Love is the best, and the more she let herself love him, the more chance was there that he would set his soul in order" (p. 205).[62] Margaret's experiences in trying to love and help Henry illuminate, too, the extent of her separation from Helen before their reconciliation. For Helen there exists a vague ideal which Henry falls irreparably short of; for Margaret there is Henry as he is and an ideal which she would like to reach, but does not set as a condition *sine qua non* for love:

And she herself – hovering as usual between the two, now accepting men as they are, now yearning with her sister for Truth. Love and Truth – their warfare seems eternal (p. 215).

[62] C.f. "Love has to be clarified and controlled to give full value, and here is where criticism may help. But one has to start with love" ("The Raison d'Etre of Criticism in the Arts" [1947], *Two Cheers for Democracy*, p. 117).

This eternal warfare is indeed a summary of the conviction which lies in Forster's mind throughout *Howards End*; yet it is nothing more than the theme we have followed through the earlier novels: the problem of reconciling ideal and reality as experience to arrive at reality as ultimate truth. But Margaret is not, in the first place, concerned for Truth, but far more for truth with a small 't', which lies somewhere between the pragmatic attitude of the businessman, Mr Wilcox, and an exaggerated version of Helen's uncompromising attitude.[63] She cannot accept the absolute positions of either world, and her vision of the rightness and wrongness of each amounts to a variation on Rickie Elliott's concept of the knowledge of good-and-evil. For this reason if truth is to be found it will only be by granting love and understanding to Henry in his obtuseness and weakness[64] and to Helen in her constancy.[65]

It is a sign of the coming reconciliation between the sisters, that Helen, in spite of her practical inability in matters of love,[66] (in her conversation with Leonard Bast at Oniton), is able, not merely to formulate the ideal but also to relate it to an ultimate reality, the reality of death.

I love Death – not morbidly, but because He explains. He shows me the emptiness of Money. Death and Money are the eternal foes. Not Death and Life (p. 222).

Commenting on Helen's argument, Forster emphasises the contrast between Love and the inner weaknesses of the "men of the world".[67]

---

[63] "No; truth, being alive, was not half-way between anything. It was only to be found by continuous excursions into either realm, and though proportion is the final secret, to espouse it at the outset is to ensure sterility" (p. 182).

[64] C.f. "Henry must be forgiven and made better by love... she, too, would pity the man who was blundering up and down their lives" (p. 227).

[65] C.f. "It all turns on affection now... Affection. Don't you see?... Surely you see. I like Helen very much, you not so much... That's all. And affection, when reciprocated, gives rights" (p. 271).

[66] See Helen's comments regarding her affair with Leonard in the last chapter, p. 314.

[67] "Men of the world may recoil from the charnel-house that they will one day enter, but Love knows better, Death is his foe, but not his peer, and in their age-long struggle the thews of Love have been strengthened, and his vision cleared, until there is no one who can stand against him" (p. 223).

Thus is the contrast between the Schlegel sisters and Henry Wilcox related to the theme of the conflict between the ideal (love) and reality (death). Within this context we may better understand Margaret's reaction when Henry finally collapses, and so contradict those critics who are opposed to the close of the novel.[68]

No sudden warmth arose in her. *She did not see* that to break him was her only hope. She did not enfold the sufferer in her arms. But all through that day and the next a new life began to move. ... Then Henry's fortress gave way. He could bear no one but his wife, he shambled up to Margaret afterwards and asked her to do what she could with him. She did what seemed easiest – she took him down to recruit at Howards End (p. 311, my italics).

Here the important fact emerges that Margaret has found an ideal which can be translated into practical action. Love works, one might suggest, is the conclusion to her compromise. Too much emphasis has surely been placed on the concept of breaking Henry so that they may live together successfully, and too little on the italicised phrase that states clearly that Margaret does not even include such thoughts within her vision of love. In other words, the world of money, property, generalisations about class and duty has failed to stand up both to the reality of experience, and to the eternal realities of truth and death; love can now take over.

Henry's situation here has a parallel in the position of Leonard at Oniton (p. 212), who has lost the visions of an unpracticable ideal contained in poetry and culture and has substituted for it an equally uncertain truth that "There always will be rich and poor" (p. 212); where he has simply exchanged Schlegel beliefs for those of the Wilcoxes.[69] At Oniton, too, Margaret it is, not Helen, who has a sufficient grasp of reality to sort out rights and duties and attitudes with a measure of certainty and proportion. In reply to Helen's insistence that Mr Wilcox has a duty to help, she replies, "Nor am I concerned with duty. I'm concerned with the characters of various people whom we know, and how, things being as they

[68] E.g. "The triumph of a kind of sexless feminity", Rex Warner, *E. M. Forster*, Writers and Their Works series (London, 1964), p. 21.
[69] C.f. Mr Wilcox's statement, "There are just rich and poor, as there always have been and always will be" (p. 179).

are, things may be made a little better" (p. 213). In the case of Leonard Bast, Margaret's "spontaneous humanity"[70] is certainly more useful and helpful than Helen's catastrophic gestures of love and sympathy for the man out of whom she has made a symbol.

Love as affection resulting from and included in the sharing of common experience is at the root of the reconciliation of the two sisters; a reconciliation which is never, not even in terms of the plot, ever seriously endangered by being carried out in opposition to Wilcox wishes, and which, more significantly, is staged at Howards End, the symbol of the inner life sanctified by the past. Although at the outset (p. 275) affection cannot comfort them for the loss of ease of communication, the true coming together is established on the basis of memories of childhood and a shred of instinctive feeling for the house where they are, things which are summed up (p. 278) as "trivialities" and remind us of Mrs Failing's insistence in *Journey* that the small things of life are the truly important.

Explanations and appeals had failed; they had tried for a common meeting-ground, and had only made each other unhappy. And all the time their salvation was lying round them – the past sanctifying the present; ... They looked into each other's eyes. The inner life had paid (p. 278).

Since the inner life has paid and the outer life has crumbled in the face of the reality of experience, the two sisters emerge triumphant and dominate the close of the novel. For they personify the still optimistic viewpoint that Forster maintains: that love, affection, personal relations are more real than the tangible, pressing realities of property and success, social relationships, and class differences.

The close of the novel belongs to Margaret,[71] the extent of whose flexibility in matters of compromising the ideal is shown in her reaction to the news that Mrs Wilcox's wishes with regard to leaving the house to her had been suppressed: "Nothing has been done

---

[70] McDowell, "'The Mild Intellectual Light'...", p. 459; c.f. Crews, p. 121.

[71] Critics who have assumed that the child who will finally inherit Howards End is the clue to the novel, or the key to the conclusion, have rightly criticised it as theoretical and even as ridiculous, but they have failed to see that the child is only important in terms of the overall symbolism of the novel. C.f. Thomas Churchill, "Place and Personality in *Howards End*", *Critique*, V (1962), p. 72; Cox, p. 93; Hannah, p. 175.

wrong" (p. 319). Shortly before, Margaret and Helen return once again to the subject of love and the difficulties of reconciling experience with the ideal; Margaret is the first of Forster's 'searchers after truth' to have found an answer. For her it lies in the diversity of the human race; ideals so often tend to imply uniformity, but the true ideal is that which takes individuals into account:

It is only that people are far more different than is pretended. All over the world men and women are worrying because they cannot develop as they are supposed to develop. Here and there they have the matter out, and it comforts them. Don't fret yourself, Helen. Develop what you have; love your child... (p. 314).

We may, therefore, conclude by noting, in contrast to some other critics,[72] the prevailing optimism as regards both the ideal, love and personal relations, and the abilities of individuals to make the ideal relevant and practicable. Even though the creeping suburbs do encroach upon the rural idyll in the last chapter, Margaret is still able to utter the hope:

Because a thing is going strong now, it need not go strong for ever... This craze for motion has only set in during the last hundred years. It may be followed by a civilization that won't be a movement, because it will rest on the earth... I feel that our house is the future as well as the past (p. 316).[73]

In only one sense can *Howards End* be suggested to be pessimistic in tone or outcome: namely that Forster has rejected much of the out-and-out optimism and high ideals of, say, *Where Angels Fear to Tread*. The spirit which pervades the fourth novel is not one of

[72] C.f. Doughty, p. 547; Hall, p. 75; Alex Zwerdling, "The Novels of E. M. Forster", *Twentieth Century Literature*, II (1957), p. 179. Shusterman's evaluation, though somewhat imaginative, certainly points the way from *Howards End* to the true pessimism of *Passage*: "It seems possible, even probable, that by the time [Forster] had finished *Howards End*, he was convinced that perfection could never be reached" (Shusterman, p. 157).

[73] C.f. "The city that is 'creeping' upon the countryside in the final scene... represents a principle that cannot in the nature of things support the life of private affairs and personal relations that has been nurtured there and if this is to endure in the future, it must be sustained by the transcendent power of love" (Hoy, p. 135).

judgement, however ironical, or categorization of sheep and goats (there is no Harriet, no Mrs Herriton, no Cecil Vyse or Mr Eager, no Herbert Pembroke or Mrs Failing here); rather the prevailing spirit is neither unadulterated liberalism, humanism, or Love, but tolerant affection. That is the note on which *Howards End* closes.

8

THE YEARS BETWEEN: 1910-1924[1]

> In 1914 there was an explosion at
> the heart of Christendom whose effects
> are incalculable.

E. M. Forster[2]

The years which separate *Howards End* from *A Passage to India* were anything but unproductive; during them Forster published five books and one hundred and fifty-four pieces of miscellaneous prose.[3] It is this last body of writing that will be our main interest in this chapter; a collection of articles and reviews which is dominated, as was Forster's own life during this period, by the East.[4] Forster visited India with his friends Dickinson and R. C. Trevelyan from October 1912 to March 1913, and has recorded his "bewilderment and pleasure at plunging into an unknown world".[5] In his letters home he mentions that conversation turned to religion,[6] considera-

---

[1] This study was completed in manuscript before the posthumous publication of *Maurice* in 1971. Although this novel reveals further preoccupations during the years 1913-14 it in no way significantly alters or adds to the views documented and expressed in this chapter. Philip Toynbee's review of *Maurice* supports Forster's own doubts as to the novel's value, and his evaluation of the book can only meet with our agreement: "novelettish, ill-written, humourless and deeply embarassing" (Philip Toynbee, "Forsters' Love Story", *Observer*, 10.10.1971, p. 32).

[2] "Missionaries", *Athenaeum*, 22.10.1920, p. 545.

[3] For a full listing see B. J. Kirkpatrick, *A Bibliography of E. M. Forster*, 2nd. ed. (London, 1968).

[4] Miss Kirkpatrick lists eleven articles and twenty review pieces on India and thirty articles and reviews dealing with Egypt.

[5] *The Hill of Devi*, p. 9.

[6] *The Hill of Devi*, p. 25.

tion of which, in both its historical and contemporary perspectives, was to be uppermost in Forster's mind for much of this interim period.

This first visit to India started Forster off on his fifth and last novel, which was begun during this visit.[7] Certainly the qualification of having visited India, however briefly, led to a spate of articles on that country, and more particularly reviewing commissions from *The New Weekly*. A year after the outbreak of the First World War,[8] Forster went, as an officer in the Red Cross, to Egypt where he stayed for just over three years (November 1915-January 1919), and where he wrote a continual flow of articles for the *Egyptian Mail*, the majority of which are both uncollected and virtually unobtainable. More particularly, this lengthy stay was the source of two less important, but nevertheless singular books, the guide to Alexandria, with its informal historical survey, and the collection of essays, *Pharos and Pharillon*. We shall not be concerned with either of these books in the remainder of this chapter, which will centre on the Indian writings, and on others only in so far as they seem to have a bearing on the general development of Forster's position. We may, therefore, note here that the theme which runs through the history of Alexandria is a distrust of Christianity,[9] mixed with an admiration for that element in the early Christian

---

[7] McDowell, in the chronology preceding the main part of his book on Forster, places the beginning of work on *Passage* in 1913 and Stallybrass's account of the manuscripts of the novel would seem to support this. Stone, on the other hand, suggests 1912-1913. C.f. McDowell, p. 16; Oliver Stallybrass, "Forster's 'Wobblings': The manuscripts of *A Passage to India*", *Aspects of E. M. Forster*, p. 149; Stone, *The Cave and the Mountain*, p. 281. Forster himself, in the *Paris Review* interview, says that he began it in 1912, c.f. Furbank and Haskell, "The Art of Fiction, I: E. M. Forster", p. 33. Forster's diary entries for 1912-1913 contain several remarks and accounts of events which later appear in *Passage*. C.f. "Indian Entries", *Encounter*, January 1962, pp. 20-27. In *The Hill of Devi*, Forster merely writes: "Before my 1921 visit" (p. 153), with reference to the starting of work on *Passage*.

[8] Forster later notes that before this, for "some months" in 1914 he worked at the National Gallery as "amateur watchman and amateur catalogue compiler" (c.f. "Mr C. H. Collins Baker", *Times*, 14.7.1959, p. 9).

[9] "It is worth noting that the decline of science at Alexandria exactly coincides with the rise of Christianity"; "The idea that one religion is false, and another true is essentially Christian" (*Alexandria: A History and Guide*, pp. 45 & 20).

Church which Forster sees as the work of the Greek scholars of Alexandria: "The characteristic of early orthodoxy was a belief in Christ as the link between God and man. A humanizing belief".[10] In addition, we may note Forster's affection for the city, or at least for its past, as having to do with its relation to his ideal: "She did cling to the idea of Love, and much ... must be pardoned to those who maintain that the best thing on earth is likely to be the best in heaven."[11]

Forster returned to England in 1919, and in the following year he became Siegfried Sassoon's successor as literary editor on *The Daily Herald*, writing regular, but mostly undistinguished, review articles for that paper.[12] Then came the second, longer visit to India from March to October 1921, when Forster went back to the state of Dewas as private secretary to the Maharajah. It is letters and memories of this stay that make up the bulk of *The Hill of Devi*, and which supplied the material for the last section of *Passage to India*.[13] Once again Forster was fascinated, and yet also irritated, by the country which he now got to know more intimately from the inside. The doomed native state with all its inefficiencies and contradictions was for him "indescribable and unimaginable – really a wonderful experience, for it is the fag-end of a vanished civilization".[14] At the centre of the experience was, again, a personal relation to the ruler himself, who became a lifelong friend, until the Maharajah's death in 1937, and to whom a later edition of *Passage to India* was to be dedicated.[15] Forster's last letter from India on this occasion con-

[10] *Alexandria...*, p. 79.

[11] *Alexandria...*, p. 84.

[12] The comparative unimportance of this post can be seen from Sassoon's account of his work at the *Daily Herald*, c.f. Siegfried Sassoon, *Siegfried's Journey* (London, 1945), pp. 138-146.

[13] The descriptions of the Festival of Gokul Ashtami in both books are almost indentical. C.f. *Hill of Devi*, pp. 103-112; *Passage to India*, pp. 279-286.

[14] *Hill of Devi*, p. 67.

[15] *Hill of Devi*, p. 154, See, too, Forster's tribute to the ruler on his death: "He possessed incomparable qualities as an individual; he was witty, gay, charming, hospitable, imaginative, and devoted, and he had above all a living sense of religion which enabled him to transcend the barriers of his creed and to make contacts with all forms of belief and disbelief" ("Sir Tokoji Rao Puar", *Times*, 28.12.1937, p. 14).

cludes with a statement indicative of the discovery that is central to the novel which was to emerge from his experiences of India:

English manners out here have improved wonderfully in the last eight years. Some people are frightened, others seem really to have undergone a change of heart. But it's too late. Indians don't long for social intercourse with Englishmen any longer. They have made a life of their own.[16]

Between his return to England and the end of 1921 and the publication of *Passage* in June 1924, Forster devoted himself to preparing his works on Egypt for the press and in reviewing and article writing.

For Forster the supreme event of this interim period was not, however, the experience of the East, but the experience, albeit at some distance, of war. It is only against the background of human destruction and human hate that Forster's pessimism in *Passage to India* becomes finally comprehensible. At first, during the war itself, Forster is able to rationalise and discuss the significance of war as an abstract problem. Yet even here the note of hopelessness and disillusion creeps in. In 1915, Forster writes to the *Westminster Gazette* about the work of the Quakers in the devasted areas of Flanders; invasion is for him more than just killing and pain, "It is the herald of spiritual death"; even so Forster is able to rationalise to the extent of seeing the chief evil of war as being despair rather than death,[17] which suggests that he may well have recognized the symptoms of this despair in himself. Once the war was over, however, Forster's view of it becomes bleaker and gives every indication of being a reflection of the influence the events of 1914-1918 have had upon his own view of life. In January 1920 he writes:

As the war recedes it becomes even uglier than it was. It is like an island which when first sighted had a certain savage majesty, but in retrospect is discovered to be ignoble and obscene... The world is a globe over whose curves the human species are crawling, hatred and stupidity in their hearts, and whose surface they scratch with results unknown to the other animals, for they get mustard gas out of the globe and Lewisite. *Si monumentum requiris...*[18]

16 *Hill of Devi*, p. 153.
17 "Reconstruction in the Marne and the Meuse", pp. 1-2.
18 "Civilization", *Daily Herald*, 12.1.1920, p. 8. See, too, his harshly ironical

Nowhere is Forster the humanist so violent, so filled with pessimism about humanity as in this passage from an obscure review article. But his basic attitude never changes; the war of 1914-1918 is continually seen by him as profoundly disturbing and as an event whose effects are incalculable. Looking back on it from the early thirties Forster writes:

We only know that it shakes us up and shakes us about, and shakes what we have been accustomed to regard as the solid earth – frontiers, forms of government, standards of conduct and of living, all are shaken by unrest.[19]

This then is the state of mind which is in the background of Forster's second contact with India and which, more important, lies at the back of the pessimism with which *Passage to India* is so concerned.

The remaining non-Indian writings of this period are of lesser importance for our over-all theme. Reality is presented as a concept outside the ordinary self which Forster, the writer, sees as the enemy of well-made plans, in his essay on "Inspiration",[20] and in the same year, 1912, as the hard facts of life in the allegory we have quoted earlier. The reminder of reality, the traction engine, symbol in itself of the destructive force of a modern mechanized civilization, warns, "I shall pass often enough in the future", and leaves with a general gloomy prophecy, "There's a bad time coming".[21] In spite of the prevailing pessimism, Forster does insist on the necessity, however, for being interested in people,[22] although this serves very much to underline the contrast that seems to exist between what he would like to believe and what remains possible. This mental con-

---

comment on army generals: "Generals are so seldom killed, it being their duty not to die but to be the cause of death in others" ("Literary Notes", *Daily Herald*, 14.4.1920, p. 8).

[19] "Tales of Unrest", *Listener*, 14.12.1932, p. 869. C.f. "Missionaries", *Athenaeum*, 22.10.1920, p. 545; "Wilfred Blunt 2: The later Diaries" (1920), *Abinger Harvest*, p. 317.

[20] See p. 60 above.

[21] "An allegory", p. 7.

[22] Although at the same time Forster sees that the search for truth or reality is a greater and far more difficult task: "To realize humanity is one thing; to find out the truth is another" ("Tolstoy at the St. James's", *Athenaeum*, 10.10.1919, p. 1011).

flict leads Forster to a suspicion about humanity, which he voices in a review of H. G. Well's *Outline of History*: "Wells sees that humanity is creative. He cannot see that there may be an incurable defect in us ... that renders us incapable of putting to good use what we have created",[23] a comment that seems very much to echo Forster's doubts resulting from the war.

The Indian writings of the interim years may be divided into three groups: comments on India in general, upon Englishmen in India, and discourses upon Indian religion, in particular Hinduism and Islam. Reviewing A. S. Wadia's *Reflections on the Problems of India* in the spring of 1914, Forster, with his first visit to India a year behind him, is left with a sense of mystery rather than with a feeling that anything has become clearer about India. His remarks here are significant when we think of the sense of muddle, confusion, and mystery which pervades the India of *Passage*: "He leaves us with the sense of a mind infinitely remote from ours – a mind patriotic and sensitive – and it may be powerful, but with little idea of logic or facts we retire baffled, and, indeed, exasperated."[24] It is not only the otherness of India and the Indian mind which confused Forster, but the very confusion of the country itself. In a passage which is reminiscent of Professor Godbole at his most unreal, Forster talks of his difficulties with the driver who was taking him to visit the ruins of Ujjain. The resulting remarks remind one of the sort of spirit that envelops Mrs Moore after the cave episode:

One confusion enveloped Ujjain and all things. Why differentiate? I asked the driver what kind of trees those were, and he answered "Trees"; what was the name of that bird, and he said "Bird"; and the plain, interminable, murmured, "Old buildings are buildings, ruins are ruins."[25]

---

[23] "A Great History", *Athenaeum*, 9.7.1920, p. 43. These doubts are expressed with an almost bitter severity in Forster's letter to the press complaining that people are incapable of distinguishing between reality and sensationalism. Referring to the hysterical enthusiasm over the aviation feats of Mr Hawker, Forster writes "This planet is passing through the supreme crisis of its history. It is being decided whether we shall be governed openly, like a free people, or secretly, as in the past. And how the cynics who govern us secretly must have gloated over the hysterics of last Tuesday" ("Hawkeritis", *Daily Herald*, 30.5.1919, p. 4).
[24] "The Indian Mind", *New Weekly*, 28.3.1914, p. 55.
[25] "Adrift in India: The Nine Gems of Ujjain" (1914), *Abinger Harvest*, p. 341.

The untiring curiosity of the West meets here the Eastern approach to reality, that which is, is, and there is nothing more to know. It is out of this frustration that Forster, in his own way, will build up a new answer to the gloom that at present has settled round him.

Of the Indians themselves Forster notes, apart from their passing but intense spirit of self-sacrifice,[26] which reminds us of the behaviour of Aziz and some of his friends at the time of his arrest and trial, their preoccupation with religion, which may well have much to do with the particular attitude to reality, as he understands it. In "The Mind of the Indian Native State", Forster notes that "much of the spiritual life of the Indian" exists in a "broad border region between reality and dreams".[27] This comment brings with it the realization that Forster is here encountering a concept of an ultimate reality which is foreign to him, since his own humanist outlook allows for no such region as is here described. However, it is clear that he is, at least, being confronted with ideal material for the fictionalization of his problem regarding the search for this reality. Two years earlier, Forster had noticed one further preoccupation, that of the poets, particularly the Islamic, with politics, and in a review of some English translations of Indian poetry, he writes what in fact amounts to a summary of the political theme of *Passage to India*, particularly as revealed in Aziz' behaviour in turning against the British, his love of Islamic poetry and the past traditions of his people, and his final meeting with Fielding.

Poets in India cannot be parted from politics. Would that they could! there is no hope in the present circumstances... As for the politics, they are triangular. There are two chief communities – Hindu and Moslem – and a ruling class of Englishmen. Owing to their common subjection and common Orientalism, the two communities sometimes draw together and oppose the English; owing to their different religions and to racial and social differences, they sometimes fly asunder. The English view these oscillations with cynicism, but they spring from instincts, deep if contradictory, that exist in every Indian heart. Shall the Indian look to the land he lives in, and try to make it a nation? Or shall he look to his own particular past... and find in that his inspiration for the future?[28]

[26] "Reflections in India. II: The Prince's Progress", *Nation and Athenaeum*, 28.1.1922, p. 645.
[27] *Abinger Harvest*, p. 371 (1922).
[28] "The Poetry of Iqbal", *Athenaeum*, 10.12.1920, p. 803.

Forster's particular concern for the future of the confused and in-scrutable country he had obviously 'fallen in love with' is symp-tomatic; it echoes through the closing pages of *Passage* and is to reappear in articles written much later in life.[29]

Although Forster's Indian experiences were almost entirely spent among Indians and, therefore, one may infer that his knowledge of Anglo-India was less intimate, this does not save the English in India from stringent criticism. Forster acknowledges their superior knowledge, their longer aquaintance with India, but refuses to share their attitudes,[30] even if this may result in his arrival at disillusion-ment. Surprisingly enough, Forster pays tribute to the superior knowledge of the missionaries who, he points out, are in touch with native opinion as no Government official can be, since "The official need only learn how people can be governed. The missionary, since he wants to alter them, must learn what they are."[31] A view which is not so surprising when one remembers the comparatively sympathetic picture of Mr Graysford and Mr Sorley in *Passage to India*.[32] It is this attitude, too, on the part of the average Anglo-Indian that Forster picks out for particular criticism: their lack of humanity and the resulting refusal to treat the Indians as equal human beings. As he points out, "They are in India not to live but to rule, and in consequence their experiences are curtailed, and their powers of observation atrophied".[33] It is characteristic of Forster that he sees the wider perspective and does not merely castigate the Anglo-Indians for their behaviour towards the natives but points out the results in terms of general humanity. Of further particular relevance to the novel that was to develop out of these years are Forster's comments on the true sphere of life in which the English were most guilty of faulty behaviour: "The decent Anglo-Indian of today realizes that the great blunder of the past is neither political

[29] C.f. "Mahatma Ghandi", *E. M. Forster: A Tribute*, pp. 79-81; "India Again", *Two Cheers for Democracy*, pp. 327-335.
[30] "Salute to the Orient" (1923), *Abinger Harvest*, p. 288.
[31] "Missionaries", p. 545.
[32] C.f. *Passage to India*, p. 38.
[33] "Luso-India", *Athenaeum*, 27.8.1920, p. 268. C.f. Ronny Heaslop's statement to Mrs Moore, "We're not out here for the purpose of behaving pleasantly... We're out here to do justice and keep the peace" (*Passage to India*, p. 49).

nor economic nor educational, but social."[34] Which reminds us of
the hopeless failure of the 'bridge party' in *Passage* and numerous
smaller incidents throughout the first part of the book. Moreover,
in this social relationship with India, Forster supports the contention, as he was later to do in the novel, that the women were, if
anything, more to blame than the men.[35] Earlier Forster had noted
that the Indians resent such blundering behaviour (particularly that
of the Anglo-Indian to the educated native), and was to express his
sympathy for the Indians in this case.[36] Forster concludes, more
hopefully than in his novel, that the only hope for friendship will
not be between the two races but rather between individuals. The
passage is worth quoting, for, although written only two years
earlier, it marks a contrast to the conclusion reached in *Passage to
India*: "Though friendship between individuals will continue and
courtesies between high officials increase, there is little hope now
of spontaneous intercourse between the two races."[37] This is, admittedly, hardly hopeful, but the situation at the end of the novel is
certainly less so.[38]

Professor Crews has already noted that Forster has a preoccupa-

---

[34] "Reflections in India. I: Too Late?", *Nation and Athenaeum*, 21.1.1922, p.
614.

[35] *Nation and Athenaeum*, 21.1.1922, p. 615.

[36] "The Indian Mind", p. 55.

[37] "Reflections in India, II: The Prince's Progress", p. 614.

[38] In this context it is interesting to note that, although Forster himself has
written of *Passage*, "my main purpose was not political, was not even sociological" (Prefatory Note to the 1957 Everyman edition), a number of critics have
interpreted this novel as though it had been written as a political tract condemning colonialism. More surprising, however, is such a complete misunderstanding
as the following, which we may compare with the passage just quoted about
social relations in India. "The book's tacit but confident assumption that Indo-
British relations presented a problem of personal behaviour and could be tackled
on the personal plane" (Nirad C. Chaudhuri, "Passage to and from India",
Encounter, June 1954, p. 23). We may also note that Chaudhuri sees the novel
as a "satire on the British official in India", p. 19. In spite of the range of Forster's writings on India, and that *Passage* was largely written and completed
during and after his 1921 visit, another Indian critic insists that the India
portrayed is the India of pre-1914. Maybe this is the result of national self-
consciousness not wishing to see the weaknesses portrayed in his countrymen?
C.f. Natwar-Singh, "Only Connect... Forster and India", *Aspects of E. M. Forster*, p. 45.

tion with matters theological although, as a humanist, he has no religion or theology with which to deal with these problems.[39] So it is not surprising when we discover that much of Forster's Indian writing of the 1910-1924 period is concerned with religion. Forster himself suggests another reason for this when he points out that, India being an essentially religious country, "the Indian who is not interested in religion will never take us much beyond Bombay".[40] This leads him on to discuss various aspects of Mohemmedanism and Hinduism often seen in contrast to English Christianity and compared to each other and to Forster's own standpoint. To both religions, as readers of *Passage* will realise, Forster is sympathetic, as far as he can be to any form of organised religion. Islam is for Forster much more than a religion, as he puts it in a post-war article:

Islam is more than a religion, and both its opponents and its supporters have wronged it by their hard legalistic insistence on the Faith. It is an attitude towards life which has produced durable and exquisite civilizations, an attitude threatened by Europe's remorseless crusade today.[41]

Here one notices a hint at the criteria by which Forster judges religions, not by their efficacy in promoting contact with God, or revealing Him, but by that which they produce in the way of human groupings, culture, and civilization; the word "exquisite" is significant here, suggesting as it does an aesthetic approach to religious matters.[42] It is just this attitude to life which suggests, in its paraphrase, Forster's own substitute for religious faith of the organized variety. Therefore, too, his concern for the alienation of such people becomes very real.[43] When he turns to Hinduism, Forster sees first of all a contrast to Protestantism with its concern for conduct and morality: "The Hindu is concerned not with conduct but with vision. To realise what God is seems more important than

[39] Crews, p. 14.
[40] "The Indian Mind", p. 55.
[41] "India and the Turk", *Nation and Athenaeum*, 30.9.1922, p. 884. C.f. "Islam, an attitude towards life both exquisite and durable...", *Passage to India*, p. 20.
[42] C.f. W. A. S. Keir, "*A Passage to India* Reconsidered", *Cambridge Journal*, V (1952), p. 434.
[43] C.f. "The Rose Show", *New Weekly*, 11.7.1914, p. 119.

to do what God wants."[44] When one considers that in his earlier
novels Forster had been so concerned with the liberal humanist's
struggle against middle-class English moral conventions, this remark takes on an interesting significance for the later work. It
hints at Forster's affection for India being based on the very lack
of ethical preoccupations, and suggests, too, the reason for granting
the Hindu, Professor Godbole, so prominent a part in the closing
section of *Passage*. Yet, at the same time (and in the same article),
Forster sees the weakness of Hinduism which is the same as that of
Protestantism:

Hinduism can pull itself to supply the human demand for Morality just
as Protestantism at a pinch can meet the human desire for the infinite
and the incomprehensible. But the effort is in neither case congenial.
Left to itself each lapses – the one into mysticism, the other into ethics.[45]

It is this essential nature of Hinduism, as mysticism, that marks the
limit to Forster's acceptance, for, as he writes elsewhere during
this period, mysticism may "be selfish or erroneous".[46] Later in his
life, at the beginning of the second World War, Forster goes further,
and says outright that mysticism is sterile.[47]

A letter written home from India during his second visit suggests
the relation Islam and Hinduism have to each other for Forster:
"I do like Islam, though I have had to come through Hinduism to
discover it."[48] But his attitude seems to fluctuate; in 1940, he sees
Hindu art not only as remarkable but also as an achievement that
"I might interpret in view of my own experience and needs",[49] and
in comparing Hindu forms of worship to the Christian, Forster is
obviously attracted by the fact that Hinduism is an individual, as
opposed to a congregational, religion. In conclusion one may suggest that intellectually and aesthetically Forster can be understood
to have a preference for Hinduism, whereas humanly and emotionally his sympathies tend towards Islam. Thus when in *Passage* he

[44] "The Gods of India", *New Weekly*, 30.5.1914, p. 338.
[45] Ibid.
[46] "A Great History", p. 43.
[47] "Omega and Alpha", p. 140.
[48] *The Hill of Devi*, p. 124.
[49] "The Individual and his God", p. 802.

comes to bring the religions of East and West into a situation where again preferences may be stated,[50] he wavers between Godbole and Aziz, both of whom have their place and their function, neither of whom finally succeed in satisfying Forster's needs of the time, and who ultimately appear as complementary aspects of an India which remains unmoved and incomprehensible.

What conclusions may one draw from the reading of Forster's output of the years between *Howards End* and *Passage*? One notices first of all that the almost desperate optimism of the conclusion of *Howards End* has worn thin and is being replaced, particularly as a result of the First World War, by an equally sincere conviction that humanity is tainted and that personal relations, though capable of much, will have to be confined to the individual sphere, to the inner life where they are relevant as opposed to their irrelevance to the 'outer life'. This attitude which in later years was to be called his "disillusioned sincerity"[51] pervades the last novel and has led critics to note Forster's pessimism.[52] And it is this attitude, too, that is noted by Forster's friends and aquaintances during this period. D. H. Lawrence regards him as a prisoner of his own pessimistic outlook,[53] and in a letter of December 1925, T.E. Lawrence describes a visit to Cambridge: "There E. M. F. sat, large as life, but sad-looking, wasted almost, in another man's rooms in King's."[54] This second description is the more moving one, with its suggestion of withdrawn physical suffering which the newly found pessimism brings with it.

Yet in the middle of the gloom one becomes aware both of a determination not to let go of beliefs which have become essential and which Forster refuses to see as outworn, and, as another friend described him, one notes his "curiosity, adaptability and independence",[55] but above all his adaptability. Which brings us back, as

[50] C.f. Langbaum, "A New Look at E. M. Forster", p. 34.
[51] C.f. Zabel, "E. M. Forster", p. 416.
[52] C.f., as representative, Traversi, "The Novels of E. M. Forster", p. 30.
[53] *Collected Letters of D. H. Lawrence*, ed. Harry T. Moore (London, 1962), p. 317.
[54] *The Letters of T. E. Lawrence*, ed. David Garnett (London, 1938), p. 486.
[55] William Plomer, *At Home* (London, 1958), p. 145, and also p. 110. C.f. "The world, perforce, grows older, and we must grow old with it, or lose touch" ("The Boy who never Grew Up", *Daily Herald*, 9.6.1920, p. 7).

in the case of *Howards End*, to the need for compromise. It will be our contention in the chapter which follows that, whereas in *Howards End* Forster was exploring the possibilities and effects of compromising the ideal in order to bring liberal cultured individuals and materialist economic persons together, in *Passage to India* the connection he attempts will be between the private world of the individual and the public world of society, nation, and race. In the latter novel the compromise cannot be effected nor could it work, and Forster, while allowing room for reason in his attempts to reconcile extreme positions and assertions,[56] always falls back upon affection and emotion even when he knows that they, too, will not work.

One of the most fascinating accounts of what could have been happening to Forster during the fourteen years' interim is given in a review of *Passage*, to which we shall return in the next chapter, by John Middleton Murry.

Evidently the best part of those fourteen years was occupied not in writing this very fine novel, but in wondering whether there was indeed anything on earth, or in the heavens above, or in the waters under the earth, worth writing about. And even then, in that long space of years, Mr Forster did not *decide* that there was. No, the balance faintly inclined, the pointer dribbled over towards "To be", and the silence was interrupted.[57]

Murry's suggestion that Forster was only just able to find something worth writing about is a fairly accurate summary of the position Forster had reached by the time he was completing *Passage*. The confrontation with war, where the individual was sacrificed to mass interest; the confrontation with India, where individuals went under and were not noticed; and the encounter with mysticism and religious ecstasy, which brought in the confrontation with nothing, all seemed to have served to shake the very foundations of Forster's beliefs. *Passage* is an account of what remained and what could be effective. In essence it becomes the story of the love that failed.

[56] C.f. George A. Panichas, "E. M. Forster and D. H. Lawrence: Their Views on Education", *Renaissance and Modern Essays*, ed. G. R. Hibbard (London, 1966), p. 210.

[57] John Middleton Murry, "Bou-oum or Ou-Boum", *Adelphi*, II (July 1924), pp. 150-151.

9

THE LOVE THAT FAILED: *A PASSAGE TO INDIA*

> To the Indian nothing is real and
> nothing is separable: elephants and
> flowers and diamonds all blend and
> are part of the veil of illusion
> which severs unhappy mortals from
> the truth.
>
> E. M. Forster[1]

1

A Passage to India does not suggest that the ideals of Forster's first four novels have changed, but sets these ideals against yet another set of values which make up the testing reality of experience. Whereas in *Howards End* these were the values of English public life in the form of material, economic and social considerations, in *Passage* the attempt is made to test the ideal by confrontation with the greater 'outer' life of another race, the values of diplomacy and international relations, and the aesthetic and mystical appeals of Islam and Hinduism. Forster's concerns are, therefore, the same in both novels: to discover the validity of an ideal, till now related to private life and intercourse between individuals, to the public sphere, to intercourse between social or, in this case, racial groups.[2] The critical view which sees *Passage* as an implied criticism of the

---

[1] Foreword to Constance Sitwell, *Flowers and Elephants* (London, 1927), p. 8.
[2] Thus we are in disagreement with suggestions that Forster's *concerns* in the two novels are different; it is the setting, the nature of experience, which is different, and the conclusions that are reached which change. C.f. John Dixon Hunt, "Muddle and Mystery in *Passage to India*", *ELH* XXXIII (1966), p. 497.

conclusions reached in *Howards End*, or even as an epilogue to that novel, suggests the correct perspectives within which Forster's development may be viewed.[3]

At the centre of this last novel is India itself, not as protagonist but as all-embracing atmosphere and setting; India as a symbol of the stage that Forster has reached in his development towards middle-aged disillusion.[4] It is in this setting that Forster asks the major questions of the novel about the meaning of life, the validity of religious belief, the potentialities of private values in public life, and the possibility of friendship between Indian and Englishman. Moreover, although the setting is of itself confused and confusing, there is no doubt that Forster does arrive at a clearly established stand on these major issues.[5] The scope within which Forster is working is once again the realm of the two realities, and, as Gertrude White puts it in her penetrating study of the novel, Forster almost succeeds in the "attempt to fuse the real world of social comedy and human conflict with the meaning and value of the universe which that world mirrors".[6]

Any attempt to 'interpret' the novel will inevitably be less than the novel itself, and, similarly, it is true that all the critical comments, however wide of the mark some of them may be, form a total picture of the response which the novel has called forth. For this reason we may grant them validity. When, for example, Hunt suggests that "the novel's central theme... suggests that formlessness, disorder and inappropriateness are holier than British precision",[7] it is the word "central" we object to, rather than the suggestion, for such ideas certainly play their part in the general atmosphere of the novel. Or, when another critic sees the main concern as being "the conflict between reality and justice",[8] one cannot say that

---

[3] C.f. Doughty, "The Novels of E. M. Forster", p. 549; Hannah, "The Limitations of Liberalism in E. M. Forster's Work", p. 166.

[4] C.f. Elaine H. Johnson, "The Intelligent Mr E. M. Forster", p. 54.

[5] For a contrary view see, A. A. Mendilow, "The Triadic World of E. M. Forster", *Studies in English Language and Literature*, ed. Alice Shalvi and A. A. Mendilow (Jerusalem, 1966), p. 280.

[6] Gertrude M. White, "*A Passage to India*: Analysis and Revaluation", *PMLA*, LXVIII(1953), p. 653.

[7] Hunt, "Muddle and Mystery in *Passage to India*", p. 503.

[8] Langbaum, "A New Look at E. M. Forster", p. 47.

such a theme has *no* place in an account of *Passage*. But such views tend to concentrate one's attention too closely on particular aspects of the novel, which, for the critic in question, may well have been of overwhelming interest.

Where so much criticism of *Passage* goes wrong is when it tends to view the novel exclusively in terms of its multi-racial plot and see it either as offering solutions to the world's problems,[9] or, more narrowly, as a tract on colonialism, imperialism, and the Indian question.[10] Surely the argument against such an approach is given by seeing *Passage* within the context of Forster's established preoccupations, and thus suggesting that the drama of the book revolves round a conflict of individual viewpoints, beliefs, and temperaments. Moreover, a political interpretation makes the roles of Godbole, Mrs Moore, and Fielding insignificant and thus open to criticism on grounds of irrelevance. Certainly Andrew Shonfield, during a discussion of *Passage* in political terms, does modify his insistence on the centrality of political conflict to some extent, when he writes: "The book, it is true, is primarily about personal relations. But its theme is about how these personal relations are distorted by politics."[11] Yet even this is not satisfactory, since it simplifies a novel in which the opposing forces are much more, and much more varied, than just politics.[12] One may, however, note that contemporary reviewers and the public understood

[9] C.f. Brander, *E. M. Forster, A Critical Study*, p. 200.

[10] Symptomatically Nirad Chaudhuri criticises just that which is the essence of the novel when he writes: "The consequences of pitting humane feelings against a political phenomenon are well illustrated in *A Passage to India*. One consequence is that it leads to pure negation." The implied criticism here indicates that the writer has overlooked or misinterpreted Forster's theme, which makes just this conflict and just this consequence indispensable for the novel as a whole. Moreover, Chaudhuri goes on to show further consequences of this attitude when he suggests that Forster wastes emotion on characters who, being "insignificant and despicable", do not deserve it (Chaudhuri, "Passage to and from India", p. 20. C.f. Brander, p. 193).

[11] Andrew Shonfield, "The Politics of Forster's India", *Encounter*, XXX (Jan. 1968), p. 63.

[12] One may further note the sort of distortions that such a view brings to Shonfield's arguments when he criticises Forster for not understanding or sympathizing with the Independence movement (p. 68). For further criticism of Shonfield's article see Harland S. Nelson, "Shonfield and Forster's India", *Encounter*, XXX (June 1968), pp. 94-5.

Passage very much as an antidote to the Kipling view of imperialism, but such interpretations rest on the assumption that Forster is writing a novel about India.[13] To suggest this is largely as irrelevant as to say that *Where Angels Fear to Tread* is a novel about Italy. For Forster, India has two qualifications as a setting for his last novel: firstly it supplied him with a continuation of a fixed society of the pre-1914 vintage in the Anglo-Indian world of the Turtons, MacBrydes and Heaslop; secondly it presented him with a racial conflict imbued with religion and politics, as the Wilcox world had supplied him with a social conflict imbued with economic and financial overtones. This would seem to be the correct perspective from which to view and to investigate *Passage to India*.

A number of critics have pointed out the role that *Passage* plays within the context of those Forsterian concerns with which we have so far been dealing. The starting point to this line of interpretation is the realisation that the novel "attempts to discover whether any of the older Forsterian humanistic values are realizable" in a world in which "value distinctions are annihilated and the cause of good and evil is communal rather than individual".[14] For a number of critics, the basic question of the novel becomes that which is discussed at the opening of Chapter 2, the question of the possibility of friendship between Indian and Englishman. The answer is seen to be in the negative, in so far as the individuals are trammelled by their political or social implications.[15] Yet this again tends to limit theme by considerations of plot. It is, perhaps, nearer the truth to go in the direction suggested by Nancy Hale, when she writes, "*Passage to India* is concerned not only with relationships but with the subject of relationship".[16] Such a suggestion has the advantage

[13] We can note the contrast between L. P. Hartley's comment, "A *Passage to India* is much more than a study of racial contrasts and disabilities", *Spectator*, 28.6.1924, and the review comments of Ralph Wright (*New Statesman*) and J. B. Priestley (*London Mercury*). All three reviews are reprinted in *E. M. Forster, A Passage to India*, ed. Malcolm Bradbury, Casebook series (London, 1970). C.f. Ellin Horowitz, "The Communal Ritual and the Dying God in E. M. Forster's *A Passage to India*", *Criticism*, VI (Winter 1964), p. 78.

[14] Alex Zwerdling, "The Novels of E. M. Forster", p. 180.

[15] C.f. Oliver, *The Art of E. M. Forster*, p. 63; Bentley, "The Novels of E. M. Forster", p. 354.

[16] Nancy Hale, "A Passage to Relationship", *Antioch Review*, XX (1960), p. 21.

that it brings Mrs Moore and Aziz, Adela and Ronny, Godbole, the stone and the wasp, Fielding and Stella, into focus as further aspects of a central theme, which is elsewhere defined as "Where is love to end?".[17] Yet, such a view, concentrating as it does on the implications of Godbole's all-inclusiveness, may well be in danger of putting too optimistic an emphasis on the burden of the novel.[18] Certainly love is, as in all the other novels, at the heart of the theme, as the ideal to be tested, yet we have already seen that by the end of *Howards End* the ideal is no longer love in all its unadulterated glory, as in *Room with a View*, but tolerant affection. Therefore, to Mr Natwar-Singh's suggestion that the popularity of *Passage* may be due to the fact that "it promotes the creed that without love you cannot 'connect' ",[19] we may counter that Forster has already proved the contrary of this in the earlier novel, and that in *Passage* he is testing the validity of the compromise he has already been forced to make. Forster tends to base his hopes on a mixture of affection and humanist rationalism, in the person of Fielding, and comes to the pessimistic conclusion that even this combination cannot surmount the barriers which men have erected between themselves.[20]

Critical discussions of *Passage* have, justifiably, paid more attention to structure than was the case in examinations of the four earlier novels. Such investigations have been concerned with the dialectical or cyclic processes of the novel; the presentation of the concepts of separation and unity, which establish the dichotomy between men as individuals and men as community or social grouping.[21] This is central to the pattern of the theme as we have

---

For a particularised version of this view seen as an advocacy of internationalism, see, Hugh Maclean, "The Structure of *A Passage to India*", *University of Toronto Quarterly*, XXII(1953), p. 160.

[17] Beer, *The Achievement of E. M. Forster*, p. 154.

[18] C.f. Mason's suggestion that the novel can, for the responsive reader, become "a journeying towards the unity of man within the spirit of love". W. H. Mason, *A Passage to India*, Notes on English Literature series (Oxford, 1965), p. 21.

[19] K. Natwar-Singh, "Only Connect... Forster and India", p. 38.

[20] C.f. Ted E. Boyle, "Adela Quested's Delusion: The Failure of Rationalism in *A Passage to India*", *College English*, XXVI (1965), pp. 478 and 480. Although Dr. Boyle uses the phrase "untempered rationalism" as opposed to the amalgam which we have suggested above.

[21] Herbert Howarth notes the two dimensions of the novel in which individuals

set it out, and is a refinement of Forster's concerns in *Howards End*, where the dimension of collective social unity was missing, in so far as the forces were of the family, rather than of a mixed society. The suggestion has also been made that the novel works not so much upon two views of man, but on two levels of presentation, literal and symbolic, which each have their own particular contribution to make to the development of the theme: "The literal level of the novel emphasises the divisions between the Indians and the Englishmen, the diversity among men; the symbolic level reveals the way to union and unity."[22] We may, however, object that the symbolic level suggests ways to unity only to certain individuals and groupings, and that, on the whole, the unity is suggested to Indians, rather than as existing between the nations.[23] The central feature of the structure of *Passage* is more clearly defined as "a sense of both unity and division [which] operates throughout the novel".[24] This sense is revealed in terms of relationships and surely Daleski is correct in seeing the novel in terms which bring together thematic and structural considerations in what he calls "a cyclic process",

which we may describe – in terms of the action – as the establishment of relationship; the break-down of relationship; and the re-establishment of relationship, with a further breakdown implied – as the end of the novel strikingly indicates.[25]

It is largely in these terms, of relationship and its ultimate break-down, that we shall consider *Passage* as the final episode in the serial investigation of the validity of the ideal, and the search for a reality which may be opposed to the so-called realities of life as it is lived, and of experience.

---

have adventures and problems tend to become collective social matters. C.f. Howarth, "E. M. Forster and the Contrite Establishment", p. 204.

[22] Pedersen, "Forster's Symbolic Form", p. 232.

[23] Consider, for example, Aziz's poetry, Godbole's vision of wasp and stone as compared to the missionaries', and the whole of the closing section. Even on a wider plane, the total symbolic structure of the novel is a unity in terms of India, and not multiracial or international.

[24] Mendilow, "The Triadic World of E. M. Forster", p. 281. C.f. Gransden, *E. M. Forster*, p. 105.

[25] H. M. Daleski, "Rhythmic and Symbolic Patterns in *Passage* to *India*", *Studies in English Language and Literature*, p. 258. C.f. Horowitz, p. 87.

2

The first chapter of *Passage*, with its "extraordinary vision of disintegration",[26] opens with a description which emphasises the shifting and relative nature of the reality of experience. Chandrapore seen from the river is described as "so abased, so monotonous",[27] whereas from the civil station, "Chandrapore appears to be a totally different place... It is a tropical pleasaunce washed by a noble river" (p. 9). The truth cannot be seen by the English from their exalted position above the town, and Forster writes that newcomers "have to be driven down to acquire disillusion" (p. 10). That is just what takes place in this novel. On the level of the plot, Adela Quested is driven down, both literally to meet the Indians and to take part, with Aziz, in the picnic expedition to the caves, and, more importantly, humanly and morally she is driven down to the position of bearing false witness against Aziz. In the context of the theme we have been following through the novels, the opening of *Passage* presents us with a summary of the whole book.[28] The search for the ultimate reality can only be pursued further by means of a confrontation with experience in the form of India, the unknown. Yet, paradoxically, this confrontation will lead not to a revelation in which ideal and reality are finally at harmony, but to the hopelessness of disillusion.

This opening chapter follows the cyclic movement from hills to hills, from caves to caves; from the caves which are "extraordinary" in the first sentence, to the hills which interrupt the expanse of the plain at the end. It is characteristic of the technique of *Passage* that Forster opens the second section of the novel with a similar brief chapter, again centering on the caves which, introducing the section which they dominate, are characterised as "characterless" (p. 124). Whereas in Chapter 1 the Marabar hills are human images – "fists and fingers" (p. 11) – in the later Chapter 12, they are "unspeak-

[26] Martin Turnell, *Modern Literature and Christian Faith* (London, 1961), p. 38. C.f. "The bitter terrible hopeless picture a cloud might have painted, of man in India" (T. E. Lawrence, *The Letters of T. E. Lawrence*, p. 462).

[27] *A Passage to India*, Penguin edition (Harmondsworth, 1952), p. 9. All further references are to this edition.

[28] C.f. Hunt, p. 505.

able", "like nothing else in the world" (p. 123). Thus we are made aware of the nature of the forces against which the ideal will struggle, and, too, of the indefinable threat of something inhuman which will destroy the power of Forster's personal relationships.

The first section of the novel is, however, predominantly positive and hopeful, though perhaps mistakenly so.[29] It stands under the overall influence of the mosque, the meeting place between East and West, symbolizing the possibilities of communication.[30] "Mosque" introduces and clarifies the important relationships of the novel: the friendship rising to affection of Aziz and Mrs Moore, the emotional position of Ronny and Adela towards each other, and the establishment of the central relationship of the novel between Fielding and Aziz. Whereas one of these relations, that between Ronny and Adela, is based on a conventional view of love resulting in marriage,[31] the other two are based on vaguer foundations although they both develop into tender affection. Aziz' confrontation with Mrs Moore is prefaced by his fierce denunciation of the English in India: "They all become exactly the same, not worse, not better. I give any Englishman two years, be he Turton or Burton... And I give any Englishwoman six months. All are exactly alike" (p. 13). Thus is the atmosphere, hostile to personal relations, to the view of people as individuals, defined. The racial situation, which views people according to their membership of a group or a race, is against friendship between East and West. Yet Aziz and Mrs Moore meet and establish a contact which is transformed first into friendship, then into affection, and finally into myth. Their meeting point is their insistence on individuals in an anti-individualistic world.

Rather surprised, she replied: "I don't think I understand people very well. I only know whether I like or dislike them."

[29] It is difficult to agree with the view that both Parts 1 and 2 are negative. C.f. Maclean, p. 159.
[30] C.f. Reuben A. Brower, "The Twilight of the Double Vision: Symbol and Irony in *A Passage to India*" (1951), *Modern British Fiction*, ed. Mark Schorer (New York, 1961), p. 212.
[31] Parallels could be drawn to the relationship between Lucy Honeychurch and Cecil Vyse in *Room*, or, with the sexes reversed, Rickie Elliott and Agnes Pembroke in *Journey*. The new couple could be seen as representatives in India of the concept of Sawston, and thus imply a further defeat of the middle class world of the early novels.

"Then you are an Oriental" (p. 24).

That is, Aziz and Mrs Moore have found common ground in their placing of the emphasis on emotion rather than reason, the heart and not the head.[32] This becomes important in a book where Western forms of reasoning and logic are continually being defeated by the elusive emotionalism and mysticism of the East.

The relationship between Aziz and Fielding is to be of much greater significance, since it is made to bear the burden of the theme of interracial friendship, and since Fielding shares the tradition of Forster's own liberal humanism. It is easy to overlook the fact that Aziz and Fielding are originally brought together by Mrs Moore, at least indirectly. When Fielding invites Miss Quested and Mrs Moore to visit him, Adela asks whether he knows Aziz and the suggestion is made that, since "Mrs Moore says he is so nice" (p. 46), he is to be included in the party. Their relationship begins under the influence of this recommendation and with the advantages of spontaneous emotion and goodwill (pp. 64-6). On the whole, Aziz is the simpler character,[33] and as such only gains in interest within the plot until Part 3 of the novel, when he stands in much greater contrast to the characters around him. The account given in these early chapters of Fielding's beliefs make it clear that he has taken over the role of such earlier creations as Mr Emerson, Ansell or Margaret Schlegel, and ultimately takes over the author's position too.

The world, he believed, is a globe of men who are trying to reach one another and can best do so by the help of good will plus culture and intelligence (p. 62).[34]

---

[32] C.f. "If the major events of A Passage to India are to take place, an initial friendship between Aziz and Mrs Moore is indispensable" (Wayne C. Booth, The Rhetoric of Fiction [Chicago, 1961], p. 107).

[33] However, to say that Aziz "thinks in terms of black and white" is not only unfair but inaccurate; c.f. Maclean, p. 160.

[34] In many ways Fielding may be said to speak with the Forsterian voice; he is described as being over forty when he first arrived in India (p. 61), the same age as Forster on his first visit (1912); at the time of the events in the novel he is middle-aged, again like Forster. Above all he continues the tradition of liberalism, humanism, and tolerance which we have come to associate with Forster and his 'good' characters. C.f. Leavis, The Common Pursuit, p. 272.

We are told later, during the first conversation with Aziz, that Fielding is "an optimist where personal relations were concerned" (p. 66), and so the novel's first message of the breakdown of such relations becomes very much an account of Fielding's partial loss of faith. The limitations of his humanism, as they are set forth in Chapter 11, are symptomatic of the position in which Forster may well have found himself, and which we have seen hinted at already in the writings of the interim period.

"I shall not really be intimate with this fellow," Fielding thought, and then "nor with anyone." That was the corollary. And he had to confess that he really didn't mind, that he was content to help people, and like them as long as they didn't object, and if they objected pass on serenely. Experience can do much, and all that he had learned in England and Europe was an assistance to him, and helped him towards clarity, but clarity prevented him from experiencing something else (p. 115).

The first part of this statement reveals a similarity between Fielding and Stephen Wonham, in *Journey*: both are content to be themselves, and in running against non-acceptance they merely "pass on serenely". The second part seems to be the hint at something seriously limiting in the postion which Forster, too, finds himself in. The contrast between clarity and experience, between Europe and India, echoes the contrasting views of Chandrapore in Chapter 1. Fielding must choose between maintaining an ideal which may be irrelevant for the world in which he finds himself, or risking the virtual destruction of the ideal in the confrontation with the reality of experience that India offers. Forster hints, too, at the problem and temptation of escapism or detachment as a means of retaining the ideal intact. This is in essence the problem that he was later to deal with in his article "The Ivory Tower", and it is at the root of a serious weakness in his attitude. For Forster, while preaching consistently the gospel of personal relations, is always careful to place himself in a position where he can choose and select those people with whom he will have these relations. Never is he exposed to the casual, accidental encounters which the majority of mankind have to face from day to day. This withdrawal may, in itself, suggest flaws in the ideal, however compromised, however much refined.[35]

Such an attitude is further reflected in Fielding's self-characterisation at the close of the first section as someone who travels light, as "a holy man minus the holiness" (p. 118).[36] Aziz is made to interpret this correctly when he notes, "So this was why Mr Fielding and a few others were so fearless! They had nothing to lose. But he himself was rooted in society and Islam" (p. 118). Fielding is the rootless wanderer with no family or social or religious ties, not even the liberal tradition can be said to bind him any more than it binds Forster.

The third relationship, that between Ronny and Adela, is much closer in tone and development to the restrained loves of Forster's earlier novels. For this reason the protagonists are of interest as a means of measuring the change in Forster's position brought about by the new setting. The uncertainty of their relationship is realized, even at this early stage, by Mrs Moore;[37] Adela, "queer, cautious girl", and Ronny, "also cautious", figure in the older woman's thoughts as probably, but not certainly, going to be married (p. 25).[38] It is, however, Chapter 8 which brings the dual crisis of this

[35] It is this limitation in Forster's attitude which has, perhaps, led to a number of negative criticisms of the man and his works. Forster is seen as congenitally unattached, a spectator rather than an active participant in the world. C.f. Lord David Cecil, *Poets and Storytellers*, pp. 181-2; Noel Annan, "Books in General", p. 239. The personal relations which Forster values so highly are, one critic notes, "almost entirely confined to the upper middle classes" (c.f. George Dangerfield, "E. M. Forster: A Man with a View", *Saturday Review of Literature*, 27.8.1938, p. 4). The emphasis Forster places on friendship is seen, too, as resulting in exclusiveness, and Forster himself as an emotional egoist, c.f. Montgomery Belgion, "The Diabolism of Mr E. M. Forster", *Criterion*, XIV (Oct. 1934), p. 72; Compton Mackenzie, *My Life and Times*, *Octave 6* (London, 1967), p. 170.

[36] To suggest, on the grounds of this remark, that "Fielding's faith [is] in man instead of God, and this faith makes him holy", is a clear case of missing the point. C.f. Pedersen, p. 243.

[37] We can see here a justification for associating Mrs Moore with Mrs Wilcox, as one who has perceptions about other people's emotions.

[38] C.f. "In a very early variant of the opening of this chapter Mrs Moore and her *daughter* have come to India, where the latter is to marry a civilian named 'Hesslop' or 'Hislop'" (Robert L. Harrison, "The Manuscripts of A Passage to India", microfilmed dissertation, Ann Arbor 1968, p. xx). We should, however, bear Forster's own comment in mind when quoting from this work: "Thanks to the wobblings of authors can we not learn something about them which they

apparently conventional relationship. In the previous chapter, Aziz has unwittingly drawn from Adela, in reply to the suggestion that she should settle in India, the spontaneous comment, "I'm afraid I can't do that" (p. 72). India as a disruptive force in the novel has already begun to work out its influence on the English. As a final prelude to the critical events of the next chapter, Chapter 7 ends with Professor Godbole's evening 'raga' to Shri Krishna: "I say to him, Come, come, come, come, come, come. He neglects to come" (p. 78). The great emotional and spiritual event becomes a non-event; the god *neglects* to come. India, the land of chance, of anti-reason, is well represented in this, her song.[39] So, too, will Adela never have the great emotional experience, so too for her and Ronny emotional revelation is not granted.[40]

Adela is the first to notice that Ronny has changed (p. 79), and pinpoints a quality which we shall later (Chapter 10) discover as characteristic of the destructive apathy which results from contact with India in this novel: "he seemed more indifferent than of old". His attitude, made all the more clear by his behaviour to Godbole and Aziz at Fielding's party, leads Adela to break off an engagement that was, at best, extremely tenuous.[41] Yet India being what it is, as soon as she has taken the step, there is no corresponding emotional or mental relief; rather "Adela will not marry Ronny. It seemed slipping away like a dream" (p. 82). Yet the whole crisis is soon revealed to have been nothing more serious than a lovers'

---

did not wish us to know? I do not think we can, for the reason that creative authors do not wobble centrally." – Review of *Authors at Work: An Address delivered by Robert H. Taylor*, New York 1957 (*Library*, 5th Series, XIII) (June 1958), p. 142; also referred to in Stallybrass, "Forster's 'Wobblings': The Manuscripts of *Passage to India*", p. 143.

[39] For further possible significances of Godbole's song for the whole novel see, George H. Thomson, *The Fiction of E. M. Forster* (Detroit, 1967), pp. 220-221.

[40] The diminishing development of the experience of love in Forster's novels is brought to a close. Lucy Honeychurch experiences two moments of spontaneous passion; Caroline Abbott feels deeply but contents herself with a protective gestures; Rickie Elliot's deepest experience is of another couple's love; Helen Schlegel never meets with anything greater than a flirtatious kiss in the dark, and Adela Quested must be content with a sympathetic handclasp.

[41] C.f. Lucy's reaction to Cecil Vyse's intolerable behaviour in *Room with a View*, p. 180.

quarrel (p. 86), a discovery they make silently under the influence
of a momentary physical contact, which is in itself as conventional
as they are: an accidental touching of hands. After the accident
with the Nawab Bahadur's car, they are united as cool Englishmen
in a scene of Oriental chaos and lack of self-control, and, no doubt
because of their under-developed hearts, make up the quarrel and
become engaged (p. 91). Yet once again, the crisis passed, Adela's
feelings do not correspond to that which has happened, instead
"She felt humiliated again, for she deprecated labels, and she felt too
that there should have been another scene between her lover and
herself at this point" (p. 91).

Later, back at the bungalow, Adela attempts to sort out the
events of the afternoon in a conversation reminiscent of that between Margaret Schlegel and Mrs Wilcox in Chapter 8 of *Howards
End*: "I feel I haven't been – frank enough, attentive enough, or
something. It's as if I got everything out of proportion" (p. 95). She
exaggerates the problem, however, and Mrs Moore evades her
question about the value of honesty. Instead the elder woman suggests that much is due to the new surroundings. Like Mrs Wilcox
before her, Mrs Moore has difficulty in articulating her intuitive
knowledge. Adela asks: "'You mean that my bothers are mixed
up with India?' 'India's –' She stopped" (p. 95). The broken off
sentence, "India's – ", suggests already the overwhelming impression that the country, through the medium of the experience of the
Marabar Caves, is to make upon Mrs Moore. India as physical
entity, and threatening presence, is felt, too, at the close of the
chapter.

Never tranquil, never perfectly dark, the night wore itself away, distinguished from other nights by two or three blasts of wind, which seemed to
fall perpendicularly out of the sky and to bounce back into it, hard and
compact, leaving no freshness behind them: the hot weather was approaching (pp. 96-7).

In India night is not perfectly dark, wind is hard and leaves no
freshness, the sun is not welcomed but seen as threatening, emotional response is out of all harmony with the event that calls it
forth, proportion does not work. Such is the nature of the reality
against which love will be measured, beside which the ideal will be

shown to be inadequate, or even irrelevant.

In the manuscript version of *Passage*, the last three chapters of the first part of the published novel were one chapter. The later division places the short Chapter 10 as an interval between Fielding's disappointment over his visit to the sick Aziz, and the establishment of friendly relations between them. Attention is thus focussed on this chapter which is seen to offer further insights into the nature of India as the reality which will serve, in this book, to negate the ideal.[42]

It matters so little to the majority of living beings what the minority, that calls itself human, desires or decides. Most of the inhabitants of India do not mind how India is governed. Nor are the lower animals of England concerned about England, but in the tropics the indifference is more prominent, the inarticulate world is closer at hand and readier to resume control as soon as men are tired (p. 111).

Again we have the insistence on the negative quality of indifference, which to someone who believes in personal relations, contact, and affection must represent an insuperable barrier. The categorising of man as the minority of living beings, and the equating of the majority of Indians with the lower animals of England, reveals an increasingly sceptical, if not cynical, view of mankind for which India is responsible. For how can one preach the private values of personal affection as a panacea for public ills when the majority of those for whom the remedy is intended are indifferent and robbed of human value? So here the "inarticulate world" slowly insinuates itself as potentially more powerful than the efforts of man. One theme that runs consistently throughout the novel is the dwarfing of man and human aspirations by this particular view of reality; the natural world as symbol of human failure and an inherent destructive will.[43] Chapter 10 closes on an even more threatening note than Chapter 8: "The sun was returning to his kingdom with

---

[42] C.f. Harrison, p. xviii. For a fuller discussion of the relation between the various manuscript versions of *Passage* and the published novel, see: June Perry Levine, "An Analysis of the Manuscripts of *A Passage to India*", *PMLA*, LXXXV (March 1970), pp. 284-294.

[43] C.f. "The caves... should be regarded as an epitome of non-human India, primal India, and as such they are set against the human endeavour that is represented by the mosque, the temple and the club" (Daleski, p. 266).

power but without beauty – that was the sinister feature. If only there had been beauty! His cruelty would have been tolerable then ... he was merely a creature, like the rest..." (p. 112-3). Here the cruelty and power of the sun foreshadow the expedition, in the heat, to the caves. By equating the sun with a creature, the rest of creation is united with it in a oneness that is itself frightening, for all come thereby to share in the cruelty and negation. Here is a vision of the world of good and evil, of equality and oneness, which we shall come to associate with Professor Godbole. This chapter acts as a prelude to the one which follows; that is, it sets up the almost insuperable barrier of the background against which, and in conflict with which, the friendship of Fielding and Aziz will develop.

The beatific view of Aziz, comforted by poetry, beauty, and affection for other men and memories of the past, brings the first section of *Passage* to a close. But Forster, who after all shares these affections, sees that there is only one region where they may exist and be enjoyed untroubled: the imagination. Thus a temporary peace is achieved with Aziz dreaming of "domes whereunder were inscribed, black against white, the ninety-nine attributes of God" (p. 119). In this fantasy he returns to the very situation where he first entered into contact with the English, the original mosque where "the ninety-nine names of God on the frieze stood out black, as the frieze stood out white against the sky" (p. 20). "Mosque" thus ends on a still hopeful note of the possibilities of communication and contact between the races, where the threats to the success of such ventures are still only threats.

3

The age of the earth, the incredible antiquity of the hills, the slow retreat of primal India are all brought into focus (p. 123) at the beginning of the second section before Forster turns his attention to the Marabar caves themselves: "Having seen one such cave, having seen two, having seen three, four, fourteen, twenty-four, the visitor returns to Chandrapore uncertain whether he has had an interesting experience or a dull one or any experience at all"

(p. 124). Once again we note Forster's insistence on the impossibility of defining India. A deliberate vagueness and uncertainty pervades the atmosphere; a vagueness and uncertainty which will torture Adela Quested until the final withdrawal of her charge against Aziz at the trial. The caves, however, will test the validity of ideals – emotional and spiritual – by standards of the unknown, where the caves become a force beyond private and public life, against which both are powerless.[44] As the organisation of this chapter suggests, the caves are inextricably bound up with the confrontation of India and England, of instinct versus rationalism.[45] This conflict is symbolized in the poetic description which Forster gives of the interior of the caves (pp. 124-5), where the flame lighted by the visitor's match and its reflection "like an imprisoned spirit" are revealed in the polished walls. The two flames cannot meet and eventually the match goes out. This is in essence an account of the process of Adela and Mrs Moore trying to get to know India, it is symbolic of the brief focussing of the light of Western rationality upon the age-old primal mysteries of India. What results are brief impressions of beauty and mystery followed by the uncertainty as to the nature of the experience, if there ever was one at all.

Right up to the moment when the party enters the first cave, Forster fills his account of the journey towards the Marabar with hints of what is about to happen. Even before the group collects at the station we learn that Aziz is troubled: "Trouble after trouble encountered him, because he had challenged the spirit of the Indian earth, which tries to keep men in compartments" (p. 127). The attempt to contact other people, to build up personal relations, the very ideal itself, are presented in opposition to the setting in which the events of the novel take place. Later, in the train, we see Mrs Moore as mentally prepared for the revulsions that the Marabar will produce within her:

---

[44] John Beer hints at the importance we are to attach to the caves in all that happens in the next three chapters: "The Marabar caves are not a revelation of reality, but a touchstone by which reality is tested." What we should point out is that in the terminology of Beer's study "reality" here corresponds more nearly to what we have termed "the ideal". C.f. Beer, p. 161; Gransden, p. 97.
[45] C.f. Boyle, "Adela Quested's Delusion...", p. 479.

She felt increasingly (vision or nightmare?) that though people are important the relations between them are not, and that in particular too much fuss has been made over marriage; centuries of carnal embracement, yet man is no nearer to understanding man (p. 134).

And yet the caves are going to assert "that the emotions, the flesh must not be denied".[46] In Mrs Moore's reflections we seem to hear the Forsterian voice itself, echoing that which was in the background of his post-1910 writings: the desperate attempt to hold on to a belief in man, though the reality of experience insists on the impossibility of contact and understanding.

The vagueness and uncertainty that the party encounters is summarised in the characterisation of India itself as "not a promise, only an appeal" (p. 135). And as the elephant bearing the guests approaches the caves, this lack of promise and sense of mystery, which could well be a muddle, is repeated.

Life went on as usual, but had no consequences, that is to say, sounds did not echo or thoughts develop. Everything seemed cut off at its root, and therefore infected with illusion... Nothing was explained, and yet there was no romance (p. 139).

The feeling builds up that none of the party are capable of coping with the experience that is to be offered. Again, as, for example, in *The Longest Journey*, a vision is to be presented, a vision which Mrs Moore accepts but cannot turn to any value for herself or others; a vision which Adela and Aziz are, each in their own way, wrongly equipped to master. Aziz himself realises this in advance and, in his reflections, points to the only character in the book who could master the experience:

His ignorance became evident, and was really rather a drawback. In spite of his gay, confident talk, he had no notion how to treat this particular aspect of India; he was lost in it, *without Professor Godbole*, like themselves (p. 140, my italics).

Godbole's qualifications for the role of interpreter of the mystery of the Marabar lies in his detachment from the reality of everyday experience and his vision of the infinite.[47] He alone of all the characters in the novel is granted that sense of proportion which is able to

---

[46] Boyle, p. 479.
[47] C.f. McConkey, *The Novels of E. M. Forster*, pp. 11-12; Gransden, p. 98.

separate reality as ideal, as truth, from the spurious realities of concrete everyday occurrences. He alone it is who is able to universalise the particular and individual, and whose religion prepares him for the disappointment of nothing.[48]

So much has been written about the experiences of the two Englishwomen in the caves that it would seem almost superfluous to add more, but it is obviously of utmost importance that these experiences should be related to the conflict between love and reality. To see the experiences in perspective one must go back to the beginning of chapter 14. Here Forster, with almost devastating sincerity, states that "Most of life is so dull that there is nothing to be said about it" (p. 132) and points out that it is only human insincerity that leads us, on the dullest of days, or in periods when our feelings seem deadened and life is truly meaningless, to express the opposite so often. In this state Mrs Moore and Adela find themselves at the outset of the expedition, with the difference that Mrs Moore "accepted her own apathy" (p. 132) and Adela did not.

It is quite clear that within the total framework of the novel Mrs Moore's experience of the caves is of far greater significance than Miss Quested's; the latter's illusions are certainly of vital importance for the furtherance of the plot, and without them the relationship between Fielding and Aziz would not develop as it does nor would the ideal be so sharply set against the background of racial hatred. However, as E. K. Brown has pointed out, "The triumph in *A Passage to India* is the presentation of the spiritual crisis through which Mrs Moore passes".[49] The recognition of the centrality of Mrs Moore's "anti-vision"[50] leads to a further observation, namely that there are two aspects of our major theme being treated in this book: on the one hand there is the consistent attempt to break down the barrier of the spurious reality of everyday and discover, not only what is behind, but to see if the revelation can be borne and accepted; in relation to this aspect Mrs Moore and Professor

[48] The sinister echo in the caves was never mentioned by Godbole in advance, "it never impressed him, perhaps" (p. 145). This suggests again his detachment and so his immunity. One of the questions the novel raises will be whether Forster can accept such detachment for himself.

[49] C.f. E. K. Brown, "E. M. Forster and the Contemplative Novel", p. 359.

[50] Crews, p. 156.

Godbole are the two extremes: the failure and success of accepting the vision. On the other hand, we have the continuation of the concerns of *Howards End* on a wider basis, where the protagonists are again divided: the brittle relationship of Ronny and Adela set off against the intenser but equally fragile relationship of Aziz and Fielding. Thus in placing any stress upon Mrs Moore's crisis at Marabar, we are turning our attention away from the personal relationships theme and concentrating, once again, on problems of reality, which in this novel assume more mystical and religious proportions than elsewhere in Forster's writing.

The crisis for both Englishwomen is precipitated by the echo in the caves, which, being a product of primal India, is illusory when one attempts to define or describe it: "Whatever is said, the same monotonous voice replies, and quivers up and down the walls until it is absorbed into the roof. 'Boum' is the sound as far as the human alphabet can express it, or 'bou-oum', or 'ou-boum', – utterly dull" (p. 145). The first effect upon Mrs Moore, on emerging into the sunlight, is a moment of clarified vision; she sees that the horrific naked thing in the cave was nothing more than a baby on its mother's hip; more important, she realises that one cave is enough and that the others can offer her nothing greater or less or more final. Lastly there is her final ambiguous remark to Aziz, to whom she is never again to speak: "Don't let so many people come with you this time. I think you may find it more convenient" (p. 147). Of the various possible interpretations of the use of "convenient" here, it would seem likely that Forster wishes to imply that Mrs Moore 'knows' that a situation must be precipitated and that her sharpened vision is gaining expression in this remark.[51]

Mrs Moore's thoughts, once she is left alone, turn momentarily to her other children at home in England and then pass to religion. That is, the experience in the cave touches two areas of known experience: personal relationships and belief in an ideal. Both are totally negated by the spirit of the caves, the reality beyond experience.[52] The vision which Mrs Moore has been granted is of an all-

[51] Harrison notes that the earlier manuscript contains further examples of foreknowledge which are all but eliminated in the final book (Harrison, p. xxv).
[52] C.f. Brower, "The Twilight of the Double Vision: Symbol and Irony in

inclusive levelling-down process: "Pathos, piety, courage – they exist, but are identical, and so is filth. Everything exists, nothing has value" (p. 147). She too, like Professor Godbole, is being challenged to work into the ideal the idea that the ideal may be seen as meaningless: "All has become one; but the one is nothing."[53] Godbole, on the other hand, as we shall later see, finds in the great moment of his religious ecstasy, that his attempts to force himself to a completeness of vision fail at the last moment (pp. 281-2), but he is able to make the effort to this completeness, which Mrs Moore is not able to do. For Mrs Moore the only definable discovery is that "the universe is muddle rather than mystery"[54] and so she arrives at the position where she can feel that nothing has any power against the vision, not even her own highest ideal: her Christian belief: "She realised that she didn't want to write to her children, didn't want to communicate with anyone, not even with God" (p. 148). Here there is no dramatic, sudden loss of faith in the accepted sense of the word, rather Forster wishes to expose the weakness of the conventional ideals which Mrs Moore, who is as typical of middle class womanhood as Mrs Wilcox before her, has accepted unthinkingly for herself.[55] Thus Forster once again demonstrates the weakness of ideals which are adopted only for the sake of conformity. The greatness of Mrs Moore, as a character, lies in her acceptance of the logical consequences of her failure to assimilate the vision. Her twin props in life – the sacredness of family and religion – have disappeared, therefore life itself becomes vague, meaningless, and of little interest. There remains only the perception she has gained into the essential apathy and sameness of the world: "She lost all interest, even in Aziz, and the affectionate and sincere words that she had spoken to him seemed no longer hers but the air's!" (p. 148). Mrs Moore, having been confronted by the nothingness

Passage to India", p. 215.

[53] C.f. White, "*A Passage to India*: Analysis and Revaluation", p. 648.

[54] *Ibid.*

[55] C.f. Mrs Moore's vague appeals to the *words* of religion during her conversation with Ronny in Chapter 5 (p. 51), where she echoes a number of Christian commonplaces about "loving one's neighbour", and also the beginning of St. Paul's praise of charity, 1. Corinthians, 13.

behind her vision of reality – akin to the "panic and emptiness" that lay beneath the Wilcox ideology – becomes silent.[56] Christianity has failed because in her case inadequate;[57] from now on, at least for her, negatively, as for Professor Godbole, positively, there will be no absolute moral values.[58] Personal relationships are of no interest anymore. They have not failed or been proved inadequate, but like Mrs Moore's Christianity, they are simply of no interest any more for the old lady and the caves come to symbolize for her, and for the novel as a whole, the breakdown of communication, the inefficacy of human relationship in a situation where love itself is as meaningful or meaningless as hate or nothing.[59]

Adela Quested's experience of the caves is more prosaic than that of the older woman. Adela's moment of perception comes before she enters the second cave:

as she toiled over a rock that resembled an inverted saucer, she thought, "What about love?" ... She and Ronny – no, they did not love each other... There was esteem and animal contact at dusk, but the emotion that links them was absent (p. 150).

Here we have a repetition of one of the themes from *Howards End*; the theme of prose and passion, beast and monk,[60] and the realisation of failed connection. The very fact that for Ronny and Adela there is no connection between respect and sexuality suggests that they are still lost, for Forster, among the unregenerate of the middle class world. Outside the second cave Adela is able to take stock of the situation coolly; it is the revelation of the nothingness beyond this realization, which the second cave brings, that almost drives her mad. One might take an account of the experience a stage further and suggest that what happens to Adela is that she receives a vision of the protest of the primal forces of nature, of the ancient powers of the Indian earth, against a union between two human

[56] C.f. Pedersen, p. 238.
[57] C.f. Trilling, p. 132.
[58] C.f. Stanley Cooperman, "The Imperial Posture and the Shrine of Darkness: Kipling's *Naulakha* and E. M. Forster's *Passage to India*", *English Literature in Transition*, VI (1963), p. 12.
[59] C.f. Brower, p. 215.
[60] C.f. *Howards End*, pp. 174-5.

beings where love and physical emotion are absent.[61] However, the exact nature of the experience, which Forster leaves deliberately vague, seems to be of minor importance.[62] What is important is that the confrontation with a reality greater and more devastating than ever before experienced overwhelms both women.

The caves expedition ends with the arrival of Fielding and immediately we are made aware of a counter-force to the destructive mystery of the Marabar: the voice of logic and intellect[63] which will stand against the destructive forces of confused interpretations of reality throughout the remainder of this section. Fielding is consistently down to earth, reducing mystery, over-emotion, poetry and hysteria to the point where they are revealed as unhealthy exaggerations. The norm is practical common sense as expressed in his recitation of his favourite proverbs as the train returns to Chandrapore in the final lull before the storm: "My proverbs are: A penny saved is a penny earned; A stitch in time saves nine; Look before you leap..." (p. 158). There seems here in the very commonplaceness of the remark something of the nature of old Mr Emerson in *Room with a View*. It is these qualities in the face of tribal or racial emotion which will bring Fielding into disrepute with his countrymen in the chapters to follow:

he had not rallied to the banner of race. He was still after facts, though the herd had decided on emotion. Nothing enrages Anglo-India more than the lantern of reason if it is exhibited for one moment after its extinction is decreed (p. 162).

The aftermath of the confrontation with the revelation of reality that the Marabar offered is what we have become used to expecting from Forster when his characters confuse the reality of experience with an ultimate reality and enter into a state of "muddledom'. The

[61] Gertrude White suggests something similar and emphasises the possible universality of the experience. C.f. White, p. 650.
[62] Although an earlier version of *Passage* gave much more evidence for the attempted rape, in the book version there is absolutely none. It seems quite clear from the wording of the close of Chapter 15 that Aziz and Adela go into separate caves (p. 151); and the conversation with the guide seems to leave no doubt about this (p. 152-3), c.f. Harrison, pp. xxv-xxvi.
[63] C.f. Maclean, p. 164; McDowell, *E. M. Forster*, p. 23.

caves have resulted, in almost all involved with the exception of
Fielding and Mrs Moore, in an opting for muddle rather than the
acceptance of the mystery of the revelation. The next part of the
book, from Chapter 17 to the end of Chapter 24, lies under the
influence of muddle or a refusal to allow that reality is perhaps
relative. The English are shown judging according to established
prejudice and the Indians, though highly provoked, are little better.
In the background are Mrs Moore "sunk in apathy and cynism"
(p. 156) and Fielding actively convinced of the correctness of his
individual interpretation of the reality of experience, as opposed to
the mass view adopted by his countrymen.

4

Against the background of racial emotionalism, rectitude and quar-
relling, comes the quiet interlude of Fielding's discussion of Aziz'
guilt or innocence with the, as yet, enigmatic figure of Professor
Godbole. The introduction of Godbole at this point in the story is
of particular significance. For at this point the world has become a
muddle and is divided into parties and races, man against man,
English against Indian, and even Hindu against Moslem with
reference to the coming feast of Mohurram. Against this Forster
opposes Godbole with his clear vision of universal harmony, of a
world where the universe "may be a mystery but is not a muddle".[64]
Thus Godbole, at this stage in the novel, may be seen as representing the uninvolved, objective norm of existence.[65] At first (p. 173)
he attempts to evade discussion and thus appears as almost heart-
less in his detachment, and stubbornly so in his insistence on discussing the minor point of a name for the school he wishes to
found. Yet, in his own way, Godbole keeps to the principle of
proportion; the school and his own future are nearest to his heart,

[64] White, p. 651.
[65] In so far we may see him as the "character equivalent of the Forsterian voice"
(McConkey, p. 11). Though this suggestion of Godbole's role would hardly seem
true of the final section of the novel, where he emerges as standing for much that
is quite unacceptable to Forster, the humanist. C.f. Shusterman, *The Quest for
Certitude...*, p. 183.

misguided emotionalism and mass sentiment could not be further from his interest. Yet, we may note that at the end of the novel the school, for lack of pupils, is turned into a granary (p. 312), a fact which is all part of the appeal of Godbole whose whole interest is focussed not upon practical achievement but upon the idea.[66] Confronted with Fielding's question as to the guilt or innocence of Aziz, Godbole, rightly, suggests that such categories, being legal, are the business of the courts. When Fielding, nearing exasperation, asks Godbole whether Aziz could have raped Miss Quested, again Godbole places the question in perspective and suggests that questions about the human capacity for evil are not so easily answered. At this point we come to realise that reason, which we have associated with Fielding up till now, is limited since it is Western reason, whereas Godbole opposes to this a penetrating detachment which not even Fielding can share.

'I am informed that an evil action was performed in the Marabar Hills, and that a highly esteemed English Lady is now seriously ill in consequence. My answer to that is this: that action was performed by Dr Aziz.' He stopped and sucked in his thin cheeks. 'It was performed by the guide.' He stopped again. 'It was performed by you.' Now he had an air of daring and of coyness. 'It was performed by me.' He looked shyly down the sleeve of his own coat. 'And by my students. It was even performed by the lady herself. When evil occurs, it expresses the whole of the universe. Similarly when good occurs' (p. 174-5).

Here we have a Hindu refinement on Rickie Elliot's knowledge of good-and-evil which, rather than being an individual seeing the rightness and wrongness of both sides, becomes, in the Indian setting, a universalising vision of humanity, the sort of vision of inclusiveness which Forster sets off against Aziz' idea of universal brotherhood.

The joint pervasive influence of Godbole and the Marabar upon Fielding remain until the end of Chapter 21 where Godbole "slipped off unmolested to his new job... he always did possess the knack of slipping off" (p. 188).[67] Fielding has by now thrown in his lot

---

[66] It is disregard of this essential feature that leads Chaudhuri to see Godbole simply as a clown. C.f. Chaudhuri, p. 21.

[67] Here we may note a detail which precedes the conversation between Godbole

with the Indians against his own countryman and so provides an early example of a later Forsterian maxim: "If I had to choose between betraying my country and betraying my friend, I hope I should have the guts to betray my country."[68] For Fielding the influence of Godbole and his own brief experience of the Marabar fill him with a sense that his chosen way of life is not as satisfactory as he had thought, and we have a passage which looks forward to the concerns of the final section of the novel:

It was the last moment of the light, and as he gazed at the Marabar Hills they seemed to move graciously towards him like a queen, and their charm became the sky's. At the moment they vanished they were everywhere, the cool benediction of the night descended, the stars sparkled, and the whole universe was a hill. Lovely, exquisite moment – but passing the Englishman with averted face and on swift wings. He experienced nothing himself; it was as if someone had told him there was such a moment, and he was obliged to believe. And he felt dubious and discontended suddenly, and wondered whether he was really and truly successful as a human being. After forty years' experience, he had learnt to manage his life and make the best of it on advanced European lines, had developed his personality, explored his limitations, controlled his passions – and he had done it all without becoming either pedantic or worldly. A creditable achievement, but as the moment passed, he felt he ought to have been working at something else the whole time – he didn't know at what, never would know, never could know, and that was why he felt sad (p. 187).

Here for the first, and last, time in the novel someone has a view of the Marabar Hills which is positive. Fielding, the man with only

---

and Fielding. At the moment of Aziz' imprisonment, at the close of Chapter 18, where Fielding has attempted to intercede on his behalf, we read as the last sentence of the chapter: "As if his prayer had been heard, there was a sudden rackety-dacket on a temple bell" (p. 169). And two pages later, where Fielding and Aziz' friends are discussing the question of a defence lawyer for Aziz: "There was a lugubrious pause. The temple bell continued to jangle harshly" (p 171). Fielding then leaves the party and two pages later occurs the conversation with Godbole. Here, surely, in the bell at the significant moment of Aziz' downfall, and as prelude to the discussion of good and evil with Godbole, we hear the first sounds of the mystery that will dominate the final section of *Passage*. "Temple" is, as it were, present, at least passively, in the novel from this moment of the bell and the subsequent articulate moments of Professor Godbole.

[68] "What I Believe", *Two Cheers for Democracy*, p. 78.

reason and logic and aesthetic sense, untrammelled by passion, racialism, nationalism or any preconceived notion of man and the universe, can see in the Marabar grace, charm, and benediction. He sees it but does not experience it. Because he can be aware of something which still remains beyond his own experience, Fielding is discontented, and the suggestion is surely justified that Forster, too, at the same age and same stage in his career and self-education, feels the same when confronted by the *mystery* that is India. The search for a reality which will also involve being "successful as a human being" is that which largely occupies Fielding from now on as it was to occupy Forster for the rest of his life.

With Fielding's preoccupations established, and with the departure of Godbole from the scene, the novel centres upon Mrs Moore until the moment of the trial. Although Mrs Moore has lost her Christian faith and her interest in people, there remains the perception of reality which enables her to see through and beyond the muddle that has been created around the memories of the Marabar excursion. In this she stands out above her fellow-countrymen in the crisis, she remains alone as an incarnation of the negation which the caves symbolised and which, for a moment. they were. Yet in spite of the uniqueness of Mrs Moore's vision, we should beware of over-emphasising and over-valuing her importance in the further events of the novel.[69] We may see in her, as some critics already have done, a contrast to the attitude of Professor Godbole as developed in the last section of the book: on the one hand a contrast in which Mrs Moore is seen as rejecting the universe and Godbole as accepting it in ever widening measure;[70] and on the other hand as "an attempt by Forster, the liberal agnostic, to get beyond his own scepticism".[71]

As she is presented to us, we see Mrs Moore very much as an

[69] Mrs Moore can neither be seen as a yardstick or touchstone by which other viewpoints may be measured, nor yet as the only answer to religious faith which the novel offers. C.f. Maclean, p. 159; Pedersen, p. 231; Hoare, *Some Studies in the Modern Novel*, p. 91. For both functions she is too completely withdrawn into her own apathy and resignation to nothingness.

[70] C.f. Keir, "*A Passage to India* Reconsidered", p. 431.

[71] C.f. Arnold Kettle, *An Introduction to the English Novel*, Vol. 2 (1953) (London, 1962), p. 170.

irritable old lady who has lost all the charm of the earlier part of the novel, and is now filled with premonitions of death and a desire for isolation. When Adela questions her about the echo in the caves which is still with her, but which, unlike the older woman she cannot interpret, Mrs Moore replies: "If you don't know, you don't know; I can't tell you" (p. 195). Which once again lays the emphasis on the individual's need to interpret and assimilate his own experience without the aid of any preconceived values or evaluations. Mrs Moore, in this and in her attitude in general, presents a rather depressing continuation of another unpleasant elderly lady, Mrs Failing, in *The Longest Journey*. Her outbursts become more violent and more startlingly negative whether they are against love and marriage (p. 197) or against Christianity (p. 200). And yet within this totally negative framework remains the perception which enables her to see from the beginning that Aziz is innocent and Adela's accusation is based on a illusion: "A bad old woman, bad, bad, detestable. I used to be good with the children growing up, also I meet this young man in his mosque, I wanted him to be happy. Good, happy, small people. They do not exist, they were a dream... But I will not help you to torture him for what he never did" (p. 200). A remark which justifies Adela's insistence to Ronny that Mrs Moore has already pronounced on Aziz' goodness and innocence (p. 198). Mrs Moore's "double vision" (p. 203) enables her to see evil and good equally, yet to see herself as bad, although in her clarity of vision she may be placed on the side of the angels in her proclamation of Aziz' innocence. This double vision connects her inextricably with Godbole in his vision of the universal responsibility for good and evil. We are reminded that, for Forster, the idea of absolute standards tends to be anathema; thus, after the experience of the caves, absolute right and absolute wrong come to be meaningless terms. For Mrs Moore personally, the experience is finally defined as: "She had come to that state where the horror of the universe and its smallness are both visible at the same time" (p. 202), and it is on this note that Mrs Moore retires from the scene and from the novel. Yet, like Mrs Wilcox before her, she leaves an indefinable presence and a memory behind, which itself becomes a symbol of the "spiritual muddledom" (p. 203) which she herself has entered upon: she becomes transformed into the mysterious deity "Esmiss Esmoor" (p. 219).

The trial itself is, in terms of the themes we are concentrating on, of small interest, it is far more a dramatic *tour de force* within the terms of the plot of the novel.[72] Adela's recantation is presented as a triumph of reason which, by Western standards, is wholly praiseworthy. "I was brought up to be honest; the trouble is it gets me nowhere" (p. 233), she tells Fielding and immediately gains his sympathy, but later Forster sees her action in terms of the people it most affects, the Indians:

Her behaviour rested on cold justice and honesty; she had felt, while she recanted, no passion of love for those whom she had wronged. Truth is not truth in that exacting land unless there go with it kindness and more kindness and kindness again (p. 238).

Here Forster touches on the overwhelming demands that India makes upon the ideal, upon love itself; requiring that it should be inexhaustible in its endeavours to bridge the gap between race and race, man and man, reality and reality.[73] So are we reminded of the scope of *Passage to India* and are forewarned that even Love will prove inadequate to the task.

Before the celebration party for Aziz' acquittal at Mr Zulfiquar's house, Fielding has a moment's pause for meditation which links him once more to the Marabar caves and his own experience of them and the hills:

He lost his usual sane view of human intercourse, and felt that we exist not in ourselves, but in terms of each others minds – a notion for which logic offers no support and which had attacked him only once before,

[72] Although Adela's final withdrawal of her charge against Aziz may be seen as part of a wider acceptance of reality, or an ability to distinguish between reality and muddle. This is symbolized by the disappearance of her echo – that which has acted as "a barrier between her and the realisation she cannot quite admit". C.f. Levine, "An Analysis of the Manuscript of *Passage to India*", p. 289.

[73] C.f. "No one can ever realize how much kindness we Indians need... Kindness, more kindness, and even after that more kindness" (p. 114). This is echoed in "Indian Entries", p. 24, and in "India Again", where it becomes, "Goodwill is not enough... The only thing that cuts a little ice is affection or the possibility of affection" (*Two Cheers for Democracy*, p. 335).

the evening after the catastrophe, when from the veranda of the club he saw the fists and fingers of the Marabar swell until they included the whole sky (p. 242).

This idea is not new for Forster, we are reminded both of the argument about existence and reality at the beginning of *The Longest Journey* and the remark made by Margaret about Mrs Wilcox: "I feel that you and I and Henry are only fragments of that woman's mind."[74] The question that troubles Fielding is a basic question concerning reality and human existence: 'What is the real I? My vision of myself or other people's vision of me?' A question which, because of its very metaphysical nature, disturbs Forster, who does not wish to account for anything in terms of a metaphysical reality which cannot be grasped by reason and logic. We may note that Fielding's vision comes to him at a moment of fatigue and is contrasted strongly with his usual 'sane view' of man and his nature.

This passage serves, in accordance with the Forsterian method, as a prelude to the desultory conversation after the celebrations where Aziz announces his resolution to become anti-British, and Fielding, true to the sense of good-and-evil, pleads Miss Quested's case with him. Fielding, provoked by Aziz' attitude which he cannot understand, and hearing Aziz invoke Mrs Moore, tries to tell his friend that Mrs Moore is dead. Hamidullah interrupts, not wanting Aziz' happiness spoiled, and Fielding is again provoked to thoughts about the reality of human existence: "Facts are facts, and everyone would learn of Mrs Moore's death in the morning. But it struck him that people are not really dead until they are felt to be dead. As long as there is some misunderstanding about them, they possess a sort of immortality" (p. 247).[75] Fielding has thus gained insight into death and life and realises that immortality and human existence are but frail products of the human mind.

---

[74] *Howards End*, p. 292.
[75] A thought which, linking us with Fielding's thoughts on his way to the party, takes us forward to a later assertion of Forster's: "The people I respect most behave as if they were immortal and as if society was eternal. Both assumptions are false: both of them must be accepted as true if we are going to go on eating and working and loving, and are to keep open a few breathing holes for the human spirit." – "What I believe", *Two Cheers for Democracy*, p. 81.

The central section of the novel now moves rapidly towards its close with Fielding's departure for England via the norm of the Mediterranean.[76] However, before this point is reached we have, in Chapter 29, the important last meeting and conversation between Fielding and Adela Quested, which leads to clarification for the latter. Adela's endeavours to undo the harm she has done unwittingly are still dogged by her inability to arouse in herself affection for those she has wronged. And Fielding reveals this lack of personal concern as having been present in her since her arrival in the country: "The first time I saw you, you were wanting to see India, not Indians, and it occured to me: Ah, that won't take us far. Indians know whether they are liked or not – they cannot be fooled here" (p. 253). The inclusion of the word "here" suggests once again that India, the place, is being used in the novel as a symbol for that region of human experience where the sham, the imitation or even the well-intentioned blunder are revealed for what they are: less than the ideal, less than the ultimate reality, which in this case only the Marabar caves have revealed. The importance of this final conversation lies in that point where Fielding and Adela are in complete agreement: the question of the value of personal relations. If, as we have asserted all along, Fielding is to be taken very much as a projection (not portrait or representation) of Forster at this period in his development, then the pronouncements on this matter are of significance. Adela now recollects her experience of the caves as the moment of truth and tries to explain that which was revealed to her there in relation to her proposed marriage to Ronny:

"I entered that cave thinking: Am I fond of him? I have not yet told you that, Mr Fielding. I didn't feel justified. Tenderness, respect, personal intercourse – I tried to make them take the place – of – "
"I no longer want love," he said supplying the word.
"No more do I. My experiences here have cured me. But I want others to want it." (p. 256).

Fielding's announcement that he no longer wants love places him more or less in the position of Forster at the end of *Howards End*

---

[76] C.f. "The Mediterranean is the human norm" (p. 275).

with its stress on the values that Adela brings into her list of substitutes. Finally the two come to an agreement tacit rather than outspoken, that after all "personal relations... are temporary" (p. 257). Forster writes, as they part: "A friendliness, as of dwarfs shaking hands, was in the air", and we are told that they are both dissatisfied with the feeling of their own insignificance and the feeling that something great *may* have passed them by (p. 257). It is this, surely, that makes the final section of the novel, incongruent as it may appear, necessary. There must be a presentation of the possible alternative, friendship and affection must be shown against the greater good as well as against the background of the greater negative. For this reason, as well as for the structural, "Temple" becomes indispensable for the development and rounding off the theme of *Passage to India*.[78]

5

This final section of *Passage to India* introduces another India which is deliberately placed at a considerable distance from that we have so far experienced of Chandrapore and the Marabar: "Some hundreds of miles westward of the Marabar Hills, and two years later in time, Professor Narayan Godbole stands in the presence of God" (p. 279). At once we are transferred from the bustling, noisy quarrelsome world of the civil station and small town nationalism to what at first sight appears to be the realm of myth and legend.[79] Here the universality of muddle and chaos in human relations will be supplanted by the appeal to mystery,[80] which, however, Fielding has already defined as "a high-sounding name for a muddle" (p. 68). In short it would appear that far from offering a solution of his own to the problem of supplying a positive counterweight to the collapse of Christianity in Mrs Moore, or the somewhat resigned bewilder-

[78] C.f. Letter from Noel Annan to Wilfred Stone (Stone, *The Cave and the Mountain*, p. 333).
[79] C.f. Stone, p. 346; William H Rueckert, *Kenneth Burke and the Drama of Human Relations* (Minneapolis, 1963), p. 111.
[80] C.f. White, p. 651.

ment of Fielding, or the more drastic collapse of personal relations in Miss Quested, Forster chooses to examine what India itself offers. This is the religion and mysticism of Professor Godbole with its suggestion of "an attainment of unity not through a reconciliation of opposites which preserves separate identity but through a submergence of individual differences".[81] What Forster finally makes of this solution becomes the theme and aim of this final section; for should the Hindu vision fail, there is little else upon which man may rest.[82]

It is characteristic of Forster's India in general and of Professor Godbole in particular that his religion should, from the first, be presented as ambiguous in itself, for the God in whose presence Godbole stands is described as both unborn and born, both born already and not subject to human processes such as birth (p. 279). The description of the celebrations of the festival of Gokul Ashtami which follows serves to place certain moments of the novel in a perspective of Godbole's creation, and to highlight and summarise that which Forster feels he is able to select from Hinduism for his own purpose. Godbole himself is presented as concentrating all spiritual efforts on the attainment of a totality of acceptance of creation; a vision of a complete unity in creation; success or failure to achieve this are, however, immaterial to his religious faith and beyond the scope of Western reason.

Thus Godbole, though she was not important to him, remembered an old woman he had met in Chandrapore days. Chance brought her into his mind while it was in this heated state, he did not select her, she happened to occur among the throng of soliciting images, a tiny splinter, and he impelled her by this spiritual force to that place where completeness can be found. Completeness, not reconstruction (pp. 281-2).

This is the secret of Godbole's view of the world, the vision by which he is able to live in unaffected detachment. Completeness implies an attempt to ever widen the boundaries of the ideal, a

[81] Daleski, p. 274; c.f. Gransden, p. 103; Brower, p. 221.
[82] We should be doing Forster an injustice if we were to suppose that he is offering mystery or mysticism as a solution; rather, he wishes to show that this is what India has to offer, and, in the desperation of the situation, this answer has to be examined. C.f. Hale, p. 30; Hunt, p. 508; Keir, p. 429.

continual compromise and modification, and therefore attractive to Forster who has attempted, on a narrower plane, the same task. Opposed to this is the idea of reconstruction, which implies a starting again along the lines of strict selection of that which is acceptable; an idea not totally unacceptable to Forster. Godbole's adherence to the principle of acceptance is seen then in action and seen to fail:

His senses grew thinner, he remembered a wasp seen he forgot where, perhaps on a stone. He loved the wasp equally, he impelled it likewise, he was imitating God. And the stone where the wasp clung – could he... no, he could not, he had been wrong to attempt the stone, logic and conscious effort had seduced (p. 282).

Here we may notice that the connection to Mrs Moore is finally established, not merely by the mention of "an old woman" or of the wasp, which both have observed, but in the unity of their response. Godbole loves the wasp equally with the old woman; Mrs Moore responded with affection and admiration: "Pretty dear" (p. 35), but her Christianity has failed her. Godbole's Hinduism is also unable to go beyond the wasp because he tries to imbue it with elements of Christianity: logic and conscious effort. Since Godbole realises his failure *and* its causes, his religious belief is unaffected and he continue his dance of religious ecstasy.

The celebration ends with Godbole once again sunk in meditation, in a passage which establishes the link between himself and Fielding and which may be taken as standing for that which Forster is able to take from Godbole's Hinduism and make his own:

Covered with grease and dust, Professor Godbole had once more developed the life of his spirit.[83] He had, with increasing vividness, again seen Mrs Moore, and round her faintly clinging forms of trouble. He was a Brahman, she Christian, but it made no difference, it made no difference whether she was a trick of his memory or a telepathic appeal. It was his

[83] The emphasis is on "*his* spirit" rather than on the more abstract Christian version of the "life of *the* spirit". An indication of Forster's attraction to Hinduism for its emphasis on the individual and a reminder that Godbole is not just used as a religious type but as a person in his own right. C.f. Forster's statement of what Hinduism means to him in terms of its allowance to the individual of a place in the centre of the complexities of the world. "The World Mountain", *Listener*, 2.12.1954, p. 977-8.

duty, as it was his desire, to place himself in the position of the God and to love her, and to place himself in her position and to say to the God "Come, come, come, come." This was all he could do. How inadequate! But each according to his own capacities, and he knew that his own were small. "One old Englishwoman and one little, little wasp," he thought, as he stepped out of the temple into the grey of a pouring wet morning. "It does not seem much, still it is more than I am myself" (pp. 285-6).

This, then, is Forster's personal interpretation of Hinduism for his own use; even though, as Fielding for a moment suspected, and as Godbole notes but disregards, we are only the product of each other's minds, though we may only exist as memories, there must still be love. Here is no religious or mystical solution to the problem that India has presented,[84] for reason and spiritual insight as Godbole has consciously realised are incompatible,[85] but far more, as Gertrude White has already pointed out, the affirmation that "only 'the secret understanding of the heart', which may fail but can never be really defeated, and is our only answer to the voice of the Marabar", can save us.[86]

However, Passage to India does not end there, and we may, in fact, see this opening chapter dealing with Godbole and the festival in the same light as the opening chapters of the two earlier sections: as a prelude and a setter of tone for what comes after. That is, at the beginning of "Temple", Forster puts forward the suggestion that love, as a personal value for personal relations, for the inner life, still 'works'. The assertion almost immediately meets its own negation when Aziz and Fielding meet again after an interim of two years. Aziz the Moslem and Fielding the agnostic, both anti-pathetic to Godbole's religion, have to fight their way through to each other over yet another muddle, a well-intentioned muddle brought about by Mahmoud Ali, because, as Aziz says, "he loved me" (p. 298). Aziz is no longer able to see Fielding as an individual – as Cyril, rather than Mr Fielding – he can only recognise him as an Englishman. And, as such, "I wish no Englishman or Englishwoman to be my friend" (p. 298). Yet that which remains with Aziz after

[84] C.f. Keir, p. 434.
[85] C.f. McConkey, p. 90.
[86] White, p. 656.

the conversation is over is the memory of Mrs Moore's name, which, like that of Mrs Wilcox before her, in a similar situation where personal relations were threatened with defeat,[87] acts as a benediction upon him. The irony here is obvious, for if we recall our final vision of Mrs Moore we remember her as a bad woman, a woman who had lost her faith and was sunk in apathy and scepticism. Yet the feeling for Aziz had largely remained. Aziz can accept her, Englishwoman though she may be, for he has recreated her in his imagination, he thinks of her, half in terms of "Esmis Esmoor", the deified abstraction of the woman he had once known. She now exists as a product of his own mind and as such he can love and respect her. But this is a dismal outlook for personal relations if they can only survive as mental images.

Aziz, however, is redeemed by a spontaneity of emotion and affection; a quality which goes far towards bringing the novel to a hopeful conclusion. His closing conversation with Ralph Moore reproduces the close of Aziz' earlier encounter with Mrs Moore, Ralph's mother, in the mosque:

"Can you always tell whether a stranger is your friend?"
"Yes."
"Then you are an Oriental" (p. 306).

Once again Aziz is shown as having affection for people he can transform in his own mind; both Mrs Moore and her son become loveable when they are recognized to be a type, a type sympathetic to Aziz' way of thought. He himself notes the cycle returning: "Never be friends with the English! Mosque, caves, mosque, caves. And here he was starting again" (p. 306). And as soon as he begins to rationalise, affection retreats: "What did this eternal goodness of Mrs Moore amount to? To nothing, if brought to the test of thought' (p. 307). Thus the promise set up in the presentation of Godbole in the opening chapter comes to nothing, or almost nothing. What Forster demands and what the reader too must hope for is a workable ideal that may stand not only the test of emotion and experience but also the severer test of reason.

[87] C.f. *Howards End*, p. 292.

Much of the final conversation between Aziz and Fielding, which closes the novel, is concerned with Godbole and Hinduism. Fielding expresses his desire to penetrate beneath the chaotic surface of the festival whose close they have witnessed and to "discover its spiritual side, if it has one" (p. 314) to which Aziz replies dismissingly, "It is useless discussing Hindus with me" (p. 315) and the discussion peters out with a laughing reference to Godbole's "Come, come". Aziz gets more impatient with the direction of the conversation and they turn instead to the political problem of India's future. Thus the vision that has been offered is consciously and finally rejected. The answer for Forster most decidedly will not lie in mysticism or mystic communion; Godbole's religion is Godbole's and there it rests. The oft-quoted conclusion of the novel affirms again not so much the experience of the caves as the experience of the aftermath of that ill-fated expedition. The two would-be friends are parted by their vision of each other and the adverse circumstances in which they have come together.

"Why can't we be friends now?" said [Fielding], holding him affectionately. "It's what I want. It's what you want."
But the horses didn't want it – they swerved apart; the earth didn't want it, sending up rocks through which riders must pass single file; the temples, the tank, the jail, the palace, the birds, the carrion, the Guest House, that came into view as they issued from the gap and saw Mau beneath; they didn't want it, they said in their hundred voices, "No, not yet," and the sky said, "No, not there" (p. 317).

And thus with an emphasis on the impossibility of love and affection, of tolerance and goodwill to bridge the gap between private and public life, neither at that time nor in that place, the novel comes to its sceptical, if not pessimistic, conclusion.[88]

With the close of the last of Forster's novels we may well ask ourselves what remains of the liberal humanist position of the earlier novels: the love of the Italian stories, the assertion of a means of bridging the gap between realities, the discovery of a workable compromise of the ideal at the end of *Howards End*? Rather than

[88] Kettle, *An Introduction to the English Novel*, p. 163.

continuing to express the liberal tradition,[89] *Passage* reveals clearly
that Forster has become aware of the inadequacies of liberalism
when faced with the mystery of India and the overwhelming
presence of destructive forces in the world.[90] There is, however, no
attempt to formulate a corrective to this once held point of view.[91]
Rather Forster has painstakingly, and with destructive sincerity,
attempted to revalue his humanism in the light not only of his
experience of the almost inexplicable mystery of India, but also
against the background of the events of the First World War, and
has discovered that his faith in humanity has itself become undermined, nor can his humanism fully account for all that he has
experienced.[92] When we review the events of the novel and recon-
sider our account of them, we discover that Forster has held up
beliefs in Christianity, agnosticism, personal relations, nationalism,
love, mysticism and the need for racial understanding and acceptance, to the test of reality as experience and has found them all in
some measure or another wanting. Life in *Passage to India* is petty,[93]
and man has been reduced in stature over against the universe
around him. Surely the final thesis of the novel must be seen to be a
pessimistic one: personal relations do not work in a world where
humanity is by force of circumstances and its own nature categorized
into races, groups, classes; love cannot bridge this gap, for love is
a private virtue which cannot simply be reapplied to public situations. Man will remain separate from man.[94] Nevertheless there
may be an implied hopefulness somewhere at the back of *Passage
to India*, more specifically the hope implied in the closing remarks
of the novel: not yet and not there, which of themselves imply later
and elsewhere.[95] Forster refuses to abandon himself totally to

[89] C.f. Leavis, p. 277; Kenneth Burke, *Language as Symbolic Action* (Berkeley
and Los Angeles, 1966), p. 225.
[90] C.f. Hannah, pp. 177-8; White, p. 656.
[91] Gransden, p. 81.
[92] C.f. Cox, *The Free Spirit*, p. 101; McDowell, "E. M. Forster: Romancer or
Realist", p. 107. See, too, the suggestion that Forster is revaluing his humanism
in the new society he found in India. Barbara Hardy, *The Appropriate Form*,
p. 80.
[93] C.f. Crews, p. 142.
[94] C.f. Mendilow, p. 290.
[95] C.f. Shusterman, p. 169.

despair and pessimism; a time may come, and in another situation, maybe, love will succeed and personal relations may work. T. E. Lawrence's estimate of *Passage* as "bigger than any of the previous novels" is undoubtedly correct, but his prophecy "It's my opinion that you will yet write... something very big: bigger than the *Passage*"[96] did not come true. Forster, having taken fourteen years to come to the despairing conclusion in the face of reality, as he had experienced it, that the confirmation of love as the ideal, leading to the fulfilment of the vision of the ultimate reality, was still far away, had to wait nearly five decades for the confirmation which never came. Only Middleton Murry, at the time of the publication of *Passage to India*, was able to analyse the situation clearly and, as it has proved, correctly:

Evidently the best part of those fourteen years was occupied not in writing this very fine novel, but in wondering whether there was anything on earth, or in the heavens above, or in the waters under the earth, worth writing about. And even then, in that long space of years, Mr Forster did not *decide* that there was. No, the balance faintly inclined, the pointer dribbled over towards "To be", and the silence was interrupted. I scarcely think it will be interrupted again. The planning of Mr Forster's next novel should carry him well on to the unfamiliar side of the grave. It will take him, I imagine, a good deal more than fourteen years to find the word which will evoke a different echo from the primeval cave of Marabar.[97]

[96] Lawrence, p. 496.
[97] J. M. Murry, "'Bou-oum or Ou-Boum?' (Review of *Passage*)", p. 150.

GRIEF GENERATING ACTION:
MISCELLANEOUS PROSE

> In the realm of public battle a man is
> bound to lose his balance; in the private
> life he may keep it but at the cost of
> becoming isolated.

E. M. Forster[1]

1

The five novels reveal Forster's dissatisfaction with the world as he finds it, and more particularly with traits of the social order which he observes to be falling apart around him. In these books a variety of possible solutions are put forward which may one day lead to the "good society"[2], but which, as the novels go on, are seen to be the products of an ever weakening hopefulness about the future. One becomes increasingly aware, even if one had not read any of his non-fiction, of Forster's suspicion of the efficacy of social institutions and establishments to carry civilization as he understands it through the troubles and turmoils of a changing world.[3] As a result one aspect of Forster's novels becomes the conflict between the "good man" and the antithetical forces of society and conformity to what have been shown to be false standards.[4]

---

[1] "Notes on the Way", *Time and Tide*, 2.11.1935, p. 1571.

[2] C.f. Lunan, "The Novels of E. M. Forster", p. 52. The attempt to limit Forster's themes to that of class and social behaviour is, however, profitless and results in statements which are neither helpful nor necessarily true to the facts of the novel. C.f. Alastair A. Macdonald, "Class-consciousness in E. M. Forster", *University of Kansas City Review*, XXVII (1961), pp. 236-7.

[3] C.f. Ransom, "E. M. Forster", *Kenyon Review*, V (Autumn 1943), p. 619.

[4] C.f. "his five novels – and particularly the last two – can be taken as reflecting

Forster's consistent defence of liberal humanist values in the face of continual social and international developments which are directly opposed to them and their survival earned him the reputation that he enjoyed in the forty-five years between *Passage to India* and his death. He and his writings have continually been seen as 'contemporary', as having relevance to a particular later situation; Cyril Connolly goes further and sees even Forster's characters from the earlier novels as "the precursors of the left-wing young people of today".[5]

Yet this conflict with society may be seen as a reason for his sudden and, for most, unexpected retirement from the sphere of fiction. That very society which had formed the setting for Forster's first four novels and which, in the rigid social code of Chandrapore Civil Station is implicit in the last, had by the mid-twenties more or less disappeared. Forster, as Orwell pointed out, "was essentially pre-war"[6] and, as such, rooted in the unchanging social ethos of post-Victorian England. Forster himself states:

I think one of the reasons why I stopped writing novels is that the social aspect of the world changed so much. I had been accustomed to write about the old-fashioned world with its homes and its family life and its comparative peace. All that went, and though I can think about the new world I cannot put it into fiction.[7]

Such a statement goes a long way to explaining the apparent mystery of Forster's long silence in the field of fiction. It is certainly more

---

the advantages and the disadvantages of the humanist literary mind in an environment half hostile to it "(Bradbury, "Two Passages to India", p. 125). C.f. G. D. Klingopoulos, "Mr Forster's Good Influence", *Pelican Guide to English Literature*, Vol. VII (Harmondsworth, 1961), p. 249.

[5] Cyril Connolly, *Enemies of Promise* (1938) (Harmondsworth, 1961), p. 18; for a completely opposite view see, Anthony Burgess, *The Novel Now* (London, 1967), p. 22.

[6] George Orwell, "Inside the Whale", *Collected Essays, Journalism and Letters*, ed. Sonia Orwell and Ian Angus, Vol. I (London, 1968), p. 506.

[7] "E. M. Forster on his life and his Books", p. 11. Forster insists elsewhere that fiction depends on a fixed class structure. C.f. Toynbee, "E. M. Forster at Eighty", p. 8. Earlier Forster had noted that the young writers of the early thirties were "less flustered by social distinctions" than he and his generation had been. C.f. "Not New Books", *Listener*, 28.12.1932, p. 951. C.f., too, John McCormick, *Catastrophe and Imagination* (London, 1957), pp. 1 and 6.

satisfactory than that other explanation tendered both by himself and by his critics:[8] "I hadn't anything more I wanted to say",[9] which is patently untrue when one considers the body of writing that followed *Passage to India*.[10]

A far more useful starting point to an investigation and evaluation of the writings which follow *Passage* may be found in Forster's own words about Lowes Dickinson after the 1914-1918 war:

> Dickinson's feelings when the war broke out are best conveyed by an analogy: they resembled the feelings which arise when a promise has been broken by a person whom one loves... The shock broke something in him which was never mended, and when at the close of his life he again functioned he had evolved a new apparatus, not repaired the old.

This may now be seen as approximating fairly closely to Forster's own situation. He continues a paragraph later:

> There are two sorts of grief. There is a resentful querulous grief which throws the sufferer in on himself and makes him petty and tedious. There is a grief which expands towards the universal and generates action.[11]

It is the second sort of grief which seems to have overcome Forster after the large-scale collapse of the ideal which we have discussed above, and which generated the sort of action which it will now be our task to analyse through the writings of the next forty years.

---

[8] C.f. Oliver, p. 5. Stone characterises Forster's pre-occupation in the post-1924 period as "to be sensitive to what is going on", which is, perhaps, not as satisfactory as the epigrammatic remark of Forster's friend, Professor Sprott, "When Forster stopped writing novels he became a sage." C.f. Stone, *The Cave and the Mountain*, 347; Sprott, "Forster as a Humanist", *Aspects of E. M. Forster*, p. 73.
[9] C.f. Patrick Wilkinson, "Forster and King's", *Aspects of E. M. Forster*, p. 24. See, however, "That creative artists should be... chatty surprises me. They might be expected to have said what they wanted to say in their works, and, in the deepest sense, to have drained themselves dry" ("Recollectionism", *New Statesman & Nation*, 13.3.1937, pp. 405-6.
[10] In the period 1924-1964 Forster wrote two biographies, a pageant play and a book about India; 348 articles, reviews and letters to the press; forewords or introductions to 43 books and a filmscript; he gave evidence before two important tribunals, was interviewed at least six times, and lent his signature to 16 open letters to the press.
[11] *Goldsworthy Lowes Dickinson*, pp. 155-6.

2

After the collapse of the ideal fictionalized in *Passage to India*, Forster slowly began to establish the priorities which were to occupy his thoughts for the next forty years. In the twenties and very early thirties these may be summarised as a clinging to reason as the only possible safeguard against intellectual and emotional disintegration, a growing absorption with the notion of liberty, and a slow building up again of a compromise ideal around the twin substitutes of tolerance and personal relations.

The concern for reason is best expressed in a review article of August 1928, in which Forster is writing about the Elizabethan age and so is occupied with one of his favourite subjects, the beneficial effect of the past and considerations of the past. Forster turns to the more limited abstract "thought", which, in this context may be understood as being synonymous with reason: "Though thought may betray a man individually and bring empires to ruin, it is nevertheless the only known preservative, the only earnest of immortality."[12] What exactly Forster intends by the expression "preservative" and what he hopes to preserve is shown in a later article reviewing a broadcast discussion in which Lowes Dickinson (always the great example) had taken part.

We believe in thought, surely, for two distinct and perhaps incompatible reasons. In the first place it seems "up to us" to think; it is a noble and human activity, something that men ought to do. In the second place, we hope that by thinking we shall avert certain evils from ourselves and society, particularly the evil of war.[13]

The emphases here indicate quite clearly Forster's preoccupations: with man's humanity and with reason as a safeguard against its destruction by war and violence.[14] Thus reason, which has not always been to the fore in Forster's fiction, comes into its own as

[12] "Peeping at Elizabeth", *Nation and Athenaeum*, 8.8.1925, p. 569.
[13] "A Broadcast Debate", *Nation and Athenaeum*, 10.5.1930, p. 191.
[14] Further references to the importance of reason, particularly as an antidote to war and materialism, come in contexts where Forster is concerned with the work and writings of Lowes Dickinson. C.f. Introduction to Dickinson's, *Letters from John Chinaman*, 2nd ed. (London, 1946), p. 7; "A Great Humanist", *Listener*, 11.10.1956, p. 547.

one of the keystones of his more thoughtfully developed humanist creed. In times of crisis, which for Forster, as for most of his generation, coincided with two world wars and the struggle between communism and fascism in the thirties, the appeal is to reason and the hope, too, is in reason and man's power to think – "What I do see more clearly than I did is that reason can't solve everything, but I want it to solve as many things as it can."[15]

Reason is a principle which may be converted into action in the service of specific ideals, and which may be the motivating power for particular attitudes; in Forster's case, reason comes in to support his clear-sighted arguments for freedom which he approaches both as an artist and as an individual in his relation to the state and society around him. In the first place, Forster has consistently campaigned for the freedom of the artist from conformist moral restraint in the form of censorship, notably in the cases of Miss Radcliffe Hall's novel, *The Well of Loneliness* (1928), James Joyce's *Ulysses* (1934), and James Hanley's novel, *Boy* (1935).[16] Forster's arguments in each case and on later occasions are very much the same; only a free mind which can play at liberty over the thoughts and achievements of its age can possibly produce great literature and the mind of the artist can only be free if there is no threat of legal power hanging over him. As he puts it more colloquially in his evidence before the Select Committee on Obscene Publications in 1958: "I think it is so important that authors should have free minds and should not be worrying that they are going to be dropped on."[17] Within this narrower context of the censorship of books it is important to realise that not only does Forster's humanist distrust of conventional Christian morality feel provoked into action, but that far more it is his belief in tolerance which dictates his stand:

It is desirable that people should not be corrupted, but there is no reason why they should not be shocked, I am often shocked myself (for example

---

[15] Toynbee, *E. M. Forster at Eighty*, p. 10.
[16] C.f. "The New Censorship", p. 726; "The Censor Again?", *Author*, XLIV (Spring 1934), pp. 78-9; "Prosecution of Publishers" (letter signed jointly by Forster, A. P. Herbert, A. A. Milne, J. B. Priestley and H. G. Wells), *Spectator*, 26.4.1935, p. 696.
[17] *Report from the Select Committee on Obscene Publications*, p. 21; c.f. "The 'Censorship' of Books", p. 445.

by certain smug and loathsome advertisements of beer that defile our streets), but I bear up; everything in civilization cannot suit everybody, and as soon as possible I turn my mind and eyes elsewhere... The only possible rule here is the rule of tolerance. If a man is shocked by a particular advertisement or phrase, he should think of something else or should reason with the perpetrator; he should not call in the law to avenge his private opinions.[18]

In a wider context, Forster notes the situation of the artist in society where he has both a public and a private function, which can lead to conflict with the "powers that be". Even so freedom is the condition upon which the writer's effectivity depends; in answer to the hypothetical question as to why the artist should concern himself with the state, Forster writes: "if the right to comment is withdrawn, the power to create is mysteriously yet inevitably impaired, so that he does and must bother about the state."[19] With the advent of World War II Forster becomes more decisive in his concern to uphold the freedom of the artist, seeing the two necessities for lively literature as being freedom of expression and "freedom in discussion",[20] and summarising the whole position of the writer in his relations to the State in the sentence: "We hold that it is... the duty of the writer and the artist to express themselves, and that the State exists for its citizens, not citizens for the State."[21]

Forster's concern for freedom is not, however, confined to freedom of expression for the artist, but for freedom as one of the greatest goods for the individual whatever his profession or social situation. Through the thirties, Forster's writings show a growing conviction that freedom is diminishing and that people must be made aware of this. This viewpoint is closely connected with Forster's awareness, from 1933 onwards, that a second great war was virtually inevitable.[22] As early as December 1931 Forster sees that

[18] "The 'Censorship' of Books", pp. 444-5. C.f. Macaulay, *The Writings of E. M. Forster*, p. 294.
[19] "A Conversation", p. 269.
[20] "Books of the Year", *Listener*, 5.1.1938, p. 42.
[21] "The Freedom of the Artist" (broadcast discussion with H. V. Hodson), *Listener*, 28.3.1940, p. 639.
[22] C.f. "Madness, today, is becoming a State monopoly, beneath whose death-dealing wings the standardized individuals march to their doom" ("The English Eccentrics", *Spectator*, 19.5.1933, p. 716).

freedom of speech is menaced in England and insists that "The way out of our national difficulties lies through greater, not through less, freedom of expression and discussion."[23] And later he justifies continued concern about this matter in a further letter on D.O.R.A. (The Defence of Rights and Amusements): "There can be no reasonable doubt that the liberty of the individual has diminished, is diminishing, and will be further diminished in this country unless constant protests are made."[24] Forster analyses the situation in which individual freedom is menaced, by asserting that the organisation of the modern state has become too complex to admit the ingredient of individual liberty, and that limitation of freedom is the inevitable consequence of that form of State thinking that emphasises that "people are easier to manage when they are all alike".[25] At the same time he is forced to realise that liberty is both a nineteenth century liberal ideal and, maybe for this reason, is an ideal which in certain respects is classbound. He is aware that for the extremely poor there is little meaning in the ideal unless it can hint at a material relief of their sufferings. Yet, Forster is consistent in his thinking, in noting that "Such people cannot notice the high ideals of our civilization. And while they exist, our liberty is maimed, even inside the limits of England."[26] This realisation, while provoking to action, does not in any way revise the high value which Forster places upon liberty. Yet even in the moment of announcing this belief Forster qualifies it with the words, "I don't regard [Liberty] as a goddess."[27] During the course of this same discussion Forster underlines the reality of the situation by stating that "No individual can be absolutely free and no society could exist if he were" but this does not prevent him from insisting on the intrinsic values of liberty and pointing out his own particular reasons for holding to his belief in it. These reasons are three: liberty produces variety of character, encourages personal expres-

[23] "Are the BBC too cautious?", *Spectator*, 19.12.1931, p. 848.
[24] "D.O.R.A.", *New Statesman and Nation*, 15.10.1932, p. 442.
[25] "'Seven Days' Hard'", p. 452. See, for a confirmation of this point of view, the modern Utopias of Huxley, Orwell, and L. P. Hartley.
[26] "English Freedom", p. 791. For a less positive evaluation of Forster's view of freedom, see Cox, *The Free Spirit*, p. 87.
[27] "Efficiency and Liberty – Great Britain", p. 497.

sion, and implies the possibility to criticise.[28] Further, when we recall his devotion to the ideal of Love in the early novels and other writings, and the overwhelming pessimism which followed upon the realisation that this ideal was impracticable in the post-1918 world, it does not altogether come as a surprise to find Forster writing, on the eve of the Second World War, of "the Beloved Republic which feeds upon Freedom and lives".[29] In other words, Forster although disillusioned, although overcome with grief at the loss of the ideal, never loses sight of the "Good Place which is every poet's dream".[30]

3

Forster's concern for freedom is a part of a wider concern for what, for want of an exacter term, we may call civilization. Whereas critics have noticed either a dissatisfaction with civilization, or, more generally, an awareness of a collapse of civilization and civilised values in Forster's work,[31] one must insist that this is ultimately a view based on his novels, and on *Howards End* in particular, where modern civilization is seen as menacing nature and the old orders, as a civilization of machinery, industry, and materialism.[32] Admittedly this view reappears in the later prose writings, but it tends to be in the minority.[33] More important, as

[28] Ibid.; c.f. "What I believe", p. 79; Frederick P. W. McDowell, "E. M. Forster's Conception of the Critic", p. 96.
[29] "Freedom for What?", p. 1177. For the "Beloved Republic", see, "What I Believe", p. 79.
[30] This explains perhaps Forster's devotion to the cause of liberty in action, as seen in his membership of the National Council for Civil Liberties, the Freedom Defence Committee, and later the United India Defence Fund. For the last c.f. "Back India Appeal" (letter signed by Forster, Olaf Caroe, Barbara Ward and Guy Wint), *Spectator*, 30.11.1962, p. 856. Forster's last appearance in print was as one of the many signatories of an advertisement letter in the *Times* protesting against the war in Vietnam. C.f. *Times*, 25.4.1966, p. 7.
[31] C.f. Leavis, *The Common Pursuit*, p. 262; Hoare, *Some Studies in the Modern Novel*, pp. 84-5.
[32] C.f. *Howards End*, pp. 9, 102, 309, 316.
[33] C.f. "Recollections of Nassenheide", p. 14; "Going into Europe", *Encounter*, December 1962, p. 64.

clarifying that which Forster wishes to protect, is the definition he gives in the essay "What I believe":

> I realise that all society rests upon force. But all the great creative actions, all the decent human relations, occur during the intervals when force has not managed to come to the front. These intervals are what matter. I want them to be as frequent and as lengthy as possible, and I call them 'civilization'.[34]

This view of civilization as the creative norm of stability opposed to the moments of mass hysteria is the most constant characteristic of Forster's later liberalism and it is this view, perhaps, that was responsible for his popularity among the younger writers of the thirties and early forties.

Forster's comments on civilization may be seen as a continuation of the search for the true reality. In contrast to the ideal of a civilization the source of which is "sensitiveness and tenderness",[35] he finds a civilization in which artist and capitalist fail to communicate and connect[36] and which is perishing, perhaps because of the existence of private property.[37] The warning observation that civilization is perishing and England with it re-echoes from 1932 to 1940 with a remarkable consistency whatever the politicians of the period may have been saying. As early as January 1932 in an article on the bicentenary of William Cowper, Forster notes, "It is not an unsuitable moment for him to perish, for England is perishing, and he was English".[38] And two years later, as a contributer to a series entitled "Our Greatest Benefactor", Forster characteristically chooses an obscure doctor, James Young Simpson, who was the first practitioner of modern anaesthetics, for, as Forster points out: "With the world as it is, jostling victims and weapons together, physical suffering is assured, particularly for the poor."[39] The message is continued, notably in the "Notes on the Way" articles of 1934 and 1935, and culminates in a sad piece of recollectionism

---

[34] "What I believe", p. 80.
[35] "Notes on the Way", *Time and Tide*, 23.11.1935, p. 1704.
[36] C.f. "An Artist's Life", *Spectator*, 25.4.1931, p. 669.
[37] "Notes on the Way", *Time and Tide*, 2.6.1934, p. 696.
[38] "William Cowper, An Englishman", *Spectator*, 16.1.1932, p. 75.
[39] "Our Greatest Benefactor – IV", *Spectator*, 15.6.1934, p. 914.

in his review of Virginia Woolf's biography of their mutual friend Roger Fry in 1940:

Her readers are tempted... to reflect gloomily upon the abbreviation of civilization and the failure of hope. All that Fry cared for, and worked for, is being destroyed. Good sense has gone, so have the pursuit of the truth, peacefulness, and France. In their places stand pernicious idealism, propaganda, violence, Hitler. Courage has become the only virtue, mysticism the only victory. Sterile both of them.[40]

One notes the bitterness that has crept into Forster's writing and is reminded of his reaction to the First World War. Once the Second World War was over, Forster's direct concern for civilization in pronouncements such as those of the thirties disappears. Only once, in a contribution to a symposium conducted by *The Spectator* in 1959, does he come into the open again, once more with a word of timely warning: "The growth of secrecy and the growth of the population seem to me the twin evils that may destroy civilization, and there is little one can do against either of them."[41] This remark, like many of Forster's remarks in the later occasional journalism and letters to the press, has something of the maunderings of an old man about it. Here one is aware of his regret that the old order of his youth and maturity is past, and of a curious petulance that is hardly worthy of the man who had written so much of eminent good sense in previous years.

At the same time as the consistent warning of the imminent collapse of a civilization which for Forster is of value, come the warnings and criticisms concerning faults of a less cataclysmic nature, faults in the structure and fabric of society: a humanist liberal's pinpointing of dangerous weaknesses nearer home. In the early thirties this takes the form of an ironic comment on the mechanised nature of English enjoyment, when, writing about the ballads of the eighteenth century, Forster comments on our inability to enjoy such harmless pleasures and writes: "We must buy gramophone records instead, support British industries and keep quiet."[42]

[40] "Omega and Alpha", p. 140.
[41] "Nuisance Value", p. 431. His views expressed earlier in the same piece upon the usefulness of parliament are identical with those expressed twenty years before in "What I believe", p. 79.
[42] "The 'Osterley Park' Ballads", *Spectator*, 19.3.1932, p. 420.

It is the inexorable logic of the progression in this sentence that is typical of Forster as 'domestic' social critic at his best; a nagging insistence on seeing through the surface appearance of things and revealing somewhat sinister roots. For "keeping quiet" is one of the few 'sins' in Forster's moral code and something he consistently refuses to do. Forster ends his review of the ballads: "They make delightful reading, and may cause us to reflect what we have gained and what we have lost by organising our education and our morality."[43] It is this sense of a creeping standardization through mechanisation and organisation that Forster often sees as one of the chief menaces to civilization from within. Mass movements and mass hysteria disturb him and call forth some of his most short-tempered comments. This is true not only of political or religious movements but even of those manifestations of mass emotion which are the product of apparently harmless occasions. His reaction to the coronation of George VI is typical:

I was glad that the late king achieved his Jubilee and sorry that he died, and I value the monarchy on account of its position in the Constitution. But loyalty such as mine has today become almost treason, although it has behind it a national tradition of nearly three hundred years. No one is considered loyal now unless he is hysterical, and the hysteria is of the particularly depressing type associated with "below stairs".[44]

Later Forster characterises loyalty, "from the point of view of private ethics", as a "mean ignoble emotion, useful as a political cement, but devoid of true faithfulness or sensibility".[45] Here we notice that Forster's criterion in judging such public emotions as loyalty is the yardstick of the private life: is the emotion a product of true sensibility, is it, in fact, worthy of the name emotion at all? Many of his public utterances during this period demonstrate the impossibility of the task of trying to apply private standards to public life.

With the advent of the age of mass media in the fifties, Forster

[43] Ibid.
[44] "The Psychology of Monarchy", *New Statesman and Nation*, 22.2.1936, p. 260. The apparent class-orientated sneer at the end is, in context, meant to express that the hysteria is of that particular unmotivated, dutiful, servile kind associated with the enforced 'servant mentality' of the last century.
[45] "Royalty and Loyalty", *New Statesman and Nation*, 24.4.1937, p. 680.

turns his critical gaze upon the place of art and quality in contemporary civilization. In a long assessment of the achievements of 'quality broadcasting' on the fifth anniversary of the BBC's third programme he notes that "Quality is everywhere imperilled in contemporary life".[46] Once again this is seen as a result of standardization, of the demands the State makes upon the individual. This he relates to his concept of an "aristocracy of the sensitive, the considerate and the plucky",[47] which he had formulated thirteen years earlier:

The problem of value, the problem of maintaining and extending aristocracy in the midst of democracy... is a terrific problem with which the modern world has scarcely coped. Anxious, when it is not killing people, to feed and house them properly, it has assumed that values will look after themselves, or that what "the people" want will be *ipso facto* culture. It ignores the pioneer, the exceptional, the disinterested scientist, the meditative thinker, the difficult artist, or it contemptuously dismisses them as "superior". One trusts that they are superior. They are certainly the types who have helped the human race out of the darkness in the past. And if they vanish now, if they dissolve into the modern world's universal grey, what is to happen to the human race in the future? Into what final darkness will it disappear?[48]

Thus we find ourselves back, to some extent, among the concerns of the close of *Howards End* with Margaret's assertion concerning "the battle against sameness" and the desire that they may be "colour; sorrow perhaps, but colour in the daily grey".[49] This is in itself an indication of the path Forster has taken; the preoccupation with the ideal has retreated, or been pushed, into the background, and the foreground of activity is dominated by concerns for that which is practicable in order to ensure the survival of liberal humanist values.

While analysing weaknesses in the fabric of civilization and attempting to shore up the collapsing walls of the liberal heritage, Forster indicates where hope may lie. When, for example, he names curiosity, pleasure, and compassion as "the shaky tripod upon

[46] "Fifth Anniversary of the Third Programme", *Listener*, 4.10.1951, p. 540.
[47] "What I Believe", p. 82.
[48] "Fifth Anniversary of the Third Programme", pp. 540-541.
[49] C.f. *Howards End*, p. 314.

which any future civilization will have to rest",[50] or when comparing
the romantic attachment to early flying with the menace from the
skies of today, he states, "Romance must look further afield than
the air – or perhaps nearer at home in the unexplored tracts of the
heart",[51] he is clearly attempting a return to the ideal of the past,
of the early Forster. Compassion and the "tracts of the heart" are
clear references to the compromised ideal of *Passage to India*, the
insistence on affection, personal relations and tolerance, the qualities of the private life, the emphasis placed on the enlightened
individual rather than any reform of state or society in general.

At the very centre of Forster's statements on civilization lies,
however, a curious metaphysical belief, which, repeated twice in
Forster's writings, seems to be his personal answer to the problem
of the survival of human sanity, and the furtherance of liberal
values in a hostile world.

I am worried by thoughts of war oftener than by thoughts of my own
death, yet the line to be adopted over both these nuisances is the same.
One must behave as if one is immortal, and as if civilization is eternal.
Both statements are false – ... – both of them must be assumed to be true
if we are to go on eating and working and travelling, and keep open a
few breathing holes for the human spirit.[52]

Here, in effect, Forster returns to the problem of reality with a
vengeance and states a clear and unequivocal preference for the
ultimate reality as opposed to the reality of experience, as a guide
line to conduct and belief. Such advice is, at the same time, quite
consistent with what Forster has always advised and attempted to
practice: action and attitudes, beliefs and relations must be actuated
by considerations of eternity, of reality as ideal rather than under
the pressure of the expediency of a particular moment or situation.

4

To civilization in its organised form, as society, Forster opposes

[50] "This Worrying World", p. 865.
[51] "*The Mint* by T. E. Lawrence", *Listener*, 17.2.1955, p. 280.
[52] "Liberty in England", *Abinger Harvest*, pp. 84-5. This statement is repeated

art: "I believe that society can only represent a fragment of the human spirit, and that another fragment can only get expressed through art."[53] This fragment which art expresses is, by implication, of greater value to Forster, and it is as an artist that he often speaks through the final thirty odd years of his active life as writer and broadcaster. For it is art which brings some semblance of order into an otherwise chaotic existence,[54] and which, in the first days of gathering crisis in the thirties, though inadequate, was still seen by Forster as able to do something to restore proportion and sanity: to take the individual "into a country where the will is not everything, and braying patriots of the moment made no sound".[55] A year later Forster expresses the function of art in slightly different terms, which, once again remind us of the conflicting forms of reality: "This, it seems to me, is what great art does in these worrying times. It solves none of our bothers, personal or political, but it reveals a world where they might have been solved."[56] And the critic who may suggest that this has but small hope to offer the worrying reader, has clearly not seen the relation to an ultimate reality which is inherent in Forster's point of view here.

Central to Forster's belief that "culture matters" is his awareness of the opposition that exists between the organised state and the artist. This leads him on several occasions to examine this relationship more closely and to proclaim against the background of the realisation that the artist is being more and more assimilated into society.

Art for art's sake, study for study's sake, are not the useless undemocratic things which they sometimes appear to be. They are the powers in

---

almost word for word in "What I Believe", p. 81.

[53] "Art for Art's Sake", *Two Cheers for Democracy*, p. 103. C.f., too, "Does Culture Matter?" in the same collection, p. 112. Watt sees a close relation between Forster and G. E. Moore's "intrinsic good". C.f. Watt, "G. E. Moore and the Bloomsbury Group", p. 127.

[54] C.f. "The Challenge of our Time", *Two Cheers for Democracy*, pp. 70-71; c.f. Trilling, *E. M. Forster*, p. 154.

[55] "Notes on the Way", *Time and Tide*, 9.6.1934, p. 723.

[56] "Notes on the Way", *Time and Tide*, 2.11.1935, p. 1572. C.f. Introduction to *Two Cheers for Democracy*, p. 7.

the background without which the foreground of popular culture cannot exist.[57]

The whole question of the position of the artist within the state is nowhere so thoroughly discussed as in the article, "The Ivory Tower" (1938), in which, as the title indicates, Forster discusses the desirability and advisability of escape from society for the artist. Having given a historical survey of the problem and put forward Marcus Aurelius, Machiavelli, Karl Marx and Milton as typical Ivory Tower figures, Forster looks at the opposite view that "the duty of everyone... is to the community, and to the community as a whole", which he rejects as being based on "too simple a view of human development".[58] This Forster develops into an attack on the careless, imprecise use of words, and rewords the left-wing's demand that art should express life rather than be a means of escaping from life:

Art should be an expression of life in all its aspects, and so should include an escape from what officials call life and artists hold to be officialism. The idea that escape is, *per se*, wrong, is a bureaucratic idea.[59]

The conclusion that Forster reaches in this article is that very often the motivation of the individual's desire to retreat from the world is that he has a vision of life which is negated in society and results in horror or boredom or even disgust. The final statements of the article are a justification for a form of selfishness which is inherent in the artist's attitude. For Forster contrasts individual selfishness with the selfishness of the community in demanding conformity, and sees that the artist, through selfishness, creates "the escape into poetry, and blazes a path which others can follow".[60] Forster concludes: "We are here not to save ourselves and not to save the community, but to try to save both."[61]

The artist's role in this effort towards salvation, or rather the artist's particular competence, lies in his ability to create order, and

---

[57] "Books in 1941", *Listener*, 10.7.1941, p. 63. C.f. "The Claims of Art", *Listener*, 30.12.1943, p. 742.
[58] "The Ivory Tower", p. 54.
[59] "The Ivory Tower", p. 55.
[60] "The Ivory Tower", p. 58.
[61] *Ibid.*

since Forster as humanist cannot accept the intervention or super-imposition of divine order in human affairs, this would seem to make the artist supreme in matters of harmony.

I think there are only two forms of order in the universe; with the first we are not here concerned...- it is the Divine order, the mystic vision for those who can gain it... We *are* concerned with the second order, that which an artist can create in his own work, and that is why a work of art is important... because it is the only material object in the universe which may possess internal harmony.[62]

This "internal harmony" it is which is the last available bulwark against the conquest of the mind by force, violence and mass hysteria; it is the ability to mobilise reason and emotion, to learn the lesson of art, that Forster is attempting to bring into play, and which he holds as his own particularly relevant contribution to the salvation of mankind and civilization in time of war. It may appear ludicrously little and ineffective to us, but Forster is aware of this and sees his effort and his concerns in a different, more timeless perspective. As he says elsewhere, not of art, but of the qualities of sensitivity and openness of mind: "these are valuable qualities even in wartime, whatever the wireless says. Do they help us to conquer the Nazis? They don't. They are weapons in a larger and a longer battle."[63]

Forster makes it clear that the value of art is to the individual who is prepared to accept it, rather than indiscriminately to the mass. "Literature", he writes at the end of the fifties, "is enjoyable, it may promote individual salvation... but the time is gone when it awed Top People."[64] This view combined with what we have seen above of the particular importance Forster attaches to Art illumines that somewhat cryptic statement at the beginning of "What I Believe": "My lawgivers are Erasmus and Montaigne, not Moses and St. Paul."[65] In the course of a broadcast of 1941, Forster cites

---

[62] "The New Disorder", p. 75 (also as "Art for Art's Sake", *Two Cheers for Democracy*, pp. 100-101, a slightly different version; "The New Disorder", *Horizon*, IV (Dec. 1941), p. 381). C.f. "The Challenge of our Time", *Two Cheers for Democracy*, pp. 70-71.

[63] "Omega and Alpha", p. 141; c.f. "The Individual and his God", p. 802.

[64] "Fog over Ferney", *Listener*, 18.12.1958, p. 1030.

[65] "What I Believe", p. 77.

examples of the few great men who praised or practised tolerance.

There is the Dutch scholar Erasmus who stood apart from the religious fanaticism of the Reformation and was abused by both parties in consequence.[66] In the same century there was the Frenchman Montaigne, subtle, intelligent, witty, who lived in his quiet country house and wrote essays which still delight and confirm the civilized.[67]

Here we see the various threads of Forster's belief uniting: Erasmus and Montaigne are his "lawgivers", not only for their tolerance but for their combination of reason, willingness to retire to the "Ivory Tower" and, in Montaigne's case, because he was an artist who could "confirm the civilized".

5

Tolerance, which was already claimed both for Schlegels and by Wilcoxes in *Howards End*,[68] becomes in the thirty years from 1930 to 1960 an essential element in Forster's humanism. We have already noted it as playing a part in Forster's pleas for greater freedom for the artist in matters of censorship and Forster invokes it specifically in reviewing D. H. Lawrence's *Pornography and Obscenity* side by side with Lord Brentford's *Do we need a Censor?* in 1930:

Is not the solution to be found not in the ringing clarion calls of either camp, but in the dull drone of tolerance, tolerance, tolerance? I hope so. Nor is tolerance quite as dull as its worthy followers suggest. Tolerance has its appropriate dangers, just as much as duty or passion. It, too, can lead to disaster and death. It can do harm, like everything else... But it does less harm than anything else... It is the principle which causes society the minimum of damage, because it admits that the people who constitute society are different.[69]

[66] C.f. "[Erasmus'] rise showed that a movement of tolerance, such as humanism was, can inspire men so long as it confronts a single intolerance. And his decline showed that tolerance as an ideal no longer moves men when two opposing intolerances clamour for their loyalty. This has been the dilemma of the liberal spirit in every age since Erasmus" (J. Bronowski and Bruce Mazlish, *The Western Intellectual Tradition* [Harmondsworth, 1963], p. 84).

[67] "Tolerance", *Two Cheers for Democracy*, p. 58.

[68] *Howards End*, pp. 28 and 137.

[69] "Mr D. H. Lawrence and Lord Brentford", p. 509; c.f. "Here's Wishing", p. 18; "Tolerance", *Two Cheers for Democracy*, p. 56.

Once again, in the last sentence we recognise echoes of *Howards End* and, to some extent, of the compromised ideal in *Passage to India*.

It is in the connection with his last novel that we come to recognise the particular value this quality has for Forster: it is the public version of the private ideal. Whereas love cannot function as a public virtue, tolerance is the only practicable substitute Forster can find.[70] As Forster put it at a P. E. N. conference in 1944, to the amusement of the journalists present, "I don't believe in love in Government offices... but I believe in tolerance as a necessary part of achievement."[71] However with a further outbreak of organised violence in 1939, Forster once again becomes uncertain and in fact opens the essay "What I Believe" with the statement that, "Tolerance, good temper and sympathy are no longer enough in a world which is rent by religious and racial persecution".[72] This loss of certainty endures after the war has ended; he sees tolerance faced with "modern despair", and with reference to Samuel Butler writes, "Butler believed in tolerance and compromise, and they have not worked."[73] Yet only three years later in the Prefatory Note to *Two Cheers for Democracy*, Forster makes it clear that though tolerance may have proved largely inadequate in the immediate past, there is nothing else he knows of which may save the individual from disaster: "Though we cannot expect to love one another, we must learn to put up with one another. Otherwise we shall all of us perish."[74] This is reiterated in the interview Forster gave on television on the occasion of his eightieth birthday, where he talks of the "high value" he attaches to tolerance, among other things.[75]

For Forster, tolerance is important because it emphasises the possibility and necessity of differences among men, and thus pinpoints the individual as the important unit and not society or race or nation. Forster refuses to come down on one side or the other since very often to do so would mean shutting out one party, one

[70] C.f. "Tolerance", p. 56.
[71] "E. M. Forster's 'Intolerant Tolerance'", *Manchester Guardian*, 28.8.1944, p. 4.
[72] "What I Believe", p. 77.
[73] "Butler Approached", p. 634.
[74] *Two Cheers for Democracy*, p. 7.
[75] "E. M. Forster on his Life and his Books", p. 12.

opinion, one individual from the recognition he deserves. This not only puts him in contrast to the Western intellectual tradition in many respects,[76] but indicates that tolerance for Forster is based jointly on the perspective and proportion which reason dictates and, at the same time, on the affection of the heart for the individual human being.[77] Further, tolerance is not merely a personal whim of Forster's but is an essential part of the Victorian tradition[78] which leads him, as a humanist, to protest against intolerance in others both in questions of personal relations[79] and, more centrally, on questions of religion and belief:

To me it seems that what our tormented planet most needs at the present moment is not more faith but less faith. People believe much too ardently, and consequently desire to kill those who differ from them.[80]

6

We have already discussed Forster's humanism in contrast both to Christianity and religion in general, and earlier in this chapter we noted the importance he attaches to reason as a guide and preserver of human values. These aspects of his thought together with the emphasis on tolerance and the continued belief in personal relations

---

[76] C.f. Trilling, p. 148.

[77] Irma Rantavaara views tolerance as the direct result of "the enthronement of reason", and as such a typical Bloomsbury quality, although Forster's own note on his Bloomsbury contemporaries does not suggest this as being a notable characteristic of the group: "composed of people who hold similar opinions and like being with one another. But unkind, despite irritable protests to the contrary." In direct contrast to Miss Rantavaara's view is that of the Belgian critic, Gérard, who writes: "Le bien le plus précieux que l'imperfection humaine permette d'atteindre, c'est une compréhension personelle, humble, empreinte d'affection et de respect, et qui est toute différente de la tolérance cérébrale." Surely, as always with Forster, the truth lies within both regions, that of the heart as well as that of the head. C.f. Rantavaara, *Virginia Woolf and Bloomsbury*, p. 52; "Bloomsbury, an Early Note. February 1929", p. 10; Albert Gérard, "Edward Morgan Forster, romancier de la compréhension", *Revue générale Belge*, June 1957, p. 87.

[78] C.f. Crews, p. 4.

[79] C.f. "Portraits from Memory", p. 142.

[80] "Church, Community and State", *Listener*, 27.1.1937, p. 177.

make up the main body of Forster's humanism. Within the period with which we are now concerned, his position in relation to religious thinking and belief is clearly indicated in the following passage from his pamphlet, *Anonymity: An Enquiry* (1925):

The trees, flowers and human beings say "I really exist, not God," and continue to say so despite the admonitions to the contrary addressed to them by clergymen and scientists. To forgot its Creator is one of the functions of a Creation.[81]

The continued rejection of Christianity in the years leading up to the 1939-1945 war has two bases: Christianity, in fact faith of any kind, leads to intolerance and even cruelty,[82] and it is, as too is Communism, guilty, according to Forster, of being irrational.

Just as we reach the summit of the exposition, and our bourgeois illusions demolished, are expecting a positive goal, the exposition collapses. This collapse occurs in all religions – first the careful reasoning, the analysis of existing ills, and then the desperate jump to glory. Communism, like Christianity, jumps.[83]

However, Forster's humanism is not merely based on a negative reaction to Christianity, but far more on a positive attitude and belief in the human race and its potentialities.[84] It is for this reason that Forster finds himself so completely in agreement with Charles Mauron's theory of the triple man, which is not, as Christianity and most religions, "an ascending philosophy. It is a harmonising

---

[81] *Anonymity: An Enquiry* (London, 1925), p. 15 (reprinted in *Two Cheers for Democracy*, p. 92). It is interesting to note that "clergymen and scientists" are bracketed together in Forster's dismissal, thus reminding us of another of the objects of his criticism, which is based on the dehumanising tendency Forster professes to find in the work of scientists. C.f. "The Challenge of Our Time", p. 71; "Not New Books", p. 951.

[82] C.f. "Notes on the Way", *Time and Tide*, 16.11.1935, p. 1657.

[83] "The Long Run", *New Statesman and Nation*, 10.12.1938, p. 971. Although Forster criticises communism here, elsewhere during the late thirties he is favourable disposed towards it. C.f. "Notes on the Way", *Time and Tide*, 9.6.1934, p. 724; 16.6.1934, p. 766; 23.6.1934, p. 797; 23.11.1935, p. 1703; "The Last Parade", *Two Cheers for Democracy*, p. 18.

[84] C.f. "Notes on the Way", *Time and Tide*, 23.6.1934, p. 797; "Mahatma Ghandi", p. 80; "Fog over Ferney", p. 1030. We may note, too, his strictures on Leonard Woolf, who "though a pledged humanist... prefers animals to men" ("The Sahib from Bloomsbury", *Observer*, 5.11.1961, p. 29).

one." In reviewing Mauron's book *L'homme Triple*, Forster summarises the argument:

Man is firstly an individual animal, who shares instincts with other animals, but who is nevertheless solitary. Secondly, he is a social animal, who lives with others, develops his intelligence and likes to travel. And thirdly – scarcely developed yet – man is a spiritual personification, which leads him to be a philosopher, and artist, or a saint, and may lead him elsewhere. This triple division into animal, social and spiritual, is doubtless not new. But what is new for me in it... is the connection which the author establishes between the first man and the third, between the animal and the spiritual. [85]

Such admiration for a theory that includes man as a spiritual being may at first sight seem strange in a professed humanist, until one takes into account the particular definition of spiritual implied here which may include man's philosophical and creative faculties and so is practically synonymous with 'intellectual' rather than with 'religious'. And indeed it is the mind of man which so often motivates Forster's trust in humanity:

Curiosity cannot avert doom, but it can act as an innoculation against fear. The marvellous universe into which we have been born and where we may be contriving our death has developed one more marvel, namely the enquiring human mind. [86]

On several occasions Forster has, for himself and others, defined his concept of humanism, usually in relation to other writers and humanists, such as Gide, Lowes Dickinson, and Aldous Huxley. Its main elements are "curiosity, a free mind, belief in good taste and a belief in the human race". [87] Forster later adds "belief in reason, in integrity, tolerance, compassion, love and art" [88] and a quality which he finds missing in Aldous Huxley, "the humanist's reward of earthly warmth". [89]

---

[85] "Charles Mauron and *L'Homme Triple*", *Adam International Review*, No. 200, November 1949, p. 17.
[86] "Fog over Ferney", p. 1030.
[87] "Gide and George", *Two Cheers for Democracy*, p. 233.
[88] Introduction to Dickinson, *Letters from John Chinaman*, p. 7.
[89] "The Possessed", *Listener* 9.10.1952, p. 595.

The climax of Forster's activity as a humanist on the public stage may be seen in the statement of belief he contributed to the special "Cambridge Number" of the magazine *The Twentieth Century*. In an editorial note prefixed to the contributions from Cambridge authors (University fellows, research students, and undergraduates), the editors note the influential position Forster held in the mid-fifties: "... a distinguished Cambridge figure and an elder statesman of liberal humanism, was invited to contribute a statement of his position, a position which the majority, but by no means all, of the other contributors also hold."[90] Here Forster is elevated to the almost impossible position of being spokesman for a university and for an intellectual tradition, and, certainly nearer his own modest conception of the truth, a singularly potent influence on several generations of Cambridge students. The statement itself is characteristically intimate in tone and modest in approach. Yet in stating his belief as a humanist and in roundly refuting the exclusiveness of religion, there is no hesitancy or apology in Forster's voice:

I disbelieve in spiritual authority, however sincerely exercised and however nobly garbed... to believe anything because someone has said it or because some institution has promulgated it seems to me dead wrong.[91]

Forster concludes his letter with assertions of what humanism has meant to him over the past fifty years – "something which has made the world... exciting and valuable and sometimes comprehensible"[92] and notes that as its name suggests humanism is not merely a code of ethics or an impersonal creed, but is intimately connected with the human being, with his emotions as well as his reason. Here we slowly come full circle back to the ideal which, though we have never lost sight of it, has inevitably faded into the background since the twin cataclysms of the 1914-1918 War and the personal experiences behind *Passage to India*.

[90] *Twentieth Century*, XLVII (Feb. 1955), p. 98.
[91] "A Letter", p. 100.
[92] "A Letter", p. 101.

7

In the course of reviewing two books dealing with the effects of the Russian Revolution, Forster writes, during the last year of the Second World War, of his beliefs once again. And here, at the very centre, as the foundation of his attachment to humanity, we find the ideal, Love, again:

I myself am a sentimentalist who believes in the importance of love... I only believe that it is important in itself and that the desire to love and the desire to be loved are the twin anchor ropes which keep the human race human. [93]

Naturally love, affection and the belief in personal relations are as much a part of Forster's humanism as is tolerance, but since we are not here defining humanism but pursuing the development of the ideal we would do well to resume this theme where we left it at the end of *Passage to India*. Throughout the years which follow the ideal reappears, now as friendship, now as a simple belief in personal relations, now, rarely, as love itself, but more often as warmth of heart or affection. The position is put quite clearly in a review of *War at Wittenberg*, a play performed by the Cambridge ADC in 1925: "It moved me far more than a London production, because it is about two things I happen to care for – friendship and truth, the heart and the head – and because it is written passionately." [94] It is this contrast, "heart and head", that is so often in Forster's mind when considering not only personal relations but questions of society and the individual, belief, or civilization and freedom. In his memories of a former Cambridge teacher, Edward Carpenter, Forster writes:

It is well to remember that there are several potentialities in human nature, not one, and though it is possible to organize, organize, organize, which is what all political parties do at present, it is also possible to obey the heart's commands. [95]

[93] "A Clash of Authority", p. 686.
[94] *Nation and Athenaeum*, 19.12.1925, p. 436. It is characteristic of many of Forster's drama reviews and other literary work of the period, that his private sympathies, as here, tend to obscure his rational critical insight.
[95] "Some Memories", p. 75; c.f. "*The Mint* by T. E. Lawrence", p. 280.

Thus the obedience to the commands of the heart, friendship, love, and affection is limited to the sphere of the individual and what the individual can do, and contrasted to the standardising pressures of State and society.[96]

Not only had Forster in his last novel come to the conclusion that there is an unbridgeable gulf between private and public life, but he continues to reiterate this in the prose that follows noting that "it becomes increasingly difficult for an individual to influence events, and increasingly desirable that he should observe them",[97] which is virtually a statement of his own position at the time of writing and for three decades to follow. As we have seen it is belief in the individual as opposed to the group, the class or the mass, that lies at the centre of Forster's humanism. At which point we are inevitably brought back to Forster's statements in "What I Believe". Here personal relations, rather than love, which has proved insufficient once again, form the starting point as a breakwater against being overwhelmed by violence and cruelty and lead Forster to his famous declaration of loyalty to friendship and the individual rather than to the State ideal:

If I had to choose between betraying my country and betraying my friend, I hope I should have the guts to betray my country. ... Love and loyalty to an individual can run counter to the claims of the State. When they do – down with the State, say I, which means that the State would down me.[98]

It is worth remembering that Forster closes his article, after a determined denial of the efficacy of religion in a materialistic, violent world, with a profound vote of confidence in individualism in spite of the rise of totalitarianism and dictatorships: "The dictator-hero can grind down his citizens till they are all alike, but he cannot melt them into a single man".[99]

[96] C.f. "Tourism v. Thuggism", p. 124.
[97] "Not New Books", p. 951.
[98] "What I Believe", p. 78 (The second sentence was not in the original version).
[99] "What I Believe", p. 85. Note, too, the original ending, omitted from the collected version: "Until psychologists and biologists have done much more tinkering than seems likely, the individual remains firm and each of us must consent to be one, and to make the best of the difficult job." – "Two Cheers for Democracy", Nation (New York), p. 68.

In the background to Forster's two cheers which he allows to democracy, behind his assertion of individual value and reason and good sense, hovers the shade of the unfulfilled ideal: "Love the Beloved Republic", as yet unattained but still dictating values, imposing proportion and figuring as the true reality towards which the greater struggle will be directed. In the field of individual contact, love and willingness to show love are all important; in his conversation with Angus Wilson, Forster suggests one of the characteristics of the goats (as opposed to the sheep, or the saved, in his novels) is "the failure to love".[100] Yet, on the whole, it is affection, a more homely, less intense concept, that takes the centre of the stage in Forster's closing remarks on the subject, both when he remarks that "The true history of the human race is the history of human affection",[101] and when, having suitably come full circle, writing of his last visit to India in 1945, he concludes with words which are reminiscent of Aziz' plea for "Kindness, more kindness, and even after that more kindness":

Goodwill is not enough. Of that I am too sadly convinced. In fact, at the present moment goodwill out there is no use at all. The reactions to it are instantly cynical. The only thing that cuts a little ice is affection or the possibility of affection. Whatever the political solution, that can surely do no harm. But it must be genuine affection and liking. It must not be exercised with any ulterior motive. It must be an expression of the common humanity which in India and England and all the world over has been so thwarted of late, and so despised.[102]

---

[100] Angus Wilson, "A Conversation with E. M. Forster", *Encounter*, November 1957, p. 53.
[101] "De Senectute", p. 18.
[102] "India Again", p. 335; c.f. *Passage to India*, p. 114.

CONCLUSION

One could simply agree with Professor Cox when he writes of Forster that "Contacts with other people are the most real things he knows, and their cultivation is the source of happiness."[1] But to do so would be to limit Forster to the modest sphere of action and influence to which he himself so often attempts to retire. As we have all along suggested, what Forster is attempting in his fiction and what he goes on to attempt afterwards is that which Lowes Dickinson noticed and saw dangers in:

Your constant pre-occupation to bring realistic life into contact with values... is very difficult to bring off.[2]

And one is tempted to add that it is not merely in fiction that it is "difficult to bring off". For the aim which Forster set himself in life, even more precisely than in fiction or in art, was a total engagement in "an inner war, a struggle for truer values, a struggle of the individual towards the dark, secret place where he may find reality".[3] We have shown that this search occupied Forster for the length of his active career as a novelist, involving essential compromises and modifications both in his ideal, and in his vision of an ultimate reality which could be brought into harmony with the reality of experience. In the last chapter we followed the survival and development of various elements in Forster's beliefs, in order to see how he was able to re-deploy his reserves after the partial, if not total, defeat announced by his last novel. These writings with

[1] Cox, *The Free Spirit*, p. 80.
[2] *Goldsworthy Lowes Dickinson*, p. 216.
[3] "The Individual and his God", p. 802.

their combination of prophecy and warning of further disasters, analyses of critical situations and serious faults in the fabric of the civilised life of refined personal relations and adherence to culture, and the indefatigable proclamation of the highest practicable ideals, show Forster in unflagging action, slowly rebuilding the framework of his trust in the ideal. They are if nothing else a tribute to his emotional and intellectual resilience and a witness to the truth of Stephen Spender's judgement that Forster

is conscious of two kinds of truth. One is Truth with a big T which men sometimes think they glimpse, and the other is the truth about the Truth. The truth about it being that it can only be glimpsed.[4]

Forster's statements during the last active years of his life reinforce the impression that one has built up over the course of his very long career. There is in him a continual willingness to modify, to review beliefs and truths should the reality of experience show them to be lacking in efficacy, in freshness and validity.[5] Looking at the future in 1959 at the age of eighty, Forster sees the necessity for "altering ourselves and helping others to alter" in order to survive the foreseeable crises to come,[6] and a few months later, he recommends "improvement" (which after all implies modification and change) as a worthy goal.[7] One feels finally that Love, the Beloved Republic, is still far away, though not, in Forster's mind, unattainable. It has become the ultimate reality which dictates and guides actions, though not in itself capable of immediate transference into action in the public sphere. Here the active tenets of Forster's humanism suffice: tolerance, affection, and an adherence to reason. These can cope with the reality of experience and withstand its inroads upon the Truth. The development that has taken place in Forster through the last forty years of his writing life can be seen as a confirmation of the experience up to the close of *Passage to India*.

[4] Stephen Spender, p. 77.
[5] C.f. "I believe that all truths... ought to be picked to pieces at times in a serious way. It is a human duty" ("Fifth Anniversary of the Third Programme"), p. 540.
[6] "E. M. Forster on his Life and his Books", p. 12.
[7] "A Presidential Address", p. 8.

Forster's consolidation of experience and belief on this foundation certainly played a leading role in his emergence as an influential figure in the intellectual life of the next two decades if not for longer. One may thus see him very much as he saw Lowes Dickinson, and repeat of Forster himself:

He was an indescribably rare being, he was rare without being enigmatic, he was rare in the only direction which seems to be infinite: the direction of the Chorus Mysticus. He did not merely increase our experience: he left us more alert for what has not yet been experienced.[8]

[8] *Goldsworthy Lowes Dickinson*, p. 241.

BIBLIOGRAPHY

WORKS BY FORSTER QUOTED IN THE TEXT

The items are cited in chronological order. Exact bibliographical information may be found in B. J. Kirkpatrick, *A Bibliography of E. M. Forster*, 2nd revised edition (London, 1968).

"On Grinds", *Cambridge Review*, 1.2.1900.
"On Bicycling", *Cambridge Review*, 10.5.1900.
"A Long Day", *Basileona*, No. 1, 1.6.1900.
"Albergo Empedocle", *Temple Bar*, CXXVIII (Dec. 1903).
Where Angels Fear to Tread (1905) (Harmondsworth, 1959).
The Longest Journey (1907) (Harmondsworth, 1960).
A Room with a View (1908) (Harmondsworth, 1955).
Howards End (1910) (Harmondsworth, 1941).
"Mr Walsh's Secret History of the Victorian Movement", *Basileon Z*, XIII (June 1911).
"An Allegory (?)", *Basileon H*, XIV (June 1912).
"Inspiration", *Author*, XXII (1912).
Maurice (1913-14) (London, 1971).
"The Indian Mind", *New Weekly*, 28.3.1914.
"The Gods of India", *New Weekly*, 30.5.1914.
"The Rose Show", *New Weekly*, 11.7.1914.
"To Simply Feel", *New Weekly*, 8.8.1914.
"Reconstruction on the Marne and the Meuse", *Westminster Gazette*, 30.8.1915.
"A First Flight", *National Review*, LXXIII (March 1919).
"Hawkeritis", *Daily Herald*, 30.5.1919.
"A Flood in the Office", *Athenaeum*, 8.8.1919.
"Tolstoy at the St. James's", *Athenaeum*, 10.10.1919.
"Literature and History", *Athenaeum*, 2.1.1920.
"Civilization", *Daily Herald*, 12.1.1920.
"Where there is Nothing", *Athenaeum*, 27.2.1920.
"Literary Notes", *Daily Herald*, 14.4.1920.
"The boy who never grew up", *Daily Herald*, 9.6.1920.
"A Great History", *Athenaeum*, 9.7.1920.
"Luso-India", *Athenaeum*, 27.8.1920.
"Missionaries", *Athenaeum*, 22.10.1920.

"Mr Wells' Outline", *Athenaeum*, 19.11.1920.
"The Poetry of Iqbal", *Athenaeum*, 10.12.1920.
"In the Temple of Criticism", *Nation*, 8.1.1921.
"Victorian Writers", *Athenaeum*, 28.1.1921.
"Reflections in India, I: Too Late?", *Nation & Athenaeum*, 21.1.1922.
"Reflections in India, II: The Prince's Progress", *Nation & Athenaeum*, 28.1.1922.
"India and the Turk", *Nation & Athenaeum*, 30.9.1922.
Alexandria. A History and a Guide (1922) (New York, 1961).
Pharos and Pharillon (1923) (London, 1967).
"Eliza in Chains", *Cornhill Magazine*, NS. LVI (May 1924).
A Passage to India (1924) (Harmondsworth, 1936).
"Edward VII", *Calendar of Modern Letters*, I (April 1925).
"Introductory Notes" to Eliza Fay, *Original Letters from India* (London, 1925).
"The True Joan of Arc. Shaw's or France's", *New Leader*, 19.6.1925.
"Peeping at Elizabeth", *Nation & Athenaeum*, 8.8.1925.
"Poverty's Challenge", *New Leader*, 4.9.1925.
Anonymity: An Enquiry (London, 1925).
Review of *War at Wittenberg* by A. R. D. Watkins, *Nation and Athenaeum*, 19.12.1925.
"The Book of the Age?", *New Leader*, 12.3.1926.
"Virgil and Tommy. The Mystery of Dean Inge", *New Leader*, 17.9.1926.
"Foreword" to Constance Sitwell, *Flowers and Elephants* (London, 1927).
Aspects of the Novel (1927) (London, 1949).
"The New Censorship" (letter signed jointly with Virginia Woolf), *Nation & Athenaeum*, 8.9.1928.
"The 'Censorship' of Books", *Nineteenth Century & After*, CV (April 1929).
"Bloomsbury, an Early Note" (February 1929), *Pawn*, No. 3, November 1956.
"Mr D. H. Lawrence and Lord Brentford", *Nation & Athenaeum*, 11.1.1930.
"D. H. Lawrence", *Nation & Athenaeum*, 29.3.1930.
"D. H. Lawrence", *Nation & Athenaeum*, 12.4.1930.
"D. H. Lawrence", *Nation & Athenaeum*, 26.4.1930.
"D. H. Lawrence", *Listener*, 30.4.1930.
"A Broadcast Debate", *Nation & Athenaeum*, 10.5.1930.
"The Cult of D. H. Lawrence", *Spectator*, 18.4.1931.
"Some Memories" in Gilbert Beith, *Edward Carpenter. In Appreciation* (London, 1931).
"An Artist's Life", *Spectator*, 25.4.1931.
"The Ceremony of Being a Gentleman", *Spectator*, 27.6.1931.
"Death of a Poet: Birth of a Critic", *Listener*, 26.8.1931.
"Are the B.B.C. too Cautious?", *Spectator*, 19.12.1931.
"William Cowper, an Englishman", *Spectator*, 16.1.1932.
"The Next War", *New Statesman & Nation*, 23.1.1932.
"The 'Osterley Park' Ballads", *Spectator*, 19.3.1932.
"Mr G. Lowes Dickinson", *Times*, 6.8.1932.
"G. L. Dickinson: A Tribute", *Spectator*, 13.8.1932.
"D.O.R.A.", *New Statesman & Nation*, 15.10.1932.
"Lowes Dickinson", *Listener*, 19.10.1932.
"Tales of Unrest", *Listener*, 14.12.1932.

"Not New Books", *Listener*, 28.12.1932.

"The Future of Books", *Listener*, 18.1.1933.

"The University and the Universe", *Spectator*, 17.3.1933.

"The English Eccentrics", *Spectator*, 19.5.1933.

"BreakingUp", *Spectator*, 28.7.1933.

"'Seven Days' Hard'", *Listener*, 14.3.1934.

Goldsworthy Lowes Dickinson (1934) (London, 1962).

"The Censor Again?", *Author*, XLIV (Spring 1934).

"Our Greatest Benefactor", *Spectator*, 15.6.1934.

"Notes on the Way", *Time & Tide*, 2.6.1934.

"Notes on the Way", *Time & Tide*, 9.6.1934.

"Notes on the Way", *Time & Tide*, 16.6.1934.

"Notes on the Way", *Time & Tide*, 23.6.1934.

"E. M. Forster replies", *Time & Tide*, 30.6.1934.

"The Old School", *Spectator*, 27.7.1934.

"English Freedom", *Spectator*, 23.11.1934.

"Prosecution of Publishers" (Letter signed jointly by E. M. F., A. P. Herbert, A. A. Milne, J. B. Priestley and H. G. Wells), *Spectator*, 26.4.1935.

"International Congress of Writers", *New Statesman & Nation*, 6.7.1935.

"Notes on the Way", *Time & Tide*, 2.11.1935.

"Notes on the Way", *Time & Tide*, 9.11.1935.

"Notes on the Way", *Time & Tide*, 16.11.1935.

"Notes on the Way", *Time & Tide*, 23.11.1935.

"The Psychology of Monarchy", *New Statesman & Nation*, 22.2.1936.

Abinger Harvest (1936) (London, 1953).

"Tolstoy's 'War and Peace'", *Listener*, 13.1.1937.

"Church, Community and State", *Listener*, 27.1.1937.

"Recollectionism", *New Statesman & Nation*, 13.3.1937.

"Coronation Nightmare", *Spectator*, 19.3.1937.

"Foreword", to Alec Craig, *The Banned Books of England* (London, 1937).

"Royalty and Loyalty", *New Statesman & Nation*, 24.4.1937.

"A Smack for Russia", *Listener*, 12.5.1937.

"A Conversation", *Spectator*, 13.8.1937.

"Sir Tokoji Rao Puar", *Times*, 28.12.1937.

"Books of the Year", *Listener*, 5.1.1938.

"General Knowledge", *New Statesman & Nation*, 15.1.1938.

"Efficiency and Liberty – Great Britain", *Listener*, 9.3.1938.

"Two Cheers for Democracy", *Nation* (New York), 16.7.1938.

"Landor at Sea", *New Statesman & Nation*, 6.8.1938.

"The Long Run", *New Statesman & Nation*, 10.12.1938.

"The Ivory Tower", *Atlantic Monthly*, CLXIII (Jan. 1939).

"Here's Wishing!", *Listener*, 5.1.1939.

"Freedom for What?", *Listener*, 1.6.1939.

"The Freedom of the Artist", *Listener*, 28.3.1940.

"These 'Lost Leaders'", *Spectator*, 5.7.1940.

"English Quislings", *Spectator*, 19.7.1940.

"Omega and Alpha", *New Statesman & Nation*, 10.8.1940.

"The Individual and his God", *Listener*, 5.12.1940.

Letter, *Time & Tide*, 28.6.1941.

Letter, *Time & Tide*, 5.7.1941.

"Books in 1941", *Listener*, 10.7.1941.

"The New Disorder", *Horizon*, IV (December 1941).

"The New Disorder" in Herman Ould, ed., *Writers in Freedom* (London, 1942).

"Edward Gibbon", in George Orwell, ed. *Talking to India* (London, 1943).

"The Claims of Art", *Listener*, 30.12.1943.

"A Clash of Authority", *Listener*, 22.6.1944.

"Introduction", to G. L. Dickinson, *Letters from John Chinaman* (London, 1946).

"The N.C.C.L.", *New Statesman & Nation*, 15.5.1948.

"Freedom Defence Committee" (letter signed jointly by B. Britten, E. M. F., A. John, G. Orwell, H. Read and O. Sitwell), *Socialist Leader*, 18.9.1948 (This item is not contained in Miss Kirkpatrick's bibliography. The letter is reprinted in George Orwell, *Collected Essays, Journalism and Letters*, ed., S. Orwell and I. Angus (London, 1968), pp .446-7).

"Butler Approached", *Spectator*, 12.11.1948.

"The Raison D'Etre of Criticism", *Horizon*, XVIII (December 1948).

"Entrance to an Unwritten Novel", *Listener*, 23.12.1948.

"Mahatma Ghandi" (May 1949), in K. Natwar-Singh, ed., *E. M. Forster: A Tribute* (New York, 1964).

"Charles Mauron and *L'Homme Triple*", *Adam International Review*, No. 200, November 1949.

"The Hollywood Ten", *Author*, LXI (Spring 1951).

"Fifth Anniversary of the Third Programme", *Listener*, 4.10.1951.

Two Cheers for Democracy (London, 1951).

"The Legacy of Samuel Butler", *Listener*, 12.6.1952.

"Portraits from Memory", *Listener*, 24.7.1952.

"The Possessed", *Listener*, 9.10.1952.

"The Art and Architecture of India", *Listener*, 10.9.1953.

The Hill of Devi (1953) (Harmondsworth, 1965).

"A Magistrate's Figures", *New Statesman & Nation*, 31.10.1953.

"Dr. Trevelyan's Love of Letters", *Cambridge Review*, 13.2.1954.

"Revolution at Bayreuth", *Listener*, 4.11.1954.

"The World Mountain", *Listener*, 2.12.1954.

"A Letter", *Twentieth Century*, CLVII (February 1955).

"'The Mint' by T. E. Lawrence", *Listener*, 17.2.1955.

Letter, *Twentieth Century*, CLVII (May 1955).

"A Shrine for Diaghilev", *Observer*, 25.12.1955.

"The Swindon Classics", *Observer*, 11.3.1956.

Marianne Thornton (London, 1956).

"Goldsworthy Lowes Dickinson: A Great Humanist", *Listener*, 11.10.1956

"Henry James as Art Critic", *Listener*, 11.10.1956.

"Tourism v. Thuggism", *Listener*, 17.1.1957.

"The Charm and Strength of Mrs Gaskell", *Sunday Times*, 7.4.1957.

"On Remaining an Agnostic", *Listener*, 31.10.1957.

"De Senectute", *London Magazine*, IV (November 1957).

Prefatory Note to *Passage to India*, Everyman edition (London 1957).

Report from the Select Committee on Obscene Publications, (Evidence given by T. S. Eliot and E.M.F.), London (HMSO), 20.3.1958.

"Wolfenden Report", *Times*, 9.5.1958.
"This Worrying World", *Listener*, 22.5.1958.
Review of R. H. Taylor, *Authors at Work*, *Library*, 5th Series, XIII (June 1958).
"The Fearful Choice", in Philip Toynbee, ed., *The Fearful Choice* (London, 1958).
"A View without a Room", *Observer*, 27.7.1958.
"Fog over Ferney", *Listener*, 18.12.1958.
"E. M. Forster on his Life and his Books", *Listener*, 1.1.1959.
"Recollections of Nassenheide", *Listener*, 1.1.1959.
"Mr C. H. Collins Baker", *Times*, 14.7.1959.
"Henry James and the Young Men", *Listener*, 16.7.1959.
"Nuisance Value", *Spectator*, 2.10.1959.
"The Consett Case", *Times*, 11.12.1959.
"Introduction" to *The Longest Journey*, World's Classics edition (London, 1960).
"The Sahib from Bloomsbury", *Observer*, 5.11.1961.
"Indian Entries", *Encounter*, January 1962.
"Back India Appeal" (letter signed jointly by E.M.F., O. Caroe, B. Ward, and G. Wint), *Spectator*, 30.11.1962.
"Going into Europe" (a symposium), *Encounter*, December 1962.
"A Presidential Address", *University Humanist Federation Bulletin*, No. 11, Spring 1963.
"My First Opera", *Opera*, XIV (June 1963.)
"Where Angels Fear to Tread", *Times*, 12.7.1963.
"Arctic Summer", in Anthony Gishford, ed., *Tribute to Benjamin Britten* (London, 1963).
"E. M. Forster Points Out – Vice Versa", *Cambridge News*, 22.2.1964.
"Moonstruck", *Guardian*, 7.8.1964.
"Pylons on the March", *Times*, 5.9.1964.
"Labour Voters and Vietnam" (advertisement letter), *Times*, 25.4.1966.

OTHER WORKS CONSULTED, OR QUOTED IN THE TEXT

Anonymous, "Fiction" (Review of *Angels*), *Speaker*, 28.10.1905, p. 90.
——, "Novels" (Review of *Angels*), *Spectator*, 23.12.1905, pp. 1089-90.
——, "The Novel of the Week" (Review of *Journey*), 27.4.1907, p. 357.
——, (Review of *Journey*), *Athenaeum*, 18.5.1907, pp. 600-601.
——, "The *Bookman* Gallery. Mr E. M. Forster", *Bookman* (London), June 1907, pp. 81-2.
——, (Review of *Room*), *Athenaeum*, 19.12.1908, p. 784.
——, (Review of *Howards End*), *Spectator*, 5.11.1910, p. 757.
——, "Mr E. M. Forster's 'Intolerant Tolerance'", *Manchester Guardian*, 28.8. 1944, p. 4.
——, "Considering Mr Forster", *Times Literary Supplement*, 27.7.1951, pp. 461-2.
——, "A Qualified Tribute" (Review of *Two Cheers*), *Times Literary Supplement*, 16.11.1951, p. 724.
——, "E. M. Forster at Ninety", *Times Literary Supplement*, 2.1.1969, p. 12.
——, "Mr E. M. Forster, O.M." (Obituary notice), *Times*, 8.6.1970.

——, "E. M. Forster, English Literary Giant, Dies", *International Herald Tribune*, 8.6.1970, pp. 1 and 5.
——, "A Chalice for Youth" (Review of *Maurice*), *Times Literary Supplement*, 8.10.1971, pp. 1215-6.
Allen, Glen O., "Structure, Symbol, and Theme in E. M. Forster's *Passage to India*", *P.M.L.A.*, LXX (December 1955), pp. 934-954.
Allen, Walter, "Reassessments – *Howards End*", *New Statesman and Nation*, 19.3.1955, pp. 407-8.
——, *Tradition and Dream* (London, 1964).
Anderson, Patrick, "E. M. Forster", *Spectator*, 13.6.1970, pp. 793-4.
Annan, Noel, "Books in General", *New Statesman and Nation*, 7.10.1944, p. 239.
——, "Strands of Unbelief", *Ideas and Beliefs of the Victorians* (1949) (New York, 1966).
——, "John Stuart Mill", *The English Mind*, H. S. Davies and G. Watson, eds. (Cambridge, 1964).
Arnold, Matthew, *Irish Essays and Others* (London, 1883).
——, *Mixed Essays* (London, 1883).
——, *Culture and Anarchy*, ed., J. Dover Wilson (Cambridge, 1966).
Auden, W. H., "Lowes Dickinson" (Review of *GLD*), *Scrutiny*, III (December 1934), pp. 303-6.
——, *Collected Shorter Poems, 1930-1944* (London, 1950).
Ault, Peter, "Aspects of E. M. Forster", *Dublin Review*, October 1946, pp. 109-134.
Austin, Don, "The Problem of Continuity in three novels of E. M. Forster", *Modern Fiction Studies*, VII (Autumn 1961), pp. 217-228.
Beaumont, Ernest, "Mr E. M. Forster's Strange Mystics", *Dublin Review*, 1951, pp. 41-51.
Beebe, Maurice & Joseph Brogunier, "Criticism of E. M. Forster: A Selected Checklist", *Modern Fiction Studies*, VII (October 1961), pp. 284-292.
Beer, J. B., *The Achievement of E. M. Forster* (London, 1962).
Belgion, Montgomery, "The Diabolism of Mr E. M. Forster", *Criterion*, XIV (October 1934), pp. 54-73.
Bell, Quentin, *Bloomsbury* (London, 1968).
Bell, Vereen M., "Comic Seriousness in *Passage to India*", *South Atlantic Quarterly*, 1967, pp. 606-617.
Bennett, Arnold, *Books and Persons* (London, 1917).
Bensen, Alice R., "E. M. Forster's Dialectic: *Howards End*", *Modern Fiction Studies*, I (1955), pp. 17-22.
Bentley, Phyllis, "The Novels of E. M. Forster", *College English*, IX (April 1948), pp. 349-356.
Berland, Alwyn, "James and Forster: The Morality of Class", *Cambridge Journal*, VI (February 1953), pp. 259-80.
Blackham, H. J., *Humanism* (Harmondsworth, 1968).
Booth, Wayne C., *The Rhetoric of Fiction* (Chicago, 1961).
Bowen, Elizabeth, "Abinger Harvest" (Review of *AH*), *Spectator*, 20.3.1936, p. 521.
——, *Collected Impressions* (London, 1950).
Bowra, C. M., "Beauty in Bloomsbury", *Yale Review*, XLIV (1954-5), pp. 461-4.

Boyle, Ted E., "Adela Quested's Delusion: The Failure of Rationalism in *A Passage to India*", *College English*, XXVI (1965), pp. 478-80.

Bradbury, Malcolm, "*Howards End*", *Forster. A Collection of Critical Essays*, Malcolm Bradbury, ed. (Englewood Cliffs, 1966).

——, ed., *Forster. A Collection of Critical Essays* (Englewood Cliffs, 1966).

——, "Two Passages to India: Forster as Victorian and Modern", *Aspects of E. M. Forster*, Stallybrass, ed. (London, 1969).

——, *E. M. Forster, A Passage to India*, Casebook Series. ed. (London, 1970).

Brander, Laurence, *E. M. Forster. A Critical Study* (London, 1968).

Breit, Harvey, *The Writer Observed* (Cleveland, 1956).

Bronowski, J. & Bruce Mazlish, *The Western Intellectual Tradition* (Harmondsworth, 1963).

Brophy, Brigid. "The Saving of Maurice" (Review of *Maurice*), *Listener*, 7.10.1971, p. 481.

Brower, Reuben A., "The Twilight of the Double Vision: Symbol and Irony in *Passage to India*" (1951), *Modern British Fiction*, Mark Schorer, ed. (New York, 1961).

Brown, E. K., "E. M. Forster and the Contemplative Novel", *University of Toronto Quarterly*, III (1933-1934), pp. 349-361.

——, "The Revival of E. M. Forster" (1944), *Forms of Modern Fiction*, W. Van O'Connor, ed. (Bloomington, 1964).

——, *Rhythm in the Novel* (Toronto, 1950).

Burgess, Anthony, *The Novel Now* (London, 1967).

Burke, Kenneth, *Language as Symbolic Action* (Berkeley, & Los Angeles 1966).

Burra, Peter, "The Novels of E. M. Forster" (1934), *Forster*, Bradbury, ed. (Englewood Cliffs, 1966).

Butler, Samuel, *Notebooks*, G. Keynes and B. Hill, eds. (London, 1951).

"Caliban", "Une thèse sur la langue et le style de E. M. Forster", *Annales de la Faculté des Lettres de Toulouse*, V, NS Tome IV (1968), pp. 157-8.

Cazes, René, Reviews of *Two Cheers* and Rex Warner, *E.M.F.*, *Etudes Anglaises*, V (1952), pp. 266-8.

Cecil, Lord David, *Poets and Storytellers* (London, 1949).

Chaudhuri, Nirad C., "Passage to and from India", *Encounter*, II (June 1954), pp. 19-24.

Churchill, Thomas, "Place and Personality in *Howards End*", *Critique*, V (1962), pp. 61-73.

Cockshutt, A. O. J., *The Unbelievers* (London, 1964).

Connolly, Cyril, *Enemies of Promise* (1938) (Harmondsworth, 1961).

——, "Corydon in Croydon" (Review of *Maurice*), *Sunday Times*, 10.10.1971, p. 39.

Cooperman, Stanley, "The Imperial Posture and the Shrine of Darkness: Kipling's *Naulahka* and E. M. Forster's *Passage to India*", *English Literature in Transition*, VI (1963), pp. 9-13.

Cowling, Maurice, "Mill and Liberalism", *Mill. A Collection of Critical Essays*, J. B. Schneewind, ed. (London, 1969).

Cox, C. B., *The Free Spirit* (London, 1963).

Craig, David, "Fiction and the Rising Industrial Classes", *Essays in Criticism*, XVII (January 1967), pp. 64-74.

Crews, Frederick C., *E. M. Forster. The Perils of Humanism* (London & Princeton, 1962).

Daleski, H. M., "Rhythmic and Symbolic Patterns in *A Passage to India*", *Studies in English Language and Literature*, A. Shalvi & A. A. Mendilow, eds. (Jerusalem, 1966).

Dangerfield, George, *The Strange Death of Liberal England* (1935) (London, 1966).

——, "E. M. Forster: A Man with a View", *Saturday Review of Literature*, 27.8.1938, pp. 3 & 4, 14-16.

Decap, Roger, "Un roman pascalien: *Passage to India* de E. M. Forster", *Annales de la faculté des lettres de Toulouse*, V, Tome IV (1968), pp. 103-128.

Delbaere-Garant, J., "'Who shall inherit England?' A Comparison between *Howards End*, *Parade's End* and *Unconditional Surrender*", *English Studies*, L (1969), pp. 101-105.

Doughty, Howard N., "The Novels of E. M. Forster", *Bookman* (New York), October 1932, pp. 542-9.

Einsiedel, Wolfgang von, "Einbildungskraft des Herzens. Der Erzähler E. M. Forster", *Merkur*, IV (June 1950), pp. 629-639.

Ellmann, Richard, "Two Faces of Edward", *Edwardians and Victorians*, R. Ellmann, ed. (New York, 1960).

Fassett, I. P., Review of *Passage*, *Criterion*, III (1924-5), pp. 137-9.

Fraser, G. S., *The Modern Writer and his World* (1953) (Harmondsworth, 1964).

Fricker, Robert, *Der moderne englische Roman* (Göttingen, 1958).

Friedman, Alan, *The Turn of the Novel* (New York, 1966).

Furbank, P. N. and F. J. H. Haskell, "The Art of Fiction I: E. M. Forster", *Paris Review*, I (1953), pp. 28-41.

Garnett, David, "Books in General" (Review of *AH*), *New Statesman & Nation*, 21.3.1936, p. 459.

——, "Forster and Bloomsbury", *Aspects of E. M. Forster*, Stallybrass, ed. (London, 1969).

Garnett, Edward, Review of *Howards End*, *Nation*, 12.11.1910, pp. 282-4.

Gérard, Albert, "Edward Morgan Forster, romancier de la compréhension", *Revue générale Belge*, June 1951, pp. 77-89.

Gerber, Helmut E., "E. M. Forster: An Annotated Checklist of Writings about him", *English Literature in Transition*, Spring 1959, pp. 4-27.

Godfrey, Denis, *E. M. Forster's Other Kingdom* (London, 1968).

Goldman, Mark, "Virginia Woolf and E. M. Forster: A Critical Dialogue", *Texas Studies in Literature and Language*, VII (Winter 1966), pp. 387-400.

Gransden, K. W., "E. M. Forster at Eighty", *Encounter*, January 1959, pp. 77-81.

——, *E. M. Forster* (London, 1962).

Grubb, Frederick, "Homage to E. M. Forster", *Contemporary Review*, January 1959, pp. 20-23.

——, *A Vision of Reality* (London, 1965).

Haas, Willy, "Ein Unsterblicher stirbt", *Die Welt*, 9.6.1970.

Hale, Nancy, "A Passage to Relationship", *Antioch Review*, XX (Spring 1960), pp. 19-30.

Hall, James, "Forster's Family Reunions", *ELH*, XXV (March 1958), pp. 60-78.

Hammelmann, Hans A., "Der Romancier E. M. Forster", *Die neue Rundschau*, 1958, pp. 539-548.

Hampshire, Stuart, "Two Cheers for Mr Forster", *New York Review of Books*, 12.5.1966, pp. 14-16.

Hannah, Donald, "The Limitations of Liberalism in E. M. Forster's Work", *English Miscellany*, XIII (1962), pp. 165-178.

Hardy, Barbara, *The Appropriate Form* (London, 1964).

Hardy, John Edward, *Man in the Modern Novel* (Seattle, 1964).

Harrison, Robert L., "The Manuscripts of A Passage to India", Diss., Ann Arbor, 1968.

Hartley, L. P., Review of *Passage*, *Spectator*, 28.6.1924.

Harvey, John, "Imagination and moral theme in E. M. Forster's *The Longest Journey*", *Forster. A Collection of Critical Essays* (No. 46).

Hassall, Christopher, *Rupert Brooke* (London, 1964).

Heilbrun, Carolyn G., *The Garnett Family* (London, 1961).

Heurgon, Jacques, "Les Romans de E. M. Forster", *Revue de Paris*, XXXIV, A. II (1927), pp. 701-9.

Hoare, Dorothy M., *Some Studies in the Modern Novel* (London, 1938).

Hoffman, Frederick J., "*Howards End* and the Bogey of Progress", *Modern Fiction Studies*, VII (Autumn 1961), pp. 243-257.

Hollingsworth, Keith, "*A Passage to India*: The Echoes in the Marabar Caves", *Criticism*, IV (1962), pp. 210-224.

Holloway, David, "E. M. Forster, Influence on Literature" (Obituary notice), *Daily Telegraph*, 8.6.1970, p. 10.

Holt, Lee Ebert, "E. M. Forster and Samuel Butler", *P.M.L.A.*, LXI (1946), pp. 804-819.

Horowitz, Ellin, "The Communal Ritual and the Dying God in E. M. Forster's *Passage to India*", *Criticism*, VI (Winter 1964), pp. 70-88.

Howarth, Herbert, "E. M. Forster and the Contrite Establishment", *Journal of General Education*, October 1965, pp. 196-206.

Hoy, Cyrus, "Forster's Metaphysical Novel", *P.M.L.A.*, LXXV (March 1960), pp. 126-136.

Hunt, John Dixon, "Muddle and Mystery in *Passage to India*", *ELH*, XXXIII (1966), pp. 497-517.

Hynes, Samuel, "The Old Man at King's", *Commonweal*, LXXIX (21.2.1964), pp. 635-638.

Johnson, Elaine H., "The Intelligent Mr E. M. Forster", *Personalist*, January 1954, pp. 50-58.

Johnstone, J. K., *The Bloomsbury Group* (1954) (New York, 1963).

Jungel, Renate, "Die Zeitstruktur in den Romanen E. M. Forsters", Diss., Graz, 1953.

Junker, Rochus, "Studien zur Romanwelt von E. M. Forster", Diss., Münster, 1949.

Kaiser, Rudolf, "E. M. Forster: Gedankliche Analyse seines Romanes *Howards End* im Rahmen des Gesamtwerkes", *Die neueren Sprachen*, XI (1962), pp. 341-363.

Keir, W. A. S., "*A Passage to India* Reconsidered", *Cambridge Journal*, V (1952), pp. 426-435.

Kelvin, Norman, *E. M. Forster* (Carbondale, 1967).

Kermode, Frank, "Mr E. M. Forster as a Symbolist", *Forster. A Collection of Critical Essays*, Bradbury, ed. (Englewood Cliffs, 1966).

Kettle, Arnold, *An Introduction to the English Novel*, Vol. 2 (1953) (London, 1962).

Keynes, John Maynard, *Two Memoirs* (London, 1949).

Kirkpatrick, B. J., *A Bibliography of E. M. Forster* (London, 1965).

Klingopoulos, G. D., "Notes on the Victorian Scene", *Pelican Guide to English Literature*, Vol. 6 (Harmondsworth, 1958).

——, "E. M. Forster's Sense of History, and Cavafy", *Essays in Criticism*, VIII (April 1958), pp. 156-165.

——, "Mr Forster's Good Influence", *Pelican Guide to English Literature*, Vol. 7 (Harmondsworth, 1961).

Lacotte, C., "Études récentes sur E. M. Forster", *Etudes Anglaises*, XX (1967), pp. 425-431.

Lambert, J. W., "Mr Forster at the Play", *Sunday Times*, 4.8.1963, p. 20.

Langbaum, Robert, "A New Look at E. M. Forster", *Southern Review*, NS IV (January 1968), pp. 33-49.

Laski, Harold J., *The Rise of European Liberalism* (1936) (London, 1962).

Lawrence, A. W., ed., *Letters to T. E. Lawrence* (London, 1962).

Lawrence, D. H., *The Collected Letters of D. H. Lawrence*, Harry T. Moore, ed. (London, 1962).

Lawrence, T. E., *The Letters of T. E. Lawrence*, David Garnett, ed. (London, 1938).

Leavis, F. R., *The Common Pursuit* (1952) (London, 1958).

Leavis, Q. D., "Mr E. M. Forster" (Review of *AH*), *A Selection from Scrutiny*, F. R. Leavis, ed. (Cambridge, 1968).

Lehmann, John, *I am my Brother* (London, 1960).

Levine, June Perry, "An Analysis of the Manuscripts of *Passage to India*", *P.M.L.A.*, LXXXV (March 1970), pp. 284-294.

Lunan, N. M., "The Novels of E. M. Forster", *Durham University Journal*, XXXVII (March 1945), pp. 52-7.

Macaulay, Rose, *The Writings of E. M. Forster* (London, 1938).

McConkey, James, *The Novels of E. M. Forster* (Ithaca, 1957).

McCormick, John, *Catastrophe and Imagination* (London, 1957).

Macdonald, Alastair A., "Class-Consciousness in E. M. Forster", *University of Kansas City Review*, XXVII (Spring 1961), pp. 235-240.

McDowell, Frederick P. W., "'The Mild Intellectual Light': Idea and Theme in *Howards End*", *P.M.L.A.*, LXXIV (September 1959), pp. 453-463.

——, "Forster's many-faceted Universe: Idea and Paradox in *The Longest Journey*", *Critique*, IV (Fall/Winter 1960-61), pp. 41-63.

——, "The newest elucidations of Forster", *English Literature in Transition*, V (1962), pp. 51-8.

——, "E. M. Forster's Conception of the Critic", *Tennessee Studies in Literature*, X (1965), pp. 93-100.

——, "Forster's most recent critics", *English Literature in Transition*, VII (1965), pp. 49-62.

——, "E. M. Forster's Theory of Literature", *Criticism*, VIII (Winter 1966), pp. 19-43.

——, "E. M. Forster: Recent Extended Studies", *English Literature in Transition*, IX (1966), pp. 156-168.

—, "Bibliography, News and Notes: E. M. Forster", *English Literature in Transition*, X (1967), pp. 47-64.

—, "E. M. Forster: Romancer or Realist?", *English Literature in Transition*, XI (1968), pp. 103-122.

—, "Recent Books on Forster and Bloomsbury", *English Literature in Transition*, XII (1969), pp. 135-150.

—, *E. M. Forster* (New York, 1969).

Mackenzie, Compton, *My Life and Times*. Octave 6 (London, 1967).

Maclean, Hugh, "The Structure of *A Passage to India*", *University of Toronto Quarterly*, XXII (1952-3), pp. 157-171.

Mandrillo, Piero, "E. M. Forster e la critica", *Rivista di letterature moderne e comparate*, XVIII (1965), pp. 211-227.

Mansfield, Katherine, "Throw them Overboard" (Review of *Story of a Siren*), *Athenaeum*, 13.8.1920, p. 209.

Mason, W. H., *A Passage to India* (Oxford, 1965).

Mendilow, A. A., "The Triadic World of E. M. Forster", *Studies in English Language and Literature*, A. Shalvi and A. A. Mendilow, eds. (Jerusalem, 1966).

Miles, Hamish, "E. M. Forster" (Review of *HE, Pharos and Pharillon, Celestial Omnibus*), *Dial*, LXXVI (May 1924), pp. 452-456.

Mill, John Stuart, *Mill on Bentham and Coleridge*, F. R. Leavis, ed. (London, 1950).

—, *Utilitarianism, Liberty and Representative Government*, Everyman edition (London, 1964).

Moore, G. E., *Principia Ethica* (1903) (Cambridge, 1966).

Moore, Harry T., *E. M. Forster* (New York, 1965).

Morton, A. L., *Language of Men* (London, 1945).

Müllenbrock, Heinz-Joachim, "Gesellschaftliche Thematik in E. M. Forsters Roman *Howards End*", *Anglia*, LXXXVII (1969), pp. 367-391.

—, "Die Kunst der Eröffnung im Werk E. M. Forsters: Ein Beitrag zur Poetik seiner Romane", *G.R.M.*, XXI (1971), pp. 185-203.

Murry, J. M., "Bou-Oum or Ou-Boum?" (Review of *Passage*), *Adelphi*, II (July 1924), pp. 150-153.

Natwar-Singh, K. ed., *E. M. Forster: A Tribute* (New York, 1964).

Nelson, Harland S., "Shonfield and Forster's India. A Controversial Exchange", *Encounter*, June 1968, pp. 94-5.

Nierenberg, Edwin, "The Withered Priestess. Mrs Moore's Incomplete Passage to India", *Modern Language Quarterly*, XXV (1964), pp. 198-204.

O'Connor, William Van, "A Visit with E. M. Forster", *Western Review*, XIX (1954-5), pp. 215-219.

Oliver, Harold J., "E. M. Forster: The Early Novels", *Critique*, I (1957), pp. 15-33.

—, *The Art of E. M. Forster* (Melbourne, 1960).

Orwell, George, *Collected Essays, Journalism and Letters*, S. Orwell and I. Angus, eds. (London, 1968).

Panichas, George A., "E. M. Forster and D. H. Lawrence: Their Views on Education", *Renaissance and Modern Essays*, G. R. Hibbard, ed. (London, 1966).

Panter-Downes, Mollie, "Profiles: Kingsman", *New Yorker*, 19.9.1959, pp. 51-86.

Pedersen, Glenn, "Forster's Symbolic Form", *Kenyon Review*, XXI (Spring 1959), pp. 231-249.

Pellow, J. D. C., "The Beliefs of Mr Forster", *Theology*, XL (April 1940), pp. 276-281.

Perrott, Roy, "The Quiet Revolutionary", *Observer*, 5.1.1969, p. 21.

Plomer, William, "An Introduction to E. M. Forster", *Penguin New Writing*, XX (1944), pp. 138-141.

——, *At Home* (London, 1958).

Popkin, Richard H., and Avrum Stroll, *Philosophy made Simple* (London, 1969).

Popper, K. R., *The Open Society and its Enemies* (London, 1966).

Postel, Elisabeth, "Symbol und Leitmotiv in den Romanen E. M. Forsters" Diss., Kiel, 1959.

Price, Martin, "E.M.F. and D.H.L.", *Yale Review*, LV (1965-6), pp. 597-601.

Priestley, J. B., Review of *Passage*, *London Mercury*, X (July 1924), pp. 319-321.

Pritchett, V. S., "Mr Forster's New Year", *New Statesman & Nation*, 27.12 1958, p. 912

——, "E M. Forster" (Obituary notice), *New Statesman*, 12.6.1970, p. 840.

Pryce-Jones, Alan, "Books in General", *New Statesman & Nation*, 6.11.1943, p. 303.

Putt, S. Gorley, *Scholars of the Heart* (London, 1962).

Raleigh, John Henry, "Victorian Morals and the Modern Novel", *Partisan Review*, XXV (Spring 1958), pp. 241-264.

Ransom, John Crowe, "Gestures of Dissent" (Review of *AH*), *Yale Review*, XXVI (1936-7), pp. 181-3.

——, "E. M. Forster", *Kenyon Review*, V (Autumn 1943), pp. 618-623.

Rantavaara, Irma, "E. M. Forster ja Bloomsbury", *Valvoja*, No. 6, 1951.

——, *Virginia Woolf and Bloomsbury* (Helsinki, 1953).

Ratcliffe, Michael, "The Undeveloped Heart", (Review of *Maurice*), *Times*, 7.10.1971, p. 10.

Richards, I. A., "A Passage to Forster: Reflections on a Novelist", *Forster. A Collection of Critical Essays*, Bradbury, ed. (Englewood Cliffs, 1966).

Routh, H. V., *English Literature and Ideas in the Twentieth Century* (London, 1946).

Rueckert, William H., *Kenneth Burke and the Drama of Human Relations* (Minneapolis, 1963).

Ryan, Marjorie, "Forster, James and Flaubert: A Parallel", *Notes and Queries*, CCVI (1961), pp. 102-3.

Sassoon, Siegfried, *Siegfried's Journey* (London, 1945).

Savage, D. S., "Examination of Modern Authors: 4. E. M. Forster", *Rocky Mountain Review*, X (1946), pp. 190-204.

——, *The Withered Branch* (London, 1950).

Shahani, Ranjee G., "Some British I admire: E. M. Forster", *Asiatic Review*, XLII (July 1946), pp. 270-273.

Shonfield, Andrew, "The Politics of Forster's India", *Encounter*, XXX (1968), pp. 62-9.

Shusterman, David, *The Quest for Certitude in E. M. Forster's Fiction* (Bloomington, 1965).

Smith, H. A., "Forster's Humanism and the Nineteenth Century", *Forster. A Collection of Critical Essays*, Bradbury, ed. (Englewood Cliffs, 1966).

Spender, Stephen, *World Within World* (London, 1951).

—, *The Creative Element* (New York, 1954).

Stallybrass, Oliver, "Forster's 'Wobblings': The Manuscripts of *Passage to India*", *Aspects of E. M. Forster* (London, 1969).

—, ed., *Aspects of E. M. Forster* (London, 1969).

Stead, C. K., *The New Poetic* (London, 1964).

Stebner, Gerhard, "Edward Morgan Forster. Ein Beitrag zur Einführung in sein Werk", *Die neueren Sprachen*, NF VII (1958), pp. 449-61; 507-515.

—, "Das Phänomen des Todes im Werke E. M. Forsters", Diss., Marburg, 1960.

Stone, Wilfred, *The Cave and the Mountain* (Stanford & London 1966).

Stonier, G. W., "Books in General", (Review of *Passage*, Everyman edition), *New Statesman & Nation*, 21.11.1942, p. 341.

Swinnerton, Frank, *The Georgian Literary Scene* (1935) (London, 1938).

Tanner, Tony, (Review of Stone, *The Cave and the Mountain*), *London Magazine*, NS VI (August 1966), pp. 102-9.

Thomas, Roy and Howard Erskine-Hall, "*Passage to India*. Two Points of View", *Anglo-Welsh Review*, XV (Summer 1965), pp. 44-50.

Thomson, David, *England in the Nineteenth Century* (Harmondsworth, 1950).

Thomson, George H., "Theme and Symbol in *Howards End*", *Modern Fiction Studies*, VII (Autumn 1961), pp. 229-242.

—, *The Fiction of E. M. Forster* (Detroit, 1967).

Toynbee, Philip, "E. M. Forster at Eighty", *Observer*, 28.12.1958, pp. 8-10.

—, "Forster's Love Story", (Review of *Maurice*), *Observer*, 10.10.1971, p. 32.

Traversi, D. A., "The Novels of E. M. Forster", *Arena*, I (April 1937), pp. 28-40.

Trilling, Lionel, *Matthew Arnold* (1939) (London, 1963).

—, *E. M. Forster* (London, 1944).

—, *The Liberal Imagination* (1950) (London, 1961).

Turnell, Martin, *Modern Literature and Christian Faith* (London, 1961).

Voorhees, Richard J., "The Novels of E. M. Forster", *South Atlantic Quarterly*, LIII (January 1954), pp. 89-99.

Waggoner, Hyatt Howe, "Notes on the Uses of Coincidence in the Novels of E. M. Forster", *Forster. A Collection of Critical Essays*, Bradbury, ed. (Englewood Cliffs, 1966).

Walker, Keith, "Body Depth" (Review of *Maurice*), *New Society*, 7.10.1971, p. 680.

Warner, Rex, *E. M. Forster* (London, 1950).

Warren, Austin, *Rage for Order* (Chicago, 1948).

Watt, Donald J., "G. E. Moore and the Bloomsbury Group", *English Literature in Transition*, XII (1969), pp. 119-134.

Westburg, Barry R., "Forster's Fifth Symphony: Another Aspect of *Howards End*", *Modern Fiction Studies*, X (Winter 1964-5), pp. 359-365.

White, Gertrude M., "*A Passage to India*: Analysis and Revaluation", *P.M.L.A.*, September 1953, pp. 641-657.

Wilde, Alan, *Art and Order. A Study of E. M. Forster* (New York, 1964).

Wilkinson, Patrick, "Forster and King's", *Aspects of E. M. Forster*, Stallybrass, ed. (London, 1969).

Willey, Basil, *The English Moralists* (London, 1965).

Wilson, Angus, "A Conversation with E. M. Forster", *Encounter*, November 1957, pp. 52-7.

Wilson, Colin, "A Man's Man" (Review of *Maurice*), *Spectator*, 9.10.1971, pp. 512-3.

Woodward, A., "The Humanism of E. M. Forster", *Theoria*, XX (1963), pp. 17-34.

Woolf, Leonard, "Arch beyond Arch" (Review of *Passage*), *Nation & Athenaeum*, 14.6.1924, p. 354.

——, *Sowing* (London, 1960).

——, *Beginning Again* (London, 1964).

Woolf, Virginia, *The Death of the Moth* (1942) (Harmondsworth, 1961).

Wright, Ralph, Review of *Passage*, *New Statesman*, 21.6.1924, p. 317.

Zabel, Morton Dawen, "E. M. Forster", *Nation* (New York). 22.10.1938, pp. 412-3 & 416.

Zeh, Dieter, "Studien zur Erzählkunst in den Romanen E. M. Forsters", Diss., Frankfurt, 1970.

Zimmerman, Paul D., "E. M. Forster (1879-1970)" (Obituary notice), *Newsweek*, 22.6.1970, pp. 60-61.

Zwerdling, Alex, "The Novels of E. M. Forster", *Twentieth Century Literature*, II (1957), pp. 171-181.

INDEX